FLYING WITH DAD

YVONNE CAPUTO

INGENIUM BOOKS

ISBNs

Paperback: 978-1-989059-29-6

eBook: 978-1-989059-30-2

Hardcover: 978-1-989059-31-9

Large Print: 978-1-989059-32-6

PRAISE FOR YVONNE CAPUTO

Yvonne Caputo's remarkable, extended 'interview' of her late father, World War II B-24 Navigator Captain Michael Caputo, is a nuanced and authentic window on one man's personal experience of combat. Beyond enriching the historical record, father and daughter offer welcome insight on the veteran's humility and stoicism, and how character framed the combatant's experience of mortal adversity but is also forever changed by it.

— BRIAN MAHONEY, WORLD WAR II RESEARCHER AND CO-AUTHOR OF *RELUCTANT WITNESS: MEMOIRS FOR THE LAST YEAR OF THE EUROPEAN AIRWAR 1944-1945*

Flying With Dad is the moving story of a daughter striving to understand her father and him sharing his harrowing experiences with her as a B-24 navigator in WWII.

— JAMES BRADLEY, AUTHOR,
FLAGS OF OUR FATHERS

It's like pouring time from a bottle. Each glass reveals a lost moment all wrapped in the love of a father and daughter. Simply delightful.

— KEITH HUMMEL, MHA,
FORMER CEO FREDERICK
LIVING

For anyone who has an interest in the events leading up to and including World War II and beyond, this superb book is a must read. Yvonne Caputo brings everything to life in this very moving story.

I enjoyed the book. In a couple of places, it brought tears to my eyes. I was amazed by the accuracy and detail. Congratulations on a job well done.

Deeply personal and insightful, *Flying with Dad* is the tale of a daughter's love for a father that she yearns to know better. From the turbulent cockpit of his wartime B-24 bomber, to the tensions of their relationship, you will be "ticketed" for a courageous emotional "flight" that few of us will ever experience. Thank you Yvonne for opening your heart to remind us that forgiveness redeems and love triumphs, often when least expected!

A wonderfully inspiring read!

— WAYNE MCGAURER,
PRESIDENT, CEO PENN
FOUNDATION INC.

Memory provoking for any baby boomer whose parent returned from action in World War II. Easy-to-relate personal memories and thought provoking as Yvonne's and my father would both say, despite the depression and war, "We lived in the best of times."

— CDR. CLINT EPLEY, (USN RET)
XO/MUSEUM CURATOR,
COMMEMORATIVE AIR FORCE
CENTRAL TEXAS WING

Have now finished reading one of the best books I've read in a long time!! I have read lots of flying stories but none with the emotional connection to real life that Yvonne has captured. Everyone that has ever wondered about how high stress affects life should read this book. Everyone has to face end of life issues sooner or later, again Yvonne has included valuable guidance.. Thank you so much for the privilege of reading this powerful story....

— RICHARD WAGNER, RETIRED FORMER RECREATIONAL PILOT

Having worked with thousands of clients who long for even one deep conversation with their parent, grandparent, or uncle about their World War II experience, this book will feel very relatable. For anyone who had a difficult relationship with their silent generation dad, this will be a comfortable and comforting read. If you're lucky enough to have a World War II relative still living, this might give you the courage to ask the questions you've been wanting to ask.

— WILLIAM L. (BILL) BEIGEL,
AUTHOR OF *BURIED ON THE BATTLEFIELD: NOT MY BOY*

What grabs you in this engrossing family saga is the fierce connection forged slowly between father and daughter — a long, solo journey of small steps carried out with sensitivity and guts. Captivating! The man who loved a good story would appreciate what his daughter has done in *Flying with Dad* — as readers will too.

— JANE LATOUR, AUTHOR OF *SISTERS IN THE BROTHERHOODS: WORKING WOMEN ORGANIZING FOR EQUALITY IN NEW YORK CITY*

CONTENTS

Part III
DAD AND ME

PART I
YVONNE

A RUFFLED HEM

My mother and I sat side by side on the couch turning the pages of the photo album. My tiny forefinger slid from one photo to another, each an indelible look into how we were as a family. I loved the stories, the anecdotes, and my mother's happy voice when she said, "Do you remember when…?"

Sometimes my sister or brothers would join us in these walks down memory lane. Sometimes, my favorite times, it would be just me and Mom. We'd howl with laughter at certain photos and the memories they'd uncover. When an image prompted a sorrowful memory, we'd stay

silent and move on. We didn't acknowledge sorrow in our family, instead keeping it hidden.

Whenever I did try to find words to express a feeling other than joy, Mom would stiffen. "Yvonne, you'd be so much happier if you didn't wear your heart on your sleeve." I knew she was telling me I was too sensitive, but I didn't know how to change that.

Two photographs in particular made me sad, but at the time I didn't have a name for how I felt. My finger would brush over them, my eyes lingering only a second or two. Two black and white photographs, taken on the same day, minutes apart.

I am tiny, perhaps three years old. Dad is in a long-sleeved classy sport shirt, pleated trousers, and dark wing tips. His dark hair, beginning to thin at the temples, is combed in a soft wave over his forehead. He hasn't yet begun to put on weight; in this photo he is slim and svelte, the way he was during the war. I'm wearing a dress with puffy sleeves and a ruffled hem. On my feet are white Mary Janes and little ankle socks. My hair is as blonde as Mom's, whose hair in the photo is gathered high up and away from her face in that 1940s style. She's

wearing sling-back heels and a dark sleeveless and belted dress. She's obviously pregnant with my sister, Connie. We are on the low concrete border that surrounded a shallow reflecting pool in Nay Aug, a large park in Scranton, Pennsylvania.

In the first photo, I'm tucked between my father and mother, the top of my head coming to just below their hips. They're both smiling. Dad's right arm is wrapped protectively around Mom's shoulders, and his left hand is gently caressing my cheek. I, however, am scowling. Was the sun too bright in my eyes? Or was I unhappy having to stand still for the picture? Was Dad trying to get me to settle?

The second photo is just Dad and me. We're walking beside the reflecting pool. Dad holds my hand and looks down at me with deep affection.

The older I get, the more I wonder. What happened to that father and daughter? Why couldn't we have stayed like that forever? What

changed that I no longer experienced that tenderness from him?

I was Dad's precious baby girl just the first four years of my life. I was the second of four children. Michael, born in 1945, was the eldest. I followed in 1946. My younger siblings, Connie and Mark, came along in 1950 and 1952 respectively. With a family of six, Dad didn't have much time for tenderness.

Mark was sickly from birth. He was colicky, fussy, and wasn't gaining weight. His skin stretched tight around his dear little face, his arms and legs were scrawny, and his belly ballooned out from his tiny frame. He had trouble breathing and had to be constantly held upright. When this stopped working, my parents took Mark to the hospital emergency room, where the staff pumped a quart of phlegm from his tiny little lungs. Doctors diagnosed him with asthma and an allergy to milk. As soon as Mom changed his formula to soy milk, he began to thrive. But the all-night rocking and walking and keeping Mark's head above his lungs lasted a while.

I awoke late one summer night and came downstairs wearing a light cotton night gown. I padded down the stairs through the dining

room, into the kitchen, and back through the pantry hallway that led to the first-floor bedroom. I stood in the doorway, the air moist on my skin, the sour smell of spoiled milk wafting from the bedroom. Dad was pacing, cradling Mark, and holding him upright over his shoulder. With each step he'd bend his knees, gently bouncing Mark up and down, up and down, while whispering, "Shh, shh, shh."

I knew that Dad was missing sleep. I knew he had to go to work in the morning. I also knew that if he put Mark down in his crib, Mark wouldn't get enough air. I stood there, transfixed. The love my father was expressing to his sick son hung in the air like a grey mist.

In many ways I never left that doorway. How could I be jealous of my sick little brother? Why wasn't I worrying about him? I was confused about the conflict that was raging silently within me. Perhaps it was not jealousy at all, just wistful wishing that Dad would once again hold me in the same gentle, caring way.

2

THE FISHING TEAM

My ten-year-old ears perked right up when, from the next room, I overheard Dad talking to Mom about going fishing with my uncles and brother. Again. I listened, leaning into the space between the frame of the doorway where I was standing to where I could see them standing at the kitchen table.

Dad loved to fish. My mother's two brothers were Dad's fishing buddies. In the spring, summer, and fall the three of them would take off for a morning or an afternoon of fishing. My twelve-year-old brother was usually with them. I wasn't invited to be a part of this team.

I was part of the team of one when the guys

came back with a bucket full of fish. Dad would hand me the bucket and give me my marching orders. "Clean these."

I was pretty good at cleaning fish. Dad had set up a table in our back yard. It was an old, flat door resting on top of two saw horses. I'd cover the table with newspaper, and step by step do the job. I preferred it if the fish were already dead, because then I didn't have to whack them on the head. I'd cut off the head, slit the belly, gut and scoop out the innards, and remove all of the scales. Crappies were my favorite. Their scales slipped right off as I slid the knife from the tail to the head. Or where the head had been. Then I'd plop the cleaned fish into a bucket of clean water underneath the table.

Dad would sometimes come back to see how I was doing, silently peering over my shoulder and counting how many cleaned fish were in the bucket.

Finished, I'd wrap all the heads and gooey entrails in newspaper and deposit the mess in a garbage pail. I would take the bucket of cleaned fish into the kitchen, drain it, and rinse each fish by hand under the spigot. I'd finished the job only when the fish were either cooking on the

stove or packaged and placed in the freezer. We'd often have the freshly-caught fish for dinner, or, if the guys caught a bunch, we'd store some in the freezer for another time.

I could be a part of the team of brother and Dad if it meant going out in the deep of evening to find night crawlers. The best time was after a rain when the big, juicy worms would come up to the surface and lay atop the wet grass. Off we we'd go, Dad holding the flashlight. The trick was to shine the light on the grass to see a worm peeking out of a hole but move the light quickly away so the night crawler wouldn't shrink back into its hole so I could quickly snatch it. Squeeze or pull too hard and the earthworm would break. We wanted whole, live night crawlers. We'd keep them in a large dirt-filled coffee tin in the refrigerator, waiting for the next fishing trip.

I could be on the bait-gathering and fish-cleaning teams, but I was never invited to be on the fishing team. One day, I must have been feeling pretty brave, because I said, "Dad, I want to go along."

"No, this is something for just the guys."

But this time Mom chimed in, her voice harder than usual. "Oh Mike, take her. It's not

going to hurt anything." To my surprise and delight, this time I was on the fishing team.

One of Dad's favorite fishing places was along French Creek near Meadville, Pennsylvania, at Wilson's Chute. We walked along the hard-packed, rust-brown dirt trail by the side of the stream. The path was so narrow we had to walk in a single file, hemmed in on both sides with willowy vegetation that towered well over my head. The metal bucket I swung at my side brushed the bushes. To the left the land swept gently uphill, dense with oak and beech trees. To the right, I could hear the gentle rushing of the creek.

At intervals the vegetation would clear, and I could actually see the creek, about a hundred feet wide. Dad parked me at one of these openings and gave me a pole. He attached the red-and-white round bobber to the line, at the perfect distance from the weighted hook so the bait hung at the right depth in the stream.

I knew how to thread a slimy night crawler onto the hook without flinching, weaving them in and out of the hook and leaving a small piece free on the end. Dad showed me how to cast, and how to press the button to release the clear

fishing line. He showed me how to hold the line against the pole with my thumb, draw the fishing pole behind me, and gently swing it back to front and then release the line. I beamed as the bobber landed some distance out into the stream.

"Don't pull back on the pole right away when the bobber goes under. Wait until it's really under then give the pole a little tug. But don't pull too hard or you'll lose the fish."

It was a beautiful sunny day, and I was happy. I loved to cast and watch the bobber and bait fly in an arc out over the water. I loved the plopping sound when it hit the water, and I loved seeing it bob and weave as it drifted downstream with the current.

Apparently, I wasn't quite ready for the boys' fishing team. Dad announced that he would be leaving me on my own here, sitting on the copper-colored ground, casting my adult fishing rod with its bobbing bobber out into the sparkling stream, all by myself.

"You stay here, I don't want you to come to where we are 'cause you'll just mess up the fishing." And with that, he walked downstream to

the guys. I could no longer see him. I was very much on my own.

I knew he wasn't very far away. I was too content just to be out fishing "with the boys" to realize what he'd done. I was entertaining myself, the canopy of American chestnut, oak, and maple that shaded me from the hot sun rustling in the breeze. I cast out and focused on the bobber in the stream while letting my mind wander and daydream, simultaneously intent on catching a fish. My ten-year-old self was blissfully unaware that this might be a ripple cascading through my relationship with Dad.

And then it happened. The bobber began to bounce in the water. I knew something was nibbling and I waited, my heart racing. When the bobber went under the second time, I gave the pole a little tug. I felt it catch, and I knew I had something. I was careful to reel the line in slowly, give it some slack, then reel some more until I pulled my catch onto the bank.

"Dad!"

Silence.

"DAD!"

"What do you want?" The impatience clear in his voice.

"I caught a fish."

"Is it big enough to keep?" Did I hear a little respect in his voice? I heard his footsteps returning on the path.

"Yep." I was beaming. The fish was flopping beside me on the ground. I had done it. I had done it all by myself. I *was* on the team. I was.

He came back along the trail with a stringer in hand. This was a light metal chain that had lock snaps along its length. The snap would open, like a safety pin, and a metal wire was thread up through the fish's gill and out the mouth. Dad showed me how to use it, and he put the stringer with the fish attached back into the stream so we could keep it alive and fresh. Dad anchored the stringer into the bank beside me and set back off to his own spot by the creek.

I called him twice more.

"Dad, I got another fish."

"You know what to do?"

"Yep!" I knew *exactly* what to do.

All the way home I couldn't wait to see Mom and tell her what happened. I bounced into the kitchen, and showed her my bucket, filled with water and the three fish — that I had caught.

"How did the guys do?" Mom asked.

"They didn't get anything. Only me," I beamed.

It was only then that I realized what I had done. I stood there, pulling myself up to be as tall as I could. I was proud of myself and I wanted it to show. A smile spread across Mom's face. I turned away, allowing a silent, *Yes!* I had outdone them. And in particular, I had bested my Dad. *Don't say I can't come along. I'll show you,* I thought.

TEDDIE, TEDDY

*M*y mother hated her name: Thelma. Whenever anyone addressed her that way, her face became pinched and sour.

When telling the story of how she claimed her nickname, Teddy, her eyes would brighten. In the 1938 film *Having a Wonderful Time*, Ginger Rogers played the role of Thelma "Teddy" Shaw. When Mom saw the movie with friends, she was thrilled and took on the nickname as her own.

Mom spelled it T-E-D-D-I-E. When she met

Dad, he spelled it T-E-D-D-Y. He said he simply preferred it spelled the masculine way. Growing up, my brothers, sister, and I always saw it spelled Dad's way.

It was rare that Mom would disagree with Dad in front of us. I could tell when she wasn't pleased by something he said. Her eyes would narrow and her face would set, but I didn't hear her voice her displeasure. They never argued in front of us kids.

Mom was born Thelma Eileen McDowell Thomas on January 11, 1925 in Albion, a tiny little town in northwestern Pennsylvania. She had two older brothers and a mother who was aloof, critical, and distant.

"I'm going to see my aunts," Mom announced. "Who would like to come along?" I was the only one to say yes. My siblings preferred to stay home with Dad, perhaps because shorts and T-shirts were out of the question for this visit. Mom wore one of her best dresses, nylon stockings, her favorite espadrilles, and a touch of pink lipstick. I didn't mind donning the required skirt and blouse, Sunday-best shoes, and ankle socks. It was worth it—because I'd have Mom all to myself. There would be no

bickering about who got to ride in the front seat. That pleasure was all mine.

Mom focused on her driving while I chattered away or sang one of my songs. The road was smooth beneath us as we passed farm after farm, fields planted in corn or wheat, others dotted with grazing dairy herds. We passed through little hamlets with oak and maple tree-lined streets. When we drove through Albion, she pointed to the white two-story, wood-frame house on a corner lot with a porch stretching across the front.

"That's where I was born, right in that house." My head snapped from the disappearing view of the house back to Mom.

"You were born in a *house*?" My mouth gaped.

"In those days, Yvonne, there was no such thing as going to the hospital. Women just had their children at home." Mom smiled as I tried to wrap my head around that, imagining doctors and nurses turning a room in our home into a fully-functioning hospital room.

No road trip with Mom to visit her aunts was complete without at least one cemetery stop. The McDowell Cemetery in Summerhill Town-

ship, Pennsylvania, meant turning off of the main road. We drove beside railroad tracks that soon wound around in front of us. We crossed them with the slap-slap of tires over iron rails. A rutted dirt road lead to the cemetery, and Mom turned the car and parked on the verge.

Mom grabbed my hand as we walked under the wrought iron *McDowell* sign and hiked up the hill past multitudes of graves to the one at the very top. She was a woman on a mission, like a teacher imparting some critical lesson, marching us to the graves of her ancestors.

"Here lies my great grandfather." She knelt before the old headstone, running her fingers across the eroded and barely-legible text: *James McDowell. 1748 – 1796.* She stood and surveyed the rest of the graveyard. "Look at all of these McDowell graves."

I couldn't help but feel the tug of nostalgia, awed by the sense that my family played some important role in history, though I had no idea what that role was.

"The tiny town we passed through back there is called Dicksonburg today," Mom continued. "But it used to be McDowell's Corners."

James McDowell's father was Thomas Mc-

Dowell, my fourth-great grandfather. Thomas arrived in the United States from Northern Ireland in 1730, a sturdy and hardscrabble pioneer, settling in Lancaster, Pennsylvania. Fifty years later, James moved his family to a plot of land on the eastern side of the Susquehanna River. After raising a family, James and his sons left the women—his wife and daughters—and headed west across the Appalachian Mountains in search of a new and better homestead. They chose some land nestled at the top of one of the rolling hills in what would later become Crawford County in Summerhill Township in Western Pennsylvania. They cleared the land by hand, felling trees and using them to build a snug log cabin. Once it was finished, they returned to the Susquehanna, gathered the women and children, loaded everyone and everything onto wagon and pack horse, and made the return trek across the mountains to the new homestead. When they arrived, the new home—and the hope they'd built it with—had been burned to the ground by the Indians.

Six generations later, Mom was the fourth child born to Katheryn McDowell Thomas and Claude Howard Thomas. There are a few pho-

tographs of Mom when she was a child, with her cherub's face haloed by light blonde hair and her sad, older-than-they-should-have-been eyes.

When I was the age my Mom was in some of those sad pictures, I sat in a chair while Mom braided my hair, which was freshly washed and starting to dry. She parted it in the middle, pulling my long, silky hair very tight to make a French braid on each side of my head.

"Ouch!"

She rapped the comb lightly on the top of my head. "Yvonne, if you would quit wiggling and sit still, it wouldn't hurt."

"Mom, how did I get my name?"

"Well, when I was a girl, I named all of my baby dolls Yvonne. I always said my first little girl would be named Yvonne."

"But why did you name your baby dolls 'Yvonne'?"

Mom paused, holding three strands deftly between her fingers. "Yvonne was my sister. She died before I was born but your grandmother talked about her all the time. I thought the name was special."

"She died before you were born? Why?"

"She had a sickness called black diphtheria.

It must have been very catchy, because after she was gone all her things had to be boiled or burned. Grandma even had to burn her dolls."

"But Uncle Claude, Uncle Mac, Grandma and Grandpa—they didn't catch it, did they?"

Her voice dropped to a murmur. "No honey, they didn't, but your Grandpa died when I was eight, about the same age you are now. I remember he used to carry me around on his shoulders. I thought he was so tall! And oh how he made me laugh."

My grandfather had been an engineer on the Erie Lackawanna Railroad, and two years before he died, he was one of 7,000 laborers that helped to build the man-made Pymatuning Lake in 1931. It was designed to prevent the devastating floods that hit the region along the Pennsylvania-Ohio border near Conneaut, Ohio. Whenever we would cross the two-mile causeway joining the two states, Mom would say with obvious pride, "Your grandfather helped to build this."

My mother was determined not to be anything like her mother. Katheryn McDowell Thomas was born in 1884. The grief over her daughter Yvonne's death and the subsequent

death of my grandfather exacted a heavy toll. Suddenly she was a single mother with three mouths to feed. In the midst of the Great Depression, Grandma earned a living the only way she knew how. She made bread.

She would get up in the wee small hours to bake. The loaves were finished by the time her children awoke, and they'd be sent out to sell the bread. Food was scarce. Evening meals consisted of elbow macaroni in evaporated milk, seasoned with salt and pepper. When they were lucky, they'd get hamburger on Sundays, and an orange at Christmas was a special treat.

In her teens, Katheryn's parents caught her riding horseback astride, rather than side-saddle as was expected of "proper" girls. She avoided the punishing consequences of extra work by becoming ill. It was a pattern she repeated through much of the rest of her life. When life became unpleasant or hard, for example when her daughters or sons did something that displeased her, she'd fall ill. Doctors were never able to find a physical source for her ailments. We all believed she was faking.

When my mom was in high school, she dreaded coming home. She never knew whether

her mother would be asleep, whether she'd greet her at the door, or perhaps she'd be on the floor complaining of a heart attack or cancer. Sometimes my grandmother would be angry with Mom for going out and leaving her alone.

Mom shrunk into herself when she shared that Grandma's behavior was so severe that she had to be hospitalized in a mental institution.

"Don't you ever tell this to anyone. They diagnosed your grandmother as a hypochondriac. I don't ever want to hear about this from an outsider."

Hypochondriasis was a common psychiatric diagnosis doctors gave to people who became overly anxious about their health, convinced that minor symptoms were really a sign of major illness.

When she wasn't in bed, felled by what we believed at the time was imagined illness, my grandmother was a bright and talented woman. She wrote poetry, some of which was published in the local newspaper. She frequently read her poetry on the community radio station. She wrote her own lyrics and composed the accompanying music, most of the songs hymns.

She also had a talent for playing a wood-cut-

ting saw like a violin. I have a photograph of her in which she is seated on a hard-back chair, holding the curved handle of a saw, the tip of which is balanced on the floor. In her right hand she's holding the bow of a violin. To play, she would tuck the handle of the saw under her thigh, holding the metal end in her left hand, the jagged cutting edge pointed inward. She would draw the bow over the smooth edge of the saw, changing the arc of the saw blade to create the notes she wanted. The deeper the bend, the higher the pitch. She once played on the Major Bowes Amateur Hour on CBS radio in New York City. He gave her a ring as a prize, which she gave to me and I now treasure.

I have only one happy memory of my grandmother. She was making a batch of doughnuts. She made us kids stand well away from the stove, near a small table covered in white absorbent paper. She lifted the doughnut holes out of the fryer and held them above the pan until they no longer dripped hot oil. Then she transferred them to the paper. As soon as they cooled a little, she rolled them in sugar, and she smiled tenderly as she handed them to us. They were warm, sweet, and glorious.

Grandma came to live with us and stayed in a bedroom on the first floor in the back of our house. The room was always dark, the shades always closed, the bedside lamp throwing a circular pool of yellow light onto the edge of the bed, which Grandma was always in. She'd ring the cowbell on her bedside table when she needed something, and she didn't stop ringing until she got what she wanted. Quick as a flash, whoever was closest knew to answer it, however reluctantly. In the middle of the night the bell would wake the entire family, but Mom always got up in the night.

On top of the stove, in a white ceramic pan with a black handle, Mom would sterilize the glass syringes and hypodermic needles. On another burner, in a similar pot, was tap water. Mom would bring this to a boil, add sugar, and then let it cool. Sugar water was the serum for Grandma's injections, prescribed by her doctor. These placebos would quiet her for a while.

Grandma refused to eat what was prepared for the family. She survived on scrambled eggs and Kraft toffees. There was always a bag containing chocolate "fudgies" in gold foil and vanilla caramels in silver foil. We were never to

touch the vanilla, only the chocolate. Grandma's were the vanilla. If anyone attempted to offer her other food, besides the vanilla toffee or scrambled eggs, she would bark, "You know I can't eat that. My stomach won't tolerate it."

At a certain point, Mom could no longer take care of her four children *and* her bedridden mother. Dad found a bed for Grandma Katheryn in the county home, where she remained for the rest of her life.

Like answering the ringing bell, going to visit Grandma in that home became a duty we weren't allowed to shirk. The home was clean enough, the tile floors swept and shiny. The rooms were light-filled and tidy, but they always smelled of urine and feces. Occasionally, school and extracurricular activities would excuse us kids from a visit. But Mom never missed one, and every visit was the same. Grandma Kate was always the same, her voice shrill and whiny. "Where have you been, and when are you going to take me home?"

When Mom did respond, it was with remorse. "I can't take you home. I can't take care of you and the children as well. I'm sorry, I just can't do it." She would turn and quietly walk out

the door, her shoulders carrying a regret she couldn't shake. This scene repeated over the course of a decade until Grandma Kate passed away in 1966. But the legacy for Mom lived on, and for the rest of her life she carried two burdens: the guilt of putting her mother "away" in a nursing home, and the fear that she would become just like her.

In spite of, or perhaps because of, that family history, Mom always seemed to rise above challenges. She had acquired her mother's sharp intellect, but unlike her mother, she was tenacious. If there was something to learn, she'd learn it. If there was a problem, she would tackle and solve it.

Mom's aunt Ada was a major influence in her life. Some of her fondest memories were the childhood summers she spent with her beloved aunt. When Mom's chores were done in the morning and they met with approval from Ada's critical eye, Mom would head outside to explore the streams and woods. Aunt Ada would ring the bell hanging beside her vegetable garden when it was time for Mom to come back in for lunch or supper.

Ada was a power to be reckoned with. She

insisted on 'proper' behavior at all times. When Ada walked through town, she would cross to the other side of the street to avoid the beer hall. Church was a must, and she started each day reading from the bible. Table manners were critical, and she always cut toast into four small pieces so that she and my Mom—or any other female guests—could eat like a lady. She insisted that whatever Mom did, she do it well, which was not a cause for celebration, At the first sign of pride over a job well done, Ada would admonish, "Now, don't you get too proud."

All through school Mom was at the top of her class, an "A" student. She was an accomplished debater, winning trophies in regional debates. In her sophomore year, she learned to play trumpet in the school band. She sang in the high school choir. Later, after her children were raised, she sang bass in the local Sweet Adelines a cappella barbershop chorus.

Soon Mom was directing her own Sweet Adelines chorus and arranging her own music. She would baffle us all around the dinner table with talk of dominant and secondary seventh chords.

We ate our meals at the huge table in the

kitchen. When the table was cleared, the dishes done, and the floor swept, Mom and I would often head into the dining room. The room never really served its purpose—dining—but it did hold the old, dark, upright piano that sat against the wall. Mom would lift up the lid on the piano bench and pull out a music book of 1940s ballads. She'd play piano and I'd stand behind her to the left, reading lyrics over her shoulder. We'd both sing. Her voice, colored by years of smoking, was deep and resonant. We'd often be at the piano for hours before she shushed me off to bed.

We never knew when Mom was ill. If she had a cold, we could tell from her stuffed nasal passages and coughing, but she never complained about her health. Once when Mom was hospitalized, we only learned from another aunt staying with us that Mom was receiving a hysterectomy. What health insurance we had didn't cover all the bills. Dad's income wasn't enough. By the time I was thirteen, in 1960, my Mom went to work to help bring in more income.

The extra money was a big help, but Mom hated not being able to stay at home with us. She would have loved to have been home full

time until we had all graduated from high school. Unlike the situation with Grandma Katheryn, Mom's work wasn't the sort that she could do from home. She had to work outside the house, and we needed the money.

When Mom went to work I could no longer go with friends after school to the soda fountain at the pharmacy downtown. The minute classes released, I had to make the two-mile walk uphill to our house. It was my job to get supper on the table, which meant cooking for six to eight people depending on who was living with us at the time.

Despite working, Mom strived to be the mother she never had. Mom didn't bring friends home when she was a teen because she never knew how she would find her own mother. So, our house was a welcome spot for many of the thirty neighbourhood kids. Mom seemed to enjoy the chaos, noise, and commotion. She also wanted us under her watchful eye, where she could intervene if necessary, making sure everyone was safe. She disciplined us when we were out of line. She let us know what she considered to be right and wrong. She expected us to follow the rules, that we attend church every

Sunday unless we were sick. My older brother's underage hangover—or mine—didn't qualify.

What I wanted from Mom was emotional safety. Any little snooty remark or push from my brother, a neighborhood kid, or someone at school, and I would be a sobbing mess, tears spilling over my cheeks like a fountain. Mom might ask me what happened but, following my description, she'd send me off to my room until I could get myself together. I needed comfort and support, and I wanted her to intervene and fix it. She did none of it. Instead, what I heard was "You're just going to have to toughen up, or just don't let this stuff bother you. It will make your life so much easier."

She wouldn't intervene when my brothers or school kids would tease me. I'm not sure that I was a target any more frequently than any other kid, but it felt like it to me. Around third grade, I started to gain weight, a trend that continued into my early teens. Most of the jokes were about that, but as I entered puberty, my budding breasts became a target of jokes, too.

My siblings would tease me whenever we were all together as a family. As I grew up, I learned not to cry. Crying would only make mat-

ters worse, because then I'd get teased for cry-ing. When we were in the car, I couldn't get up and leave. I couldn't escape to the safety of my room or somewhere outside. I did the only thing I could do. I retreated into myself and went quiet.

If the teasing and laughter got too loud, Dad would yell from the driver's seat, "Knock it off you guys, just knock it off." He didn't offer any guidance for my brothers and sister or suggest that what they were doing that was unkind or hurtful.

I could see the back of Mom's head as she sat beside Dad in the front seat. I couldn't figure out why she didn't say anything. How difficult would it have been to use those moments to teach another kind of right from wrong? Mom was there to care for the slightest physical ail-ment. But anything emotional, and I was on my own.

When I was in my thirties and living in a nearby city, I had my impacted wisdom teeth re-moved. I came home for the recovery. Mom stocked the freezer with ice cream, made pud-ding, Jell-O, and milk toast. She prepared a tray and brought it downstairs to the family room

where she'd propped pillows behind me so I could sit up. "I love doing this. It reminds me of being able to take care of you when you were small."

Days later, my face no longer puffed up twice its normal size, we were sitting on the couch watching TV, her arm around my shoulder. "Oh, how I wish you were little. Then I could just pull you up on my lap." I basked in the support, but in the back of my mind I wondered why she couldn't stand up for me against the teasing.

Mom got pleasure and purpose by taking care of our physical needs, but she had no idea how to take care of our — or her own — emotional needs. She loved to learn new things or to tackle a problem, but she shied away from trying to understand her own history. Did she hate the name Thelma because it represented the stiff emptiness of growing up with an unavailable mother? Did she embrace the nickname Teddy, but not care about how it was spelled, because it represented freedom of choice? She was strident about keeping up appearances and not "airing dirty laundry," but she couldn't hide the fact that she wanted to be a better mother than her own

had been. She wanted to provide for us and nurture us but had no idea how to provide comfort if it wasn't physical. A bright, strong, compassionate, and loving woman who deserved to know those things for and about herself. That was my mom.

4

AUNT JOSEPHINE

She was a powerhouse packed into a tiny frame. Josephine Caputo, Dad's eldest sister, stood four-foot nine-inches tall. She had porcelain skin and a plain face, her black hair was parted on the right and fell in waves before being tucked into a roll at the nape of her neck. She made her own clothes—cotton dresses in blue and white print. Utilitarian pockets held the requisite white handkerchief. A simple crucifix graced her neck.

Aunt Josephine, born in Potenza, Italy in 1896, was twenty-two when she arrived in the United States. Scranton, Pennsylvania became her new home. She wanted to stay in Italy, be-

come a nun, and join a convent, but she felt she had no choice in the matter. She would tell us kids in her broken English, "You mind your mama and your papa!" No matter what, Josephine said, parents were to be obeyed. If her parents told her she was to emigrate with them, that would have been that.

When her mother died, it was Josephine's responsibility as eldest daughter to take over the running of the household. She raised her sister Rose and two brothers, one of whom was my father. She and Rose supported the family—like many Italian immigrants did—by working as seamstresses in a coat factory. No convent, no staying in Italy, and now being forced into roles as both parent and breadwinner was a disappointment.

The single ring she wore—a simple gold band with a crucifix—was symbolic of both her dream and her sacrifice. The band had been her mother's wedding ring. When I asked about the ring, she had to look up at me, as I was already a head taller. "I have cross put on ring, so when men see my hand, dey know I married to Christ." Her Italian accent was heavy.

Aunt Josephine came to live with us in 1962.

She'd already been working in the coat factory for thirty-five years by then, and she was having a few health issues. Even after all this time in the US, she thought my parents had to bribe the Italian police to allow her to stay with us. She would search the waste baskets in my parents' bedroom, looking at each slip of paper, sure she would find proof in the form of payment receipts.

Having once been in the role of a parent, helping raise my father, she continued to assert authority she didn't really have in our home. Mom would tell us to do something one way, and Josephine would step right in front of Mom and tell us to do it differently.

"Josephine, please hang the whites on the line, and put the colored things in the dryer," Mom would ask. It didn't matter. Josephine believed all clothes should hang on the line regardless of color. Mom would come home from work to find the colored items faded from the sun.

Aunt Jo was obsessed with cleanliness. When she was cleaning, she didn't like to be interrupted. One day, my sister Connie had been playing at something, coming in and out of the back door. Aunt Jo told Connie to stop and stay

out, but, either not understanding or not caring, her childhood pursuit of whatever it was trumped this demand from Aunt Jo. When Aunt Jo had had enough, she locked both the front and back doors, and my sister couldn't get in. Connie, not at all impressed, broke a window pane to let herself in. When Mom got home, she was furious.

"Don't you ever do that again!" she said, not to Connie, but to Aunt Jo. "Don't you ever lock one of my children out of the house again."

When I was in high school, my mother's brother Claude was also living with us. He and Dad had been hunting rabbit. Thank God the rabbit-cleaning job hadn't been assigned to me. Uncle Claude brought me portion-sized pieces and asked if I would cook them for him for lunch. I loved my kind, gentle Uncle Claude, and was happy to cook one of his favorite foods for him. He gave me simple instructions. "Just fry it in butter, add a little salt, but don't put anything else on it. I don't want this to go into the spaghetti sauce."

I was doing exactly what he asked when Aunt Jo came into the kitchen.

"You need to put vinegar in pan vit rabbit.

Vinegar take away vild taste." She was already reaching for the bottle of vinegar, leaning over the pan.

"No," I said, trying to move between her and the stove. "I am cooking this exactly the way Uncle Claude asked."

"Von't taste good."

I looked her straight in the eye. "I am going to do it just like I was asked."

I left the kitchen while the rabbit was cooking and ran upstairs to grab the laundry. When I returned, the smell of vinegar permeated the kitchen. I went rigid but said nothing. I was on to the next task, venting my anger by vigorously peeling potatoes at the kitchen sink for the evening's potato salad.

Uncle Claude came in and sat at the huge kitchen table behind me. I walked to the stove, took the warm rabbit out of the frying pan, and placed it on a platter in front of him.

"This is really, really good."

Aunt Josephine responded, "Tank you."

"I'm not talking to you," Claude barked uncharacteristically. "I'm talking to Yvonne. She fixed this for me."

I was careening between joy and rage. Joy

that Uncle Claude had spoken up for me, rage that Aunt Jo had gone behind my back with the vinegar and then took credit for the meal. I launched a potato as hard as I could, letting it fly from my hand. It rocketed across the room, bouncing off the Naugahyde couch and just missing the picture window before landing with a thud on the hard floor. I went to the refrigerator, slamming through its contents until I had the makings of a sandwich. Mom had walked into the kitchen and heard it all. I grabbed a book and my sandwich and stomped out of the house, across the road, and deep into the woods. My stomping continued until I reached my haven, a huge ten-foot boulder sheltered under a canopy of trees. I sat on the ground with my back resting against that sweet boulder. My lunch and my book lasted until the rage subsided.

Aunt Jo used to tell my mother, "Don't tell children dat you love them. If you do, dey will take advantage of you." I suspect Dad's economy with praise was because of the way Aunt Jo had raised him. We heard from him when something was wrong, but rarely when something was right.

Aunt Jo's fastidiousness meant we were required to do things in a certain way. She'd only drink tea out of one of two porcelain cups with tiny roses on them. One had a visible crack which Aunt Jo said made it unsanitary and unacceptable. Many times, the one perfect cup would go "missing." After a few minutes of torment, one of us kids would find a way to quietly return the good cup to its normal place.

It was from Aunt Jo that I learned the joy of true Italian cooking and the associated hospitality. The first thing she would say when anyone walked in the door was, *"Mangiare!"* Eat! She would open the refrigerator to see what was available, and with her deft hands she'd craft something delicious from nothing. I can still taste her incredible pizza, and I have no idea how she made it.

When I had grown and was living on my own, I still returned to my parent's house for free laundry services. One day I arrived with a basket filled to the brim. In a plastic bag on top of it were the makings of a man's sport coat. It was going to be a Christmas gift for my boyfriend. I was proud to show Aunt Jo how I'd made the plaid match along the seams. She said

I was ready to do the hand stitching along the collar and the lapel of the jacket, and she'd show me how to make sure it would roll the right way.

We sat in the family room, on stools in front of the fireplace. Her tiny fingers flew, making precise stitch after stitch on the hair canvas interfacing. Little Vs began to appear as she worked her way down the inside of the lapel. She handed the jacket back to me. "You do now, just da same." I did my best to do what she said, my hands clumsy by comparison, my stitches nowhere as neat and precise.

We always had one or more relatives—and friends—living with us. Friends of my father lost their home in a fire and stayed with us for a while. Both my mother's brothers, her mother, my Aunt Ada, and Aunt Jo. My parents provided shelter when there was nowhere else to go.

But Aunt Jo's interference became too much. She spent her last years with the Oblate Sisters of the Sacred Heart, and then in the John XXIII Home in Hermitage, Pennsylvania, which was run by the Benedictine Sisters. On one of Dad's many hour-and-a-half drives to visit her, he insisted that I come along. I knew

that Aunt Jo had suffered a stroke and she was no longer able to walk. I expected to see her sitting in a wheel chair.

What I didn't expect was that she'd become a sweet, and endearing little old lady, opposite of what she'd once been, except for the "little" part. The black hair of her youth had given way to white with streaks of light grey, kept in the same roll at the nape of her neck. As I listened to her delightful stories about Italy, and about my father when he was a boy, I realized that sometimes sacrifice is necessary for the sake of family, and that there is value in caring for and helping the less fortunate.

The stroke had destroyed the part of Aunt Jo's brain that had housed the paranoia and the driving need to command and control. In her mind, Aunt Jo was more than a patient at the convent. She believed she had finally become a nun.

5

THE CAMP KISS

Mom called me into the kitchen, a letter in her hand and a huge grin on her face. "You're going to camp again this year!"

I nearly dropped my school books on the floor. I thought we couldn't afford camp this year. I'd finally resigned myself to having to watch my brother and sister for the entire summer.

I'd already been in the Girl Scout troop for three or four years. When there was a little extra money at home, my parents would send me to camp. I loved it, a week away from home, living in a cabin, being outdoors, and having fun. The

camp, located on a small lake thirty miles from home, consisted of bare-boned cabins gathered in a semicircle on a large grassy lawn and shaded by oaks and maples. Each cabin had a screen door through which we had a clear view of the lake. If we had to pee during a downpour, we'd run, screaming and alive with adventure, clear across the camp to the building with the bathroom.

We did all the usual camp things: crafts, games, swimming, and singing around the night-time campfires. At meal time, we marched cabin by cabin down to the mess hall.

"It's being paid for by the troop," Mom's smile got wider as her eyes slid between the letter and my face. "And they've asked our permission for you to be a counsellor."

Being a counsellor meant I'd live in one of the cabins with the younger girls. I'd be responsible for their care. Could I handle it? I was pretty sure I could. After all, wasn't I was already thirteen? Hadn't I already been babysitting, taking care of other people's children?

I was still soaring from the promotion when Dad drove me to the drop-off point for my ride to camp. It was a warm summer day with a

cloudless blue sky, and the trees that lined the street provided a shady canopy across the sidewalk. Dad pulled over in front of the house belonging to the designated camp driver. He went to the trunk, took out my suitcase, and set it on the sidewalk. We waited a little while in silence.

When the driver and some of the other campers came out and greeted us, Dad reached over and took my hand—in front of them. "You be good and take care of those kids. Do your job. We'll see you at the end of the week. Have a good time." Then, he leaned closer and kissed my cheek.

My heart rose into my throat. I froze for what felt like minutes, not wanting to move. I wanted the moment to last forever. My father had kissed me! In front of other people! My cheek was warm where his bristly lips touched. My father had kissed me goodbye.

I arrived at camp early that year to receive training as a counsellor. This was a big deal. I could hardly get my head around the fact that I was no longer going to be one of the kids being cared for—I was going to be the one responsible for the safety and well-being of the three little girls who shared my cabin.

I learned how to make sure everything was done in a timely fashion: waking up, straightening the cabin, faces washed, teeth brushed, and at the dining hall on time. At lights out, it was my job to make sure everyone was in bed and absolutely quiet. I was supposed to know where each of my charges was at all times. It was a big responsibility.

After my week at camp, I walked into the kitchen to see Mom. She greeted me with an embrace and a huge smile. "Did you have a good time?"

My first answer wasn't about how I kept track of my cabin mates. It wasn't how hard it was to get some of the girls up and going in the morning. It wasn't about how I felt so grown up when I told them to do something and they did it.

"Mom, Dad kissed me on the cheek—in front of people—before he said goodbye!" My hand went to the very spot on my cheek, where the memory was as bright as it had been the second after it happened.

SUNDAYS AT THE LAKE

For the Caputo family, every Sunday was for church. Rain, shine, illness, it didn't matter. Even when we were away on vacation, Mom and Dad found a Catholic church and we'd attend.

For several years, going to early Mass preceded a day at the lake. We didn't complain because we loved going to the lake afterward. We'd enter the church filing down the aisle, Dad in the lead and Mom bringing up the rear. The first pew on the left was our regular spot. I felt like we were all on display, and perhaps that was my parents' intention. They expected us to behave and be silent, unless murmuring prayers or

singing hymns in the appropriate places. They tolerated no tomfoolery, dishing out a minor slap on the hand to quell any misbehavior.

Mom and Dad often sacrificed comfort so they could afford to send all four of us kids to St. Agatha's parochial school. Private education was expensive, but Mom and Dad sent us anyway.

We didn't get into bed without first dropping to our knees to say our nightly prayers.

Breakfast, lunch, and dinner started only after one of the family said grace. Picnics were no exception. When it was time to eat, Mom would call us all together. The rough wooden picnic table was laden with all kinds of mouth-watering goodies, but first everyone had to be in place, heads bowed, and grace said before one morsel was consumed.

Preparations for our lake outings always started the day before. Either in the afternoon or after supper, Mom would be busy in the kitchen, and I was her helper.

"Yvonne, put the eggs on to boil. Set the timer for twenty minutes, and while you're waiting for them to cook, chop the onions and the celery," she'd coach, and I'd try to remember

everything I was supposed to do. "The potatoes and macaroni are already in the fridge. We can throw the salads together when your things are done. I put the cake in the oven, and I'll get the burgers ready."

As soon as we got home from church, Mom and I would pack the picnic basket and the cooler. It was standard fare: hot dogs, hamburgers, potato and macaroni salad, and often cake for dessert.

Dad would have the fishing gear ready, and he and the boys would pack the blue and white Ford Fairlane station wagon. His usual speech would be ringing through the house. "What's taking so long? The day's a-wasting! It will be nightfall before we get going."

The seven-mile drive took us up a winding hill. We'd chatter or sing or play games the whole way. When the car finally crested the hill, we'd all be quiet, gazing down at the private little twenty-three-acre lake sitting in the midst of the tall yellow pines. Dad would show our family summer pass at the gate.

Chores came before play. Mom and kids transferred the food to a picnic table nestled on a carpet of pine needles, dappled shadows on the

ground from the sun shining through the trees. Mom always tried to choose a table in the shade. "It will help the cooler do its job."

Dad, on the other hand, gathered his fishing gear and headed off to the lake. "Call me when it's time to eat." He'd go far enough that we couldn't see him, but not so far that he couldn't hear the call for supper.

Mom would grab a couple of old blankets and hand each of us a towel. We walked as fast as we could to the swimming beach. Taking corners of the blankets, we stretched them until they were smooth on the hard ground. Then it was a race to see who could get into the water first, and who was brave enough to dunk fully in the chilly water. Mom kept constant vigil over us from her place on the blanket.

We swam for most of the afternoon, with the exception of forced time out of the water, when Mom insisted we be still and let our skin dry. We'd sit on the blanket or go back to the picnic table, where we'd play the board games or card games that we'd packed along with all of the gear and food.

"Dad, come and set up the camp stove. It's almost time to eat." Then, and only then, did

Dad come back to join us. He hooked up the camp stove and set about cooking the burgers and the hot dogs. He sat at the table with us, but he was quiet. The chatter swelled around him.

I was old enough to be upset about his detachment. Why was it important for us all to be together at church, if he'd then take off by himself for the entire family day at the lake? I desperately wanted to be with him, talk to him, play with him, and have fun together. Had we done something he didn't like? Was there something wrong with us? With me? Why didn't he spend some of his time with us? Most of the time, Mom seemed to love being with us. Why didn't he?

TRAINS AND PLANES

*D*ad got his first balsa wood model airplane kit when he was ten. One piece of balsa, the wings, slipped through a slot in another, the fuselage. The tail slipped into a notch at the end.

"Under the nose there was place to hook the rubber band," Dad told me one day after I'd asked him how his fascination with models got started. "I'd pull the band back as taut as it would go, then I'd let go." He mimed the remembered movements, pinching his thumb and forefinger together, drawing them back until they created an O, and then release to launch the plane.

Dad also built a model railroad that took up one whole side of our basement. The locomotives, train cars, and tiny people were made of dark plastic. Dad's steady hand would paint clothes and facial features. His tiny trains would run through a tunnel in the mountain, and past a lake in the valley. There was a rail yard with a coal chute, water tank, and turntable. There were wooden outbuildings and a depot. Trees dotted the landscape, everything perfectly to scale.

I wasn't allowed to touch anything, certainly not the controls to make the train go. But I was allowed to look. Dad put a wooden crate in front and gave me a hand to climb up so that I could see. I thought it was magic. He'd push tiny buttons and levers and transform the stationary model into a miniature full-motion replica of the real thing. I stood transfixed as the locomotive whistled by, pulling railcars around the track. I especially loved the caboose. I imagined sitting in that little caboose, a tiny version of myself, waving and smiling up at the life-sized Dad and me looking back down. My father, the magician!

For a time, Dad took up photography. He'd take pictures of anything and everything and de-

velop the photos in his basement dark room, which was always off limits. "There are too many dangerous chemicals in there, and I don't want you getting hurt," he said. What I heard was, *"You can't be trusted not to mess things up, so stay out!"*

In the beginning he was developing and printing black and white photos, but at some point we began to see his work in color. He told me he'd discovered a simpler process to print in color, and he was so excited that he approached several banks for a loan. He wanted to set up his own business, but bank after bank turned him down. He never said why, or maybe he never knew. Shortly thereafter, the sour taste of rejection dampening his enthusiasm, he lost his passion for photography.

When I was in my teens, Dad returned to his childhood love of building model airplanes. We moved into a new house my senior year. His four-by-eight-foot table dwarfed the family room and was covered with parts and pieces and paint

that would someday be the next model, and his desk drawer was filled with blueprints.

He'd lay out the plans and make templates for each part of the plane's fuselage with tracing paper, cut those parts out, and assemble. Dad's model airplanes weren't made to sit on a shelf: most had wing spans of three to four feet. Some would hang from the ceiling in the family room or garage. Others, complete with engines, were built to fly.

Good-weather Sundays and Wednesdays were fly days. When he asked me along, I jumped at the chance. Dad would load the planes, special fuel, and remote controls into the back of the van. We'd drive twenty miles to the field, which was maintained by the so-called "fly guys." A long expanse of neatly mowed grass allowed for hours of take-offs, flights, and landings.

Dad put fuel in the engine and, with his index finger, gave the propeller a twirl. (Sometimes it took several twirls until the engine caught.) He set the plane down on the close-clipped grass, picked up the hand control, and started taxiing the plane down the field. Pushing and pulling the levers, the model would pick up

speed. At just the right time, another gentle hand movement would lift the plane off the ground. I watched in awe as the model plane my dad had built climbed in the air. I watched Dad deftly move the levers on the transmitter, up or down, left or right, just a tap or more solid pressure, and in response the plane would turn, bank, descend, or ascend. At some point, Dad would bring it back around to land, unless of course it didn't.

One of the many crashes happened as I watched, the sky a crystal blue. Dad was maneuvering the plane above the tall pines—within sight but way over our heads. Suddenly the engine cut out. Nose down, the plane started to spin out, plummeting earthward and hitting the ground with a whack. The plane Dad had poured hours and weeks into building, painting, and loving lay motionless, its nose buried in the grass and pieces scattered around.

Dad walked over, bent down, and picked the plane up, nonplussed. When I asked him what happened, he said, "When I tear it apart, I'll see if I can figure it out. But, sometimes, there's no explanation. It just happens." The model went back onto his work bench. If it could be rebuilt,

Dad would find a way. If it couldn't, it was the perfect excuse for him to build a new one.

I'd watch the magic in his hands as he built these model airplanes, step by step. He'd transform flat pieces of balsa into a three-dimensional fuselage, complete with wings and a tail. He'd add the skin of the aircraft, then meticulously apply the decals and mount the engine. There, sitting on a table in our house, was a smaller—but not miniature—version of the real thing.

My awe of him and his creations did nothing to dispel my resentment. Dad could spend hours at his work table. Hours when he didn't seem to be aware of anything happening around him. He didn't notice if there was anything he could do to help Mom, and he was too focused on his table to have conversations with his children. I'd watch him, wanting nothing more than for him to stop, look at me, notice me, and talk to me.

THIRTY-FIVE CENTS

*E*ven with both parents working, money was in short supply. But Mom had ways of making the food dollars stretch. She added dry powdered milk and water in equal parts to the fresh, whole milk delivered to the house. She only went to the grocery store once per week, and never without her list. Once the food was gone, there was no more until the next week's grocery day.

Meals were a family event. Everyone was present at 5:30 p.m. sharp, which was when Dad walked through the door at the end of his work day. Meat, potatoes, and a vegetable was stan-

dard fare. Dessert was canned peaches, pineapple, or sliced bananas with milk and sugar.

We ate three square meals a day, and never went to bed hungry. Still, it was obvious to me that Mom worked as hard to stretch the food dollars as Dad did to bring them home. I didn't get an allowance, so when I needed money for something, I had to ask Dad. I would delay as long as possible, because I was sure that he was going to snap at me. I hated the confrontation.

There was a high school dance every Saturday at the YWCA. I knew my boyfriend would be there, so I *had* to go. I needed thirty-five cents to get in, and I didn't have it. Several times I approached the living room, where Dad sat working, only to turn around and go back to my chores. The clock on the kitchen wall told me I was running out of time. I still had dinner to cook, and I would need hours to bathe, iron my dress, and put on make-up. Summoning all my courage, I went and stood at the door. Dad was standing next to his desk with his back to me.

"Dad," I said. No answer. A little louder, I tried again. "Dad, can I have thirty-five cents to go to the dance tonight?"

He turned quickly, looked at me, and barked, "Thirty-five cents? What do you think I'm made of? Money?" I hated that tone. It made me afraid of him. I rarely knew why he was angry, what I'd done wrong. Or worse, had I done something stupid? What was it?

I was about to back away in defeat when he jammed his hand into his pocket, pulled out a handful of coins, and counted out the amount I'd asked for.

"Thanks, Dad." Smiling, with a huge sense of relief, I turned and left the room.

Dad was never mean, but he was often gruff. His voice was deep, resonant, and loud. The Italian members of my family would say that his manner of speech was normal. The Scotch-Irish side would characterize it quite differently. My mother's tone, even those rare times she'd yell, was nothing like his. She shared her displeasure in a look. I wasn't afraid of the look, but at the same time I knew she meant business.

One day when I got home from high school, Dad called me into the living room. He was standing very still, hands in his pockets. "Yvonne, where were you yesterday?"

"I was at the library."

His eyes grew sad and his usually-brisk tone was gone. "No, you weren't. You were seen downtown at the pharmacy with your boyfriend. I am so disappointed in you, Yvonne, I never thought you'd lie to me."

He walked past me and out into the dining room. I stood in the same spot for a long, long time. He hadn't yelled or barked. This time it was the calm, gentle tone, and the word "disappoint" that echoed over and over in my brain and shook me to the core. I had let him down. My heart was in my shoes.

SILVER FRITZ

When I was about fifteen, Dad came walking through the back door with a dirty dog following behind, its tail tucked tight to its backside and its head low. He'd seen this dog outside a house, chained on a short lead and unable to move or lay down. There was no shade and no water. Dad knocked on the door and said if they weren't going to properly care for the dog, he was.

Fritz looked more like an oversized drowned rat than a dog. He was covered in mud and skinny as a rail. After a bath, which only marginally improved his appearance, he greedily ate

what was set in front of him. Fritz didn't trust us kids, cowering whenever one of us tried to approach. His fear spoke volumes about the type of treatment he was used to. Dad told us to be patient, and little by little the dog began to understand he was safe with us. Fritz was soon one of the family.

Fritz was a beautiful Weimaraner. He was sleek, with a long snout and huge ears, a silver-grey coat, and liquid pale-blue eyes. He was gentle, consistently yielding to Bub, our beagle, who clearly had more family seniority. An over-stuffed chair in the dining room became Fritz's own—unless Bub got there first. With only a look from the much smaller dog, Fritz would leave to find somewhere else to rest.

He had a stinky habit that we simultaneously hated and found uproariously funny. Fritz would walk into a room, often the one where Mom was hosting her bridge club, and pass foul-smelling gas. Then he'd turn tail and leave. However awful his habit, he was Dad's buddy, following him from room to room. He'd also accompany Dad hunting, where he was a natural. He just picked up on what Dad wanted him to do. If Dad shot a pheasant, Fritz would retrieve

it in his soft mouth, dropping it at Dad's feet and looking up at him with those pools of sky blue. Their bond grew.

One bright summer day, in front of our house, Fritz was struck by a car and killed. Dad and Uncle Claude put Fritz's big body on the metal coil spring of a single bed and carried him up the hill behind the house to bury him.

I'd arrived home from a trip to the library, oblivious, and was about to walk up the hill to join my dad. But something about his body language made me stop. I noticed Fritz lying still on his side, Dad driving a shovel into the ground, sluicing up mounds of earth and tossing them to the side.

Transfixed, I stood and watched. I didn't know what to do. I was sick about Fritz, and I knew my father must be feeling even worse about losing his companion. As Dad turned to dump another shovel-full of black earth onto the growing pile, sunshine reflected off his wet cheeks.

The tears were a shock. I expected a brave face. If our roles were reversed, he would have told me this sort of thing happens. I was sur-

prised, yet somehow pleased to know he felt emotion the same as me.

I wanted to hug him and to comfort him. But we didn't have that kind of relationship. I turned and went back into the house. Dad never knew I'd been there or that I had seen his tears.

TURBULENCE

*D*ad loved flying models, but he loved real planes even more. If there was an airshow nearby, he'd get tickets for the family. We'd spend hours watching planes twisting and turning in gyro acrobatics that defied logic as well as gravity.

When I was thirteen, Dad took my older brother Mickey and me to New Jersey. Dad was still in the Air Force Reserves and he was scheduled for his mandatory two-week stint on active duty at McGuire Air Force Base in Burlington County, New Jersey.

My Aunt Rose lived nearby, which meant that Mickey and I could stay with her while

Dad was fulfilling his reserves obligation. On the weekend, however, Dad took us to the base for its annual air show and introduced us to the Air Force Thunderbirds. These jets screamed in formation overhead. They'd separate and loop, wispy white contrails like ghosts in their wake. I was impressed. Dad was in heaven.

It was the tarmac displays that captured me. Row after row of planes glistened in the sun. Biplanes of a bygone era, small privately-owned single-engine planes, and modern jets. The Lockheed C-130A, ninety-seven feet long with its tail thirty-eight feet high and its 137-foot wingspan made my jaw drop. It was enormous. How would that monstrosity ever get off the ground?

Sometimes we were allowed to crawl inside, sit in the seats, and touch the instrument panels. Sitting in the pilot's seat, I imagined myself taking control, taking off and flying, and then returning to land. Dad patiently answered as many questions as he could. "I really wish there was a B-24 that I could show you. It was the one I flew during the war."

Five years after that airshow reminiscence, when I was a sophomore in college, a high

school friend had arranged a blind date for me for Notre Dames' homecoming. I purchased a cheap ticket with my meager savings, and Mom and Dad drove me to the airport. Dad was grinning from ear to ear when we got out of the car at the terminal. Snow crunched under our feet.

"Mike, I don't think we should let Yvonne get on that plane," Mom said. "This is such awful weather." There'd been an unusually heavy early snowfall.

"This is the best possible weather for her to fly. The colder it is, the less turbulence she'll have." Dad was right. Oddly, Mom was right too. The plane ride was as smooth as silk, but the South Bend airport was closed due to the heavy snowfall and our flight was diverted to Chicago. My view as we prepared to land in this huge metropolis was breathtaking, with a sea of twinkling city lights. I imagined Dad looking down from his navigator's seat and felt a warm connection.

My second plane ride was ten years later. I was still single, a teacher, and grabbed any chance I could to travel. A colleague invited me to join her on a road trip to Colorado.

We took the northern route, through miles of

Missouri cornfields. I gasped as the Grand Tetons came into view in Wyoming. We traveled the southern route on the way home, and the Petrified Forest in Arizona gave me goose bumps.

To save money, we camped out under the open skies, the sunsets serving a show of shifting gold, fuchsia, and aubergine.

While my friend was visiting her brother in Denver, Colorado, I paid a visit to my great uncle in Cedaredge. To get there, I had to take a plane to Grand Junction. When I crossed the tarmac at the airport, overnight case in hand, fingers of fear tickled my heart. How was the small twin-engine plane in front of me supposed to get me over the Rocky Mountains?

For an hour that felt like ten, turbulence produced a deep thudding in my chest. I tried to distract myself by reading my book, bouncing and all. I stole a glance out the window, but that just made matters worse. Where would we make an emergency landing amongst all those peaks of jagged rock?

As though the pilot could read my thoughts, we began a descent through a mountain pass so narrow it looked to me there were only a few

inches of clearance beyond the wingtips. I hadn't been aware my flight would have to make a stop before Grand Junction. The terminal, off to my right as we approached for a landing, was a white, one-story clapboard building that suggested the horse-and-buggy era and not modern air travel.

My fears weren't realized, thankfully. The landing was smooth, and during the takeoff shortly thereafter I willed my eyes to focus on the interior of the plane and not watch the rock faces whizzing past my window. I wondered what in the world Dad saw in this thing called flying.

THE GREAT DIVIDE

*D*ad would sometimes talk about a job he had in the south in the early 1940s, before the war. He'd tell us about the boarding house he lived in, referring to the servants as "darkies," using the common vernacular of the time. But it revealed an attitude about African Americans that made me uncomfortable. I knew Dad was a blowhard, talking up a good racist line—unless he was actually standing in front of a black person, at which point he was respectful. As I grew into adulthood, we argued about race relations. A lot.

And then I accepted a teaching position in

an all-black school in Cleveland, Ohio. He was not happy.

"What the hell did you go and do that for?" he spat.

"Because I want to make a difference," I reasoned.

"You can make a difference right here in your home town."

I was tired of this now-familiar prelude to a race argument.

"I am going to do it in Cleveland," I retorted, a little more hotly than necessary.

That's how many of our conversations would go. It was like we were on a tennis court. Lob and return, lob and return. We'd deliver our words with a *whack,* and the other would smash them back with a harder, faster retort. Neither of us would back down. Neither of us would let the other win. The match would end with one of us turning forcefully and walking away.

One Thanksgiving, we had traveled to another state to spend the holiday with Dad's niece. Dad did all of the driving, mother was in the front seat beside him, and Aunt Josephine and I sat in the back. We managed the four-hour drive together without a cross word about some

social issue. In fact, there wasn't much conversation at all, which suited me just fine.

The women were in the kitchen preparing food, and the men, my niece's boys included, were in the TV room watching football. There was lots of laughter coming from both rooms. All the burners and the oven were on, condensation coating the kitchen windows like gray clouds before a rain. The house was filled with wonderful aromas of the deliciousness to come.

Nine of us gathered around the table, prepared to sit for several hours. The courses flowed according to Italian tradition. There would eventually be turkey, stuffing, sweet potato casserole, and green beans. First there was Italian wedding soup, followed by an antipasto. Next, pasta with sauce and Italian sausage. Pumpkin and apple pie along with ricotta cheese pie would finish the meal.

I never made it to the turkey course. Somehow when I wasn't looking, the conversation slipped to the subject of race.

There were plenty of hot-button race issues during that time, and Dad and I saw opposite sides of every one of them. Segregation, Martin Luther King Jr., my teaching job in Cleveland.

He swung a strong overhand serve, and I returned with a forceful backhand. Back and forth, back and forth. In good Italian fashion, the conversation got more heated and louder with each passing moment. The rest of the table fell silent. Aunt Josephine spoke up and chastised me,

"Don't you talk to your papa like that!"

That just added fuel to my fire, an explosion against his resistance to my reasoning imminent. Then my brain kicked in with a warning: *Don't say another word, Yvonne. Because if you do, it will be something you'll never be able to take back*. Where that wisdom came from, I'm not sure, but I'm grateful that it did.

I pushed my chair back from the table. "I'm going for a walk."

"Good idea," Dad said, his face red.

"You apologize to your papa first," said Aunt Josephine.

I threw a fiery look in her direction, grabbed my coat, and stormed out the kitchen door. I didn't know the neighborhood, so I kept walking around the same large block. I reached the end of one street, turned right, turned right again and again until I passed the house. I was

locked in my own head and didn't notice anyone or anything else. Over and over I played with all the things I could have said, should have said, wished I'd said. How could he — in this day and age — continue to believe those things? How could he, who had suffered at the end of the prejudicial stick for being Italian, continue to say what he said?

The sky had begun to darken when I finally headed back inside. The walk had helped my anger subside but it was replaced with a deep, aching sadness. How could I be this man's daughter? He could talk up a good racist line in white company, then be perfectly decent and re-spectful when any black person — or other ethnic minority — was actually standing in front of him looking him in the eye. Was he being insincere? Or, as I suspected was the case, was he a walking contradiction?

I must have been gone for hours. By the time I arrived back at the house, the table had been cleared, and the dishes were done. The dining room was dark. Mom was sitting on the couch, but she looked up when I came into the room.

"I've been waiting for you. Your father has gone to bed, as have the others."

"I had to leave before I said something really hurtful."

Her face was sober, her eyes clear but sad. "Yvonne, if you want to know your father, you will have to go to him. He isn't going to change. If you are ever to have the relationship you want with him, you'll have to make that happen."

I took her words to heart, and little by little I shifted how I responded to Dad. I tried to meet him where he was.

I avoided anything that might trigger an argument. I talked about things I knew would interest him. I asked his advice. Slowly, the tension between us eased. We weren't yet where I wanted us to be, but we were closer than we'd been.

Several years later, when it was very clear that my dying car could no longer take care of me, Dad suggested it was time I buy a new one. And he knew where I could get a really good deal.

"Your cousin Tony owns a dealership. Why don't you call him and see what he might have? I think you'd get a really good deal."

It was good advice. Tony gave me a sweet deal

on a 1972 Dodge Dart with a slant-six engine. It was a deep forest green with a black vinyl roof. It wasn't my style, but I wasn't prepared to say no to either man. Besides, Tony kept reassuring both Dad and me that the car was safe and reliable.

It was true. What the car lacked in sportiness or elegance it made up for in dependability. It took me back and forth to work, and it was good in the snow. So good that my friends and I always took my car when we went cross-country skiing.

One summer, I called Dad.

"I want to come home this weekend. I'm learning to work on the Dart. Is it okay if I grab your tool box?"

"You're learning to work on your car?" His voice was tinged with disbelief.

"Yup. The spark plugs and oil need to be changed."

That Saturday, a sparkling June day with clear blue skies and a gentle breeze, I raised the garage door and backed the car halfway in. I grabbed Dad's tool box and went to work.

I was loosening one of the spark plugs when Dad came out and leaned on the front left

fender, peering under the hood to see if I knew what I was doing.

"You know, it always bothered me that you went to your mother for advice and you didn't come to me," Dad said. "I know it's because you don't want to hear what I have to say."

I pulled out the first spark plug, turned to face him and looked him in the eye.

"No Dad, it wasn't that. It was that you didn't *talk* to me. You were always yelling."

I had come to where he was that day. He and I had crossed a great divide. And the gruff tone that had made me afraid disappeared—mostly— into the rear-view mirror.

DUST IN THE WIND

*M*y baby brother Mark had a rough start in life. And his life was hard.

It was February 18, 1952. Dad took Mom to the hospital in the morning when she started labor. He then left to go to work, telling her he'd be back periodically to check on her. The hours kept passing, and her doctor came in several times. He told her that everything was fine, but this birth might take a while.

Having been through labor and delivery three times before, Mom knew something wasn't right.

"Mike, something is really wrong," Mom said when Dad returned. "I know what I'm sup-

posed to feel. The doctor says I'm fine. But I'm not fine, and I'm scared."

Dad turned on his heels to go find the obstetrician. He returned instead with our family doctor.

The doctor examined Mom. When he was finished, he pulled Dad aside out of Mom's hearing. "Mike, the baby is turned sideways. It can't be delivered that way, and Teddy is exhausted. I will do my best to turn it, but at this point if I can't do it, I am not sure either of them will make it."

It took four attempts at kneading and manipulating Mom's huge belly, but the baby did finally turn. Mark was born.

Despite the traumatic birth and being terribly sick as an infant, Mark was a cheerful kid. As a toddler, his short little legs would propel him quickly across the lawn, his diaper drooping and a smile radiating on his round face.

Things began to shift as he reached sixth grade. He wasn't doing well academically. It wasn't that he didn't understand the material. He was so bright that he was bored. He hated having to go over the same things time and again. And homework was a battle.

"I already know this stuff, why do I have to do it again?"

Mom started to think Mark's teachers were part of the problem.

"I will not have the nuns comparing him to his brother and sisters in front of the class. He is not Mickey, or Yvonne, or Connie. He is himself." And she yanked him out of Catholic school.

With that, Mark became the only Caputo sibling to attend public school. It helped, but only marginally. His grades were adequate, but they certainly weren't the straight A's he was capable of achieving. At one point he was suspended from high school after a verbal battle with a teacher. In true Caputo fashion, Mark refused to back down from an argument.

He and Dad began to fight, too, most often over political issues. If the government believed that we should be at war, Dad believed we should be a war. Mark, however, was on the opposite side. The country was knee-deep in the Vietnam War, and Dad and Mark's arguments were bitter and divisive. Mark was always on the liberal side of a social issue and Dad was on the conservative side. The battles often happened at the dinner ta-

ble, and Mark would get up, go to his room, and pick up his guitar. He turned to music for comfort.

Somehow, he managed to turn his grades around and get into college. During the first semester of his freshman year, Mom called to tell me Mark had been found unconscious on the floor of his dorm room, a bottle of pills by his side. He was rushed to the hospital where doctors pumped his stomach and saved his life.

I went home to be with Mom and Dad. I sat on the sofa in the living room, with a view of the front lawn. The leaves on the maple trees had turned to amber, ochre, and russet. The lawn was still a lush green, and Mom's pink roses were in bloom all along the driveway. Dad was seated in the amber cushy chair on the right side of the window. Mom was on the left.

"The psychiatrist said that Mark showed some signs of depression and anxiety, but the bigger problem was his anger," Dad said.

We talked some more, but there didn't seem to be anything else to explain Mark's brush with death.

"If I've ever done anything to hurt you kids, I'm so sorry."

I'd never heard Dad say anything like that before. He wasn't one to say sorry to anyone about anything.

It told me that despite what I had believed, Dad thought about his relationship with his children. It told me that sometimes he questioned what and how he did as a father. This was a side of him I'd never seen. He'd shown both compassion and vulnerability.

Dad pulled Mark out of college and brought him home. Mark complained of being tired all of the time, and Dad objected to Mark's taking prescription drugs to combat the so-called anxiety. Dad insisted on another medical opinion and a complete physical. When the new doctor checked Mark's blood pressure, he said that it was way too high for Mark's age. He then checked the pressure in the opposite arm and in both of his legs. He couldn't get a pressure reading in either leg. Further tests revealed that Mark had a congenital narrowing of the aorta, which resulted in insufficient blood supply to his legs. This—not anxiety or depression—was the cause of Mark's tiredness.

Mom was sick with guilt. "I can't believe all

these years I believed his teachers. I believed them when they said he was just plain lazy."

Surgery corrected the problem.

"I can't believe my feet feel so warm," Mark said during a visit shortly after. "I thought it was normal to have cold feet all the time."

Mark never went back to college. He spent the next years working in janitorial and manufacturing jobs. He moved around, living with sister Connie in Wisconsin and brother Michael in Alabama. He moved back to Meadville, married, and two short years later divorced.

There was, however, a shift in Mark's relationship with Dad. Perhaps it started with Dad's insistence on the complete physical. Maybe it helped Mark and Dad see each other in a new light. They began to spend more time together. As often as they could manage, they were off hunting in the woods or fishing on the lake.

Mark continued playing the guitar in several bands and he started to teach at a local music school. He called me with the news.

"Sis, I'm going back to school," Mark said, the words tumbling out of his mouth. "I've been accepted at Mercyhurst College in the music program. I'm going to be a music teacher!"

I was elated. He'd found a life purpose, and he was going to use his God-given intelligence. I was secretly thrilled that he was following in my steps. Teaching was sacred to me. Had he listened to me, finally? I'd been telling him, for years, that if he wanted to change the world, he would have to do it *within* the system instead of throwing rocks at it. I knew once Mark stood in front of a classroom, he'd begin to change the world one student at a time.

Shortly afterward, at his invitation, I visited Mark over a weekend in Pittsburgh. I stayed with his girlfriend, Mary Catherine, who was also my best friend. We took in a Gordon Lightfoot concert on Friday. On Saturday we shopped at the largest music store in Pittsburgh.

Mark bought the sheet music for "Dust in the Wind," a song released the year before by the group Kansas. I loved the melody and the orchestration, but the words, about nothing lasting forever and that we humans are only dust in the wind, I found depressing.

We visited the Carnegie Mellon Art Museum and walked slowly around a three-dimensional display in a riot of color. We had a dinner of pizza and beer, then went back to the apartment.

I curled up on the couch in the living room and Mark sat on the floor with his back to the door. He picked up his classical guitar and started to play. I was mesmerized, awed by his ability. I hadn't known how good he was. The strumming guitar lulled me to a blissful sleep.

Mark's warm and gentle smile, crystal clear and in slow motion, was with me as I sped back toward my parents' home. The memory gave reassurance that all was finally well in his life and all was well with us.

When I got home Sunday night, I called Mark and Mary Catherine to thank them for one of the best weekends of my life.

"Oh Mark, it was so wonderful. I loved all of it. I loved being with you and hearing you play. You're incredible."

"It was good, wasn't it? I mean the weekend *and* my playing," he teased.

"I love you, Mark. Thanks again."

"I love you too, sis. See you soon."

My phone started to ring at dawn a few days later, on April 19, 1978. I was annoyed as I

threw off the covers and climbed out of bed. My roommates were closer—why didn't they answer it? The phone was on the wall near the kitchen sink. My annoyance rose to anger as I looked at the dirty dishes my roommates had left. Again. When were they ever going to clean up after themselves?

The sun was rising and a blue sky predicted a wonderful spring day. I could see the brick house next door out the kitchen window. It was so close that had I opened the window I could have touched it with a broom.

I answered the phone. It was Dad.

"Yvonne." Something in his tone made me pull in my breath.

"Mark was killed last night in an automobile accident."

I froze. Then my whole body began to shudder. I couldn't move. I couldn't speak. The silence in the rest of the apartment was deafening. How could my brother be dead, and my roommates remain asleep?

Mom and Dad had received a call from the coroner. Mark had been driving to Mary Catherine's again in Pittsburgh. He lost control of his car, hitting a bridge abutment head on.

The impact of the crash pushed the engine forward into the front seat. He died instantly.

Dad's voice broke on the phone. When I recovered my own, I said I would leave right away and come home.

It was the shortest and longest phone call in my life, because time seemed to stand still. Mark couldn't be gone. We had just been together for a whole weekend. He was turning his life around. He wanted to teach. My dear brother. Gone?

One of my roommates wrapped a blanket around me. I had jumped out of bed partially dressed. Another offered to drive me to my parents' house. The hour's drive was mostly silent, as I tried to take in the news.

I never saw the scenery whizzing past the passenger window.

"I love you, Mark. Thanks again."
"I love you too, sis. See you soon."

Those had been our last words, and they were my only comfort on that long trip home. We pulled into the drive that led to the house. My roommate took my suitcase out and set it on

the ground. He gave me a hug and said to call if I needed anything. I stood near the front steps wanting and not wanting to go in. I turned the knob on the door, wondering why my parents had painted it such an ugly shade of green. It clashed with the gold brick. The door always stuck a little, and I had to push to get it to open.

Dad stood at the top of the steps in front of Mom's organ, wearing a slight smile as if he'd forgotten the reason I'd come. It quickly faded, and as I closed the door, tears started to cascade down his cheeks and his body was wracked with sobs. He pulled me to him and we sobbed together.

It was the start of the Dad/Grandad bear hug. It wasn't rough or hard or forced. It was safety and love and thank you and sorry all wrapped into one. It became the way we greeted each other and the way we said goodbye.

Most of the days that followed were a blur. We were on autopilot. My brother and sister arrived from out of state. We made funeral arrangements with the church. We began to receive sympathy wishes from friends and neighbors. We contacted Mark's close friends and asked them to be pall bearers. We made final

plans with the funeral home, and we selected Mark's casket.

Mother and I took the stairs to the basement of the funeral home. We wandered down the rows and rows of caskets, as if this was just a normal thing one did. We were looking for just the right casket. "Mom, it has to be one made of wood. Mark loved the outdoors and anything other than wood wouldn't feel right."

"What do you think of this one?" Mom fingered the label. Cherry wood.

Mom never cried, at least not in front of us. She seemed to move through the air, her body upright and purposeful.

Mark's funeral was held at the family Roman Catholic Church, St. Agatha's. There was comfort in the ritual we knew so well. We responded to the familiar prayers. We knelt, stood, and genuflected at the appropriate times. The priest gently swung the metal censer up three times on its chain. He repeated the ritual all around the casket, releasing the plume of incense and filling the air with the woody aroma.

When we began the Lord's Prayer, I reached for my father's hand on my right and for my other brother's hand on my left. They in turn

reached for the hands of those standing beside them. We were at once a solid family facing this horrific thing. From that day, no matter how many of us are together, the Lord's Prayer has us holding hands.

Back at the house after the burial, the house was filled with people, food, well-wishers, and an oddly festive air. It was such a relief from the somber day. I thought all five of us, the remaining family members, appreciated the kindness of those present and the respite from sorrow.

The vocal quartet Mom coached came to the house. They stood in our living room and serenaded us. My brother Michael, sister Connie, and Mom and I loved it. What a sweet, kind thing to do. The barbershop harmonies and the quartet's enthusiasm brought much needed smiles to our faces.

But Dad stormed off. Later he said, "Why in hell didn't those people know it was time to leave? Enough is enough."

Dad was very clear about his way of dealing with it.

"I'm not like your mother. I can't talk to you about what's happened. That's just not my way."

Somehow I understood what he meant without feeling dismissed or hurt. He was just being Dad. And so, we didn't talk about it.

Later, Mary Catherine gave Dad an opportunity to listen. Mom, Dad, Mary Catherine, and I were sitting in the living room. Three of us were sharing Mark stories. Dad didn't walk away this time, and he looked like he was enjoying what was being said.

"Mike, there's something you need to know," Mary Catherine said. "Mark talked about you a lot."

She told him that on several occasions Mark had said, "The older I get, the more I know that Dad was just plain right about some things. I never would have believed that years ago, but now I do. He was just right about stuff."

Dad's eyes grew wide and moist, and he smiled sadly.

Mark's death changed something else in how we were as a family. We agreed that we'd end every visit and phone call by saying, "I love you." It wasn't a cliché anymore. We knew that every parting might be our last, that we might never have another opportunity.

CHRISTMAS CACTUS

In the February following Mark's death and a few days after his birthday, I drove down to spend the weekend with Mom and Dad. Mom was standing at the top of the stairs as I walked through the door. She was smiling and excited, and her voice rang, "Yvonne, you have to come see."

She took me by the hand and pulled me gently down the narrow hall. The first bedroom on the left had been Mark's, and it was still decorated as if he were there. The dresser and the narrow single trundle bed stood against the long wall. On top of the dresser was a ceramic statue of a boy holding a guitar. Mom had painted it

for him as a Christmas present a few years be-
fore. On the opposite wall was a crucifix over
the lamp table. Hanging from the only window
in the room was a Christmas cactus in full
bloom. I thought it strange that it would be
blooming at that time of the year.

Mother was a woman of prayer. It was the
glue that held her together. She was brighter
than I had seen her in months.

"I had to know that Mark was okay," Mom
said. "I prayed day after day for some kind of a
sign, and I was specific as to what the sign had
to be. Mark loved this Christmas cactus, so I
asked that it start to bloom for his birthday to
tell me he is okay, and that it stay blooming until
the anniversary of his death." Her eyes misted
for only a moment. "Now I know for sure he's at
peace."

The buds had appeared a week before
Mark's birthday, and some of them began to
bloom on his birthday. And, just as Mom had
asked, the plant continued to bloom until April
and the anniversary of his death.

Mom and Dad came across the state to my
home for the Christmas holiday. When they
walked in the door, Mom presented me with my

very own cactus, a small one, filled with lovely white flowers.

A year or so later, Mom called to say that Dad had seen the doctor and a quadruple by-pass had been scheduled for the following week. I said I'd come home.

As my husband and I were packing the car, I glanced over to the large bay window in the dining room. There was my Christmas gift, the little cactus. It had one single white bloom. I went home with the assurance that Dad would be fine.

Ten years after Mark's death, the entire family was together on vacation. Connie and Michael had each brought their respective chil-dren. There was even a great grandchild present. We rented a sixty-foot-long houseboat and cruised around a man-made lake on the Tennessee border. The boat accommodated all twelve of us and offered all of the modern con-veniences. There was a full kitchen including a microwave. The air conditioning kept us com-fortable when we weren't outside. The water slide at the end of the boat entertained the kids for hours.

When we weren't cruising, the boat was tied

to the shore. One afternoon, Mom asked if I'd like to go for a walk with her. We headed into the woods that lined the lake. It was a glorious, sun-filled day. The breeze rustled through the trees, and the ground crackled as we stepped on the blanket of leaves beneath our feet. It was just the two of us.

"Oh, how Mark would have loved this." Her eyes filled with tears. Then her face became rigid as she pulled back the tears, gritted her teeth and looked at the ground.

"Oh, Teddy, stop this. You should be over this by now." Her self-chastising words stung as they left her mouth.

"Mom please don't say that. You shouldn't be over this. It hurts me to hear you say that. No parent ever gets over losing a child. Sometimes it gets easier, but at other times when something reminds you, the hurt and sorrow bounces back like it never went anywhere."

My advice was carried away on the breeze. It was as if she had never heard it. She turned and started to walk back to the boat. She simply wouldn't accept that the grief over Mark's death would be with her for the rest of her life.

Yes, Mark loved being outside. He loved the

trees and the sound of the breeze through the leaves. So, it is on the breeze, or in the sunshine, that I sometimes feel Mark's presence. He is also there in the song "Dust in the Wind." It will randomly play on the radio, or sometimes just in my head, when I need reassurance that all is, or will be, well.

ALL THE APPLESAUCE

By the time Mom's health issues became serious, my brother Michael had his PhD in Clinical Pathology, Connie was a registered nurse, and I had completed my master's degree in Clinical Psychology. Whenever a new issue arose, the sibling with the appropriate knowledge would step in to support.

There was Mom's hysterectomy and then diverticulitis. She had surgeries to lift her bladder, repair a rotator cuff, remove bone spurs in her shoulder, and fuse two cervical vertebrae. As her osteoporosis became more severe, a falling lamp broke her arm, and an attempt to open windows

left her with cracked vertebrae. Once she was hospitalized with severe bursitis in her shoulder.

Doctors prescribed Percocet for pain. When my brother Michael found out how many she'd been taking, he obtained her pharmacy records and discovered that she had been prescribed 3,200 tablets in eighteen months. At the time, Michael was the assistant administrator in a Kentucky rehabilitation hospital, and he arranged for Mom to go there to be weaned from the drug.

When Mom needed a cardiac catheterization, the procedure was done at my sister's hospital in Wisconsin.

Mom also discovered that she was sensitive to wheat and yeast, so she followed a strict diet. When doctors recommended exercise for her joint and bone problems, she joined a gym, lifting weights and using the pool for aqua-size classes. She continued to work and volunteer, despite all her health issues. She was Grandma Teddy to a class of third graders. She delivered Meals on Wheels, and she taught a woman to read.

One day, as she walked across the parking lot toward her car, she stepped off the curb and

fell. Her bones were so fragile she broke her hip. She didn't need a hip replacement, but she did need surgery to insert pins into her hip joint. After that, she stopped going out, and her dementia began to show.

She would frequently pass out, requiring a trip by ambulance to the emergency room. This time, my sister Connie stepped in. She took Mom's list of prescriptions to a geriatrician in her hospital, who noted that one of Mom's medications was contraindicated in a woman her age. Once Mom stopped taking it, the fainting stopped.

When doctors diagnosed her with colon cancer, we all came home. After Mom's surgery, it became clear that Dad would no longer be able to care for her. She was weak and needed specialized assistance. Her short-term memory was gone; she couldn't remember what had happened ten minutes ago.

By this time, I'd changed careers from teaching and was working in a retirement community that had a nursing wing, and I began the search for an appropriate placement. I reviewed survey results and visited facilities close to Dad. I could tell by walking through the door

whether one would be at the top or the bottom of my list. I was grateful the one at the top of the list was a five-minute drive from Dad's house.

My work in a retirement community gave me first-hand experience of how families are impacted by the level of care for aging parents. Michael, Connie, and I never seemed to struggle with each other. There were never cross words. I do believe the teamwork training those long years ago at our parents' hands set us on that path.

When I was in my teens, convinced that noon would be a good time to get up on a Saturday, Dad's booming voice would bark orders through our house. It was how he set things in motion.

"Let's get crackin', times a-wastin', the day's half over!"

Sleeping in was not an option. We were allowed to have breakfast, but then there were chores. We each had assigned duties and the fun part of the weekend started when—and only when— those were completed.

Before the boys were old enough to take over for him, Dad's chores took him outside where he'd do yard work or clear the snow. In-

side, Mom became the drill sergeant. There were no white gloves, but a finger over a dusty window sill or the top of a dresser would be noted, and correction required. Early afternoon on Saturdays, only when Mom finished her inspection, could we think about going out, meeting friends, or attending a dance.

None of us children were excused from chores. Our responsibilities increased when Mom went to work. Each of us was expected to contribute according to our abilities. We'd often offer to do the chores we liked. Mark loved riding the lawn mower, and I loved ironing Dad's dress shirts. If we were grounded for some infraction, extra chores might be added to our list. Michael was an expert at finding a project that would reduce grounding from a month to a week and a half.

Picking up our rooms, collecting laundry, dusting, and vacuuming were standard. There was no automatic dishwasher in the house, because, as Mom said, "I have four dishwashers of my own." Chores weren't divided by gender. Our assignments would change from week to week, and complaints about having to clean the bathroom were ignored. We were all taught to

use the washer and dryer and how to fold clothes. Spring cleaning had us taking down curtains, washing baseboards, removing mattresses, and scrubbing bed frames.

What Dad created through his marching orders, and Mom supported through her inspections, was a well-oiled team. It was the team that would eventually coordinate, oversee, and provide care to both parents as they aged.

BY THE TIME Mom's short-term memory had slipped, Dad had to drive her everywhere. Otherwise, for awhile, she was able to care for herself. She bathed, dressed and fed herself all on her own. She prepared her own breakfast and lunch, and my parents generally ate out every evening. Her osteoarthritis caused pain, but she rarely complained.

Soon, things shifted. Mom was aware of her memory loss, and she was frightened much of the time. She'd ask Dad the same question over and over again. If he left the family room to go to the bathroom, she would scream wanting to know where he was. Many times, she'd scream out of shear frustration, and

yelling back at her was the only way Dad could get her to settle.

During the night Dad would feel Mom pulling his big toe, "Mike are you there? Are you alive?" Her dementia robbed her of the ability to understand that her husband was sleeping. She feared he was dead.

She spent most of the time in her recliner near the brick fireplace watching TV. The heating pad would be on and against her spine. It was the one thing that gave her some relief. Dad could then be in the room with her at his work bench building his latest model or tinkering with one of his radios. His computer was right there, so he was able answer email or Skype.

Dad hated it when, otherwise quiet and still, she'd turn to him and ask, "Do we have children?"

"Four—" and he'd catch himself just in time. "Yes, honey, we have three children."

"What are their names?" she'd ask. Then he'd have to figure out whether to add "Mark" after Michael, Yvonne, and Connie. He never knew how she'd react, so he left Mark out.

I went to visit Mom in the nursing home on

Thanksgiving. When I sat on the edge of the bed, she recognized me. For a second. Then, in the time it would take to snap my fingers, the elderly woman I knew was gone. In her place was an eight-year-old girl. Mom recalled hurt after hurt from her childhood. Her mother was never there for her. Her mother would rather be on the radio reading her poetry or playing the saw for the Major Bowe's Talent Show. Her mother never knew she was around. Aunt Ada was more of a mother to her than her own mom.

In that conversation, Mom consistently used her mother's first name, Kate. She carried on like this for fifteen minutes. I listened until she quieted. "You really didn't get the mom that you needed, did you?

"No," she said, her eyes misted with tears.

"You just wanted to be loved, and noticed, and made to feel special. You didn't get that, did you?"

She shook her head.

"Well, you are loved now. Daddy loves you, Michael loves you, and Connie loves you. And, of course, I love you a bunch."

In that moment, I understood what she

wanted to be and do for her children. She wanted to be the mother she never had.

Dad tolerated Mom being in a nursing home for only so long. He visited daily and was pleased with her care—until he wasn't. He called me one afternoon in a blind rage, using the voice that had terrified me as a child.

"Your mother had a doctor's appointment and I told the nursing home that I would meet them at the doctor's office. When I got there, she was sitting in a wheelchair and she was all alone. Not one person was in the office, and whoever drove her just dumped her."

"Dad I understand you're really angry, but sometimes mistakes happen. Did you talk to the nursing home?

"I did, and they apologized. I let the doctor's office staff have it too, but they whined they were on their lunch break."

"Was Mom hurt in any way?"

"Dammit, Yvonne, that doesn't matter."

I'd said the wrong thing, fueled the fire, and now I couldn't talk him down. He was angry. I listened to my father's raging frustration at the lack of one-on-one care he felt my mother de-

served. He felt that no one could take care of her as well as he.

"Yvonne, I yanked her out of that nursing home and brought her home."

Dad took care of Mom at home, all right. He also started yelling at her. He found it difficult to manage Mom's dementia. I was concerned. I raised the issue with him several times, giving him suggestions on how to handle things.

It was the disappearance of ice cream from the freezer that pushed his buttons. "Dad she doesn't remember she has already eaten another ice cream cup."

"I know she doesn't, but I don't know what else to do. I told her there were twelve cups in the freezer this morning. I told her if there were only eight left, she must have eaten four. Yvonne, she asks me the same things over and over again! If I yell, she settles down for a while. It's the only thing that seems to work."

Mom and Dad's marriage wasn't one I would've wanted. They didn't have the type of friendship I enjoy with my husband, Kirk. They didn't seek solace in one another. They didn't seem to have deep conversations between them. Hugs and holding hands? Never. They did

things together, of course. They went out to dinner every evening, because Mom didn't like to cook, even before her dementia set in. They watched television together when there was a program they both enjoyed. They went to Sunday Mass together every week. But they didn't share another pastime or a hobby. They both volunteered, but Mom with Meals on Wheels, and Dad with the Red Cross. They each had friendships outside the marriage centered on their separate activities.

They didn't seem to share the deepest parts of themselves. I never knew them to say what they felt, or why they felt the way they did. I never saw them fight about anything. I know they disagreed, but I didn't see them talk about those things, at least not in front of us.

My father actively gave his love to my mother, that much was clear. He took care of her until the end. He saw to her needs in the only way he knew how, and he kept her in her beloved home.

Easter of 2002 was the last profound exchange that I had with Mom. I went home for the holiday and we were sitting together in the family room. She was enveloped in her recliner

by the fireplace and the TV was on. The heating pad was tucked behind her back, and she turned to me with a serious face. I could feel something important was coming, so I picked up the remote and turned the sound down on the TV. With sadness in her eyes she said, "Yvonne, I want to go."

I inched forward on the couch so my feet could rest flat on the floor, my spine ramrod straight, my training and experience overruling the panic I felt at the thought of losing her. What she needed from me was that I listen, validate, and respond with all the care I could muster.

"What makes you say that?"

"I can't remember things. I think my mind is going and I hurt all the time. I'm scared."

"It is scary not to remember things. And I know you're in pain because you aren't doing any of the things you love to do."

A pause. Then, "I just want to go."

"Mom, it's okay. I think I understand. It is okay with me too! I will miss you like crazy. Talk to God about what you want. You two decide together." She got silent for a while, then repeated that she wanted to go.

Less than a month later, she was hospitalized again. Her dementia was causing severe behavioral problems. Mom's screaming finally forced Dad to pick up the phone and call her doctor.

"Mike, bring her in," the doctor said. "I'm going to admit her, as much for you as for her. You need time to rest and recuperate. Your own health is in danger."

Dad told me he was relieved, in a way, because he'd be able to get some sleep.

Dad visited every day, but every time he went to leave, the screaming would start all over again. The nurses would force him out the door of her room telling him to go. Mom's doctor called him and asked him not to visit for several days, saying it would be better for them both if he stayed away.

A few days later, Dad was in town getting groceries and filling his prescriptions. He was about to head home when his van seemed to automatically head in the direction of the hospital.

When he walked in, Mom was sitting up in bed, her dinner on the tray in front of her.

"Hey, hon, is there anything I can do for you?" Dad asked.

"Can you help me eat? I would like some of the applesauce."

He put spoon after spoon into her mouth, and she told Dad how good it tasted. After she'd eaten all the applesauce, Mom turned to Dad.

"It's time for you to go home," Mom said. "I know you don't like driving in the dark and I want you to be safe."

Dad kissed her on the forehead and told her he would be back to see her soon. He picked up some dinner and took it home. He tested his blood sugar, gave himself his shot of insulin, and ate with a sense of peace he hadn't felt for a long, long time.

Dad's phone rang in the early hours of the morning. It was the hospital. Mom had passed away in her sleep. She was gone.

No one was with her, and as angry as I first was about that, I later understood that this was exactly the way she wanted it. She didn't want to be seen when she was sick, and she didn't want to be seen when she died.

PART II
MICHAEL

CAPUTO WITH A "C"

In 1939, the country was in the throes of the Great Depression. The Caputo patriarch, Dominick, couldn't lift the family out of poverty because he was ill and unable to work. Michael's two sisters were the breadwinners of the family, earning not much as seamstresses in the coat factory. His older brother had been forced to quit school at fourteen in order to go find work. Dominick himself had little formal education, so, Michael's graduation from Scranton Technical High School was a big deal.

When Michael entered school, he could speak only a few words in English. He sat in the

back of the classroom, not participating because he didn't understand much. His teacher allowed him to spend his time drawing, which he loved, so he didn't feel isolated. When he was just eleven years old, his mother Angelina suffered a massive stroke and died. The only clock in the small house never worked again after her death, and the family took it as a sign of Angelina's spunk and spark having left this earth. Into the motherhood vacuum stepped Josephine and Rose.

Michael was the only one of the Caputo children who was an American citizen by birth. By the time he reached high school, he was on the honor roll. His father told him time and again that it was important to have a trade, and even more important to have a high school diploma. Michael knew the pressure on him to finish school was related to his father's own dreams. But rather than rebel against the pressure, Michael embraced it. He wanted to make his father proud, to help Dominick feel that his immigration to the United States had indeed been worth the sacrifice. Life for the Caputos was going to be better here.

During the Great Depression, there wasn't

much money for anyone to build anything and as such not much work for a stonemason, even a talented one like Dominick.

Michael and his brother Joe would pull a wagon seven miles across Scranton to get the weekly allotment of twenty-five pounds of flour, the foundation of the family's standard meal: pasta fagioli (pasta and beans.)

Dominick did whatever he could to provide for the family. He brought bathtubs into the basement of the house and used them to make wine. It was bootleg stuff, of course, because of prohibition. Sunday evenings were poker nights at the house, complete with beverages provided by Dominick. There was little concern about getting caught because the mayor and police chief were regular players at those Sunday night poker games, and they enjoyed their wine.

Scranton High was on Adams Avenue, two and a half miles across town. Every day, Michael left the rented duplex and its fake asphalt brick siding on South Ninth Street and walked through the familiar neighborhood of Little Italy. He crossed

the railroad tracks and the Lackawanna River, passed through the center of Scranton, scurrying quickly through a neighborhood of palatial homes he couldn't relate to, and along North Washington Street. The high school was an imposing four-story building, with grey mottled stone walls and a row of arched windows on the fourth floor. Michael's dark eyes, skin, and hair —and the fact that Italian was his first language —set him apart from the other students in the school.

Michael's father suffered from cirrhosis of the liver. He was weak and jaundiced and in incredible pain. It was Michael's responsibility to provide the nightly morphine shots that would permit his father a little respite and sleep. It didn't matter where Michael was, who he was with, or what he was doing, he had to be home by 11:00 p.m. every night to administer the medication. It had been a long while since Michael saw his father up and about, and even longer since he had left the house.

On the night of Michael's graduation, he was astonished to see his father get out of bed and put on a crisp white shirt and tie with his heavy winter wool blue serge suit.

"Poppa, what are you doing?" Michael asked, concerned because he knew how sick and in pain he was.

"I'm coming to see my son graduate." Dominick forced himself to stand up tall.

Michael worried his father would have to leave the ceremony early. There were 1,300 students in the school, and a few hundred in the graduating class! But he was a Caputo so he hoped Dominick could stay until he was called to the stage to receive his diploma.

He needn't have worried.

Dominick sat all the way through from A to Z. He met Michael outside the school when it was over. "Have fun at the prom tonight, and I have someone else lined up to give me my shot," said Dominick, his often cold, piercing blue eyes softening as he handed his son a fifty-dollar bill.

Michael stood there for a long while watching his father as he walked away, slow and lurching. Had those been tears forming in his father's eyes? He couldn't figure out what astonished him more: that his father had managed to come to the graduation, or that he'd just given

him an incredible sum. He pinched himself, just to be sure he was truly awake, and then headed to the prom.

Michael's father Dominick died two weeks later.

It was July 4, 1939.

BUST 'EM UP

Michael's graduation from high school lay like bricks on his shoulders. At least his father wasn't around to see that his diploma hadn't helped him get a job. The fact that many of his friends were in the same unemployed boat didn't make him feel any less disillusioned.

His sister Rose, now thirty, was about to marry. She was thrilled. Outwardly, Mike shared Rose's joy. Inwardly, he felt a sense of gloom. Instead of having two steady sources of income from the coat factory where Rose and Josephine worked, the household would soon be down to one. They couldn't continue to sur-

vive on pasta and beans. Something, anything, had to happen. Mike needed a job, any job.

With a new sense of determination, he walked to the Public Assistance Office on Penn Avenue in the center of Scranton. Looking up at the imposing three-story red-brick structure, he gathered up his pride, filled his lungs, and entered. The state welfare office was the last place he wanted to be, but perhaps, just perhaps, something good lay beyond the door.

He learned about the National Youth Administration, a New Deal program. Eleanor Roosevelt had pushed her husband to come up with a solution to the problem of unemployment for America's youth. She was the public champion of the NYA and it was created by President Roosevelt's executive order in 1935. The program offered options for technical training to unemployed youth between ages sixteen and twenty-five.

Running down a list of choices for a possible trade, Mike's eyes locked and widened. The straight set of his mouth opened into a broad smile. His career jumped off the page at him. He didn't think twice.

Airplane repair.

With every model airplane he'd built, without realizing it, he'd dreamed about working on the real thing.

Model after model appeared in his head like a series of images in a movie. Mike saw every model plane he'd ever built, starting with his first at age six. The models were simple at first. Soon, though, all he needed were the blueprints and he could build any model plane. He loved it, and knew he was a whiz. But until now he never dreamed his hobby could become his career.

Would his talent translate to the real thing? Would he really be any good at working on real airplanes? He forced the self-doubt back into the shadows of his mind.

While the words, in black and white, captured his attention, his head was spinning with the possibility of earning twenty-seven dollars a week. It was an enormous sum. He calculated what it meant: a loaf of bread was ten cents and a pound of ground beef cost twenty cents. He felt rich just thinking about it. He filled out his application, feeling an odd sense of destiny, as though the paperwork was a simple formality. This was what he was meant to do.

Mike returned the following week to learn

he'd been accepted into the program. On the way home, the bricks that had been weighing his shoulders down lay in a heap outside the Public Assistance doors. He didn't notice the distance or any of his surroundings on his way home. He didn't notice the game of pick-up underway as he passed the ball field, and he didn't hear the guys calling out for him to join the game the way he had many times before. He didn't remember crossing the river or the railroad tracks, or arriving back in Little Italy, until all of a sudden, he was opening his front door.

He opened his mouth to holler "Hello!" but then stopped. His sisters were not yet home, and his father had been gone for over a year. A small grin softened his face and his eyes moistened when he thought, "Oh, Pop, you'd be so pleased. I think my grades and my diploma helped me get accepted. I know I'll make you proud."

His grin vanished as quickly as it had come as he realized that his new circumstances meant he would have to leave Scranton, his home, and his sisters.

He settled, however, on the fact that he could now look forward to Rose's marriage, and his income would help support Josephine. She

wouldn't have to worry anymore about paying the rent or purchasing food. There'd be enough for her to serve meat several times a week. Perhaps she'd even be able to buy her favorite lamb chops once in a while. Again, he realized how much Josephine had done for him since his mom died, and he whispered a "thank you" into the empty hallway.

Mike's journey to learn how to repair aircraft, formally known as Aviation Technical Training, began at Middletown Depot near Harrisburg, Pennsylvania at Olmsted Air Field, which would later become the Harrisburg International Airport in 1969. It was adjacent to the repair depot, a storage facility for military equipment and supplies built on farmland that had once belonged to the Heinz family, makers of "the fifty-seven varieties." The airfield and the depot together extended over an area of 500 acres and was the largest Air Corp installation in Pennsylvania.

Although Mike was itching to pick up tools and work on repairing planes, he had been told what to expect when he reported to the National Youth Administration Center in Harrisburg on January 13, 1941. He would have to learn to

live in barracks with all of the other trainees, share a room, and eat all meals in the mess hall.

During his first six months, he felt like he'd never left high school. It was a long parade of classroom sessions where he had to prove he had the required basics in reading, writing, and arithmetic, as well as higher levels of mathematics before he'd be transferred to the base.

He hadn't expected that he'd be working side by side with women. He loved women, of course, and had dated a few. He'd been raised by women. But he couldn't imagine his sisters wearing pants and boots and being prepared to do the kind of work he was about to do.

Mike passed all his tests, and soon he was released from the barracks. He found his own lodgings in a duplex on Liberty Street that reminded him of his home on South Ninth Street in Scranton. It was on a similarly narrow tree-lined street. His daily walk to the bus stop took him past the thirty-five-acre Harrisburg Cemetery, filled with old oaks and maples and head stones. Once he reached State Street, he was awed by the granite façade, the grand columns and dome of the State Capitol building off to his right.

On June 9, 1941, he boarded the bus that would take him along the Susquehanna River to the warehouse at Middletown Depot for the next phase of his training. With each bump on the road he bounced between apprehension and excitement. He arrived and, along with the other trainees, reported to an enormous dome-shaped building.

The warehouse superintendent greeted them at the door.

"Welcome, you are about to enter the building where we store every conceivable item that is needed to repair and service the damaged airplanes that come our way. There are 250,000 items from paper clips to engines. You will not get to the next phase of learning to repair planes until you can locate each and every item at a moment's notice."

Mike's knees weakened, his feet anchored like lead bricks as he stood, momentarily unable to move before he entered the building which was the size of a football stadium. Row after row of wooden crates organized by size, were stacked as high as four or five men standing on each other's shoulders. Tall stalls held whole aircraft wings. Not daunted, Mike knew he could

memorize the location of every piece. "The quicker I learn this stuff, the quicker I can learn to repair."

The days passed in a blur as he found items by their stock number and memorized their location. Mike worked hard, studied harder, and was exhausted at the end of every shift, often a graveyard shift in those early days where he'd be responsible for gathering parts for the next day's repair work.

When he worked the day shift, his new landlady, Mrs. Mullahy, sent him off after a breakfast of piping hot oatmeal, cold cereal, or creamed chip beef on toast. When he worked the grave yard shift, he was often greeted by the delightful aroma of the hot meal she had prepared for him. She told him the meal would make up for the proper supper he missed. His favorite was pork chops and fried potatoes. It was a luxury he didn't experience when he lived with his sister.

On August 7, 1941, he received the news he was being transferred from the warehouse to the sheet metal department. Finally, he'd get his hands on the tools! He loved tearing down the planes that had been damaged and then fixing

them. He learned to weld and rivet wings and fuselages. Sometimes, when a particular part was out of stock and couldn't be ordered from any of the other depots, his creative juices activated, and he'd find a way to make what he needed.

Every so often the shop foreman would call out, "Okay folks, the hangar is going to be opened and one of the planes you repaired will be taken out. Come see what you've accomplished."

Mike watched as the tractor towed the reconditioned plane out onto the tarmac. When it was in the appropriate position, the test pilot climbed aboard, started the engines, and taxied the plane to the end of the runway. Beyond the airstrip, Mike could just see the edge of the Susquehanna River.

The plane began to pick up speed and it slowly lifted into the air, the sun glistening off its wings. The pilot banked, turning the plane to rise ever upward. When it was no longer in sight, Mike heard the foreman call out. "Back to work, there are plenty more where that one came from."

Mike's head felt as light as the breeze that

surrounded him, and he felt six inches taller. As he walked back to his station, he thought, *A part of me is up there, too.*

As intimately as he had known the model airplanes he had built growing up, he now knew the Douglas B-18, the Bell P-39, the Curtis P-40, the North American P-51 and the first Consolidated B-24.

In early April 1942, he was focused on the piece of sheet metal he was shaping when he heard the shop assistant call out, "Hey Mike, you're wanted in the foreman's office."

Walking to the office in the Air Material area, he wondered why he had been summoned. Had he done something wrong? Made a mistake? His foreman had often been complimentary of his skills. When he had made mistakes, he had learned to correct them. He had no idea what would be so bad he was called to the office. He forced a confident expression onto his face, walked in, and stood tall.

"Mike, you're being transferred to the sub-depot at Daniel Field in Augusta, Georgia. Nice work."

Mike's thoughts jumped to what had happened at Pearl Harbor the previous December.

With a confidence that surprised him, he said, "Sir, with due respect, I would like to be transferred to the depot at Pearl Harbor."

The foreman's response was quick and sharp. "No way, son. Daniel Field's depot is third echelon; Pearl Harbor is not. Mechanics are needed when planes come back badly beaten up. Pilots are trained at Daniel Field and that's where you're heading."

"Yes, sir. Thank you, sir." He turned on his heel and left the office, as if floating on a cloud.

Training was over, and for the first time, Mike had a job. A real job. The elation was temporary, though, as soon as he realized he'd once again be leaving for a new home. He signed his release paperwork and received the train ticket that would whisk him to Augusta, Georgia and Daniel Field, 700 miles away in the deep south.

PACKED WITH PLANES

\mathcal{M}ike reported to Daniel Field and immediately understood why he was there. Every available open space, whether a field of hard-packed earth or green grass, was packed with planes. Many seemed in good state of repair, but he could tell that others would require a ton of work if they were ever to fly again. The air around the base was filled with a sense of "the job should have been finished yesterday."

In 1924 the city of Augusta leased 302 acres of cornfield to create an airport at a cost of $110,000. The lease was pushed by its mayor,

Raleigh Daniel, and despite his protests the project leaders named the field after him. The citizens of Augusta thought the expense outrageous and success so improbable that Daniel lost the next election, and it ended his political career. In 1927, there were 35,000 people at the dedication ceremony, and the airfield was used to provide passenger and mail service. As the citizenry feared, at times the airfield struggled with profitability.

President Roosevelt understood the South's financial problems. During his many visits to Georgia he saw firsthand the economic challenges in the region, made worse by the Great Depression. He saw the New Deal and the Works Progress Administration as a way to improve conditions and combat unemployment and poverty. Roosevelt wanted to restore prosperity to Americans and, during the Great Depression, instituted a series of programs and projects, bundled them up, and called the bundle the New Deal.

In 1938, Daniel Field was the beneficiary of the New Deal. The funding paved runways, upgraded drainage, and a host of other improve-

ments. In 1940, the federal government stepped in again. Alarmed by the fall of France, Congress funded the strengthening of the Army Air Corp by nearly doubling the number of air bases across the country. The quickest way to do that was to use existing civilian airports. In 1941, construction to turn Daniel Field into a military base began. Crews lengthened existing runways and built new ones. They added frame-constructed plywood and tarpaper hangars and support buildings because they were not meant to be long term.

Military leaders originally intended to train fighter pilots at the base, but geographical restrictions such as the ravine to the west and the city to the east meant they couldn't extend all the runways. New taxi ways, a large parking apron, and a control tower were used for transport and observational squadrons. As other airfields became available after August of 1942, Daniel Army Field became a repair and replacement depot for the Army Air Force. Planes came to Daniel Field when they needed heavy repair. The depot was now considered both third and fourth echelon, which meant it needed to house

large pieces of shop equipment and specialized mechanics in order to perform the major aircraft overhauls or modifications.

The get-it-done-yesterday mantra became Mike's new reality, and the exhaustion he felt during training now seemed like child's play. The days passed in a blur as he patched and welded plane after plane coming through the hangar. He loved the work and the deep focus it forced on him, and he jerked when he heard someone call his name.

"Mike, you're wanted in the shop office." He didn't recognize the speaker.

"What for?"

"Don't know," replied the messenger in a deep southern drawl that still sounded strange to Mike's ears.

Mike reported to the office, too tired to care very much about the reason for the summons.

"Mike, we've watched you work. You know what you're doing, and we need someone to oversee the work coming out of your department. Think you can handle it?"

"Yes sir, but you'll have to tell me just what I am supposed to do."

"Continue to do what you're doing. At the same time watch what the others are doing. If you see something that could be done better, show people. If something needs to be corrected, correct it. Is that clear enough?"

"Yes sir. When do I start?"

"Now. We'll let folks on the floor know."

Mike knew he could handle the additional responsibility, in fact he revelled in it. But he wasn't ready for the twist that hit him square in the face like a right jab.

There, signing in at the employee desk, was a woman. Her hair was pinned up and secure, but she was wearing a skirt! There was no way he could allow her to work dressed like that. The level of comfort with women he had developed while he was training blew out the front door of the hangar. How was he supposed to handle this one? He'd just have to tell it like it is.

He asked the young woman to step outside, far enough away from other ears that they could talk in private. "Miss, I am going to have to send you home."

"Why? I just got here. What have I done wrong?"

"You need to change into a pair of pants. Your job requires you to be in awkward positions, like crawling all over a wing. There's just no way that you can do that decently in a skirt. Please, report back when you have changed."

Her blush started at the collar of her blouse and swept up the rest of her face as she turned and walked away. Mike walked out on the tarmac and looked at the open sky, thinking, *Fixin' planes is one thing. Telling a woman to get out of her skirt? That is something else.*

Climbing on the bus at the end of the day and sinking into his seat, he sighed so loud others turned around to look. He wanted to be home, now, and his stop was all the way at the southern end of the Augusta National Golf Club. To keep from falling asleep and missing his stop, he pictured the azaleas the golf club was famous for. Mike's arrival to Augusta had coincided with the blossoming of white, pink, rose, and purple bushes all along the fairways. Even as the blooms faded, the fairways were beautiful, soothing Mike's weariness and aching muscles as he walked past.

One day as Mike passed the club, eyes on the ground and the azaleas, he looked up when

he nearly bumped into Bob Jones. There he was, his picture often in the newspaper and one of the most famous golfers of all time. Jones was legendary. He won the Grand Slam in 1930, the only amateur golfer ever to do so.

"Excuse me, sir," Mike said, embarrassed.

"No harm done," Jones replied, and kept walking.

Mike stood still for several seconds. He wasn't a golfer, but he did love sports. His embarrassment melted as he thought about how, when he got home, he'd tell the story of nearly running down Bob Jones.

The Bon Air Hotel, a block away along Walton Road, was Mike's source of respite after a weary day at work. He never ceased to marvel at the grand structure. The hotel, built by the Vanderbilt's, was massive and elegant, sitting up on the hill overlooking the heart of downtown Augusta.

Mike dragged himself up several flights of stairs to the lobby, walking across the polished wood floors under crystal chandeliers and brass fixtures and into the bar. He was now a regular and he didn't have to order. One of the pretty waitresses, also a sight he looked forward to,

would bring him his new favorite drink: a mint julip.

Glancing at his Waltham wristwatch, he calculated how much time he needed to change for dinner, which was served at the boarding house at the same time every evening. He didn't like to keep the thirty or so other boarders waiting. More than that, he didn't want to draw attention to himself by coming in late, with everyone already seated around the expansive dining room table. And he didn't want to offend his new landlady.

As a civil servant, Mike was responsible for finding his own lodgings. He couldn't believe his luck when he arrived at 817 Hickman Road. There in front of him was a white clapboard southern mansion. It could have been a set in the movie, *Gone with the Wind*. It was three stories tall. The first story had a porch that went half the length of the house and around the right corner. The windows of the second and third floors were flanked by shutters. The room Mike rented for thirty-five dollars a month was one of

twenty-two rooms in the mansion. *If folks could see me now,* he thought.

Mike had never lived in such a large house, and he was new to all things southern. There were seven black people who lived in a cottage at the back of the property and waited on him and the other boarders. When Mrs. Watkins first showed him to his room she asked, "Mike, do you drink?"

"I do, why? Is that not allowed?"

Mrs. Watkins turned to look at the door, making sure no one was around. "No, but I want to caution you. If you keep liquor in your room, you will need to hide it well. My darkies have been known to pour some out of the bottle and replace what they have taken with water."

A few weeks later, Mike walked into his room, and his toe kicked up the edge of the carpet to reveal a pile of dust. He found Mrs. Watkins and asked for a broom and a dust pan.

"Whatever on earth do you need those for?"

"There's a pile of dust under the corner of my carpet. I just want to clean it up."

"Absolutely not! That's what my darkies are for. I'll send someone up to take care of it." With

that she turned on her heel and went down the hall.

Another time, Mike used the back entrance to the house, which also had stairs to the second and third floors. He looked up and noticed Fanny, the head maid, coming down with a large load of laundry in her hands. She stopped and pulled the corners of the bundle in more tightly when she noticed him, and she pulled herself closer to the wall. She stood very still.

One voice in Mike's head told him that it was right for her to stand by and wait for him to pass. He was the paying customer, but more than that, he was white, and she was black. The other voice in his head said she was a woman, carrying a heavy load, and letting her pass first was the right thing to do.

"Fanny, come down," he called up. "Your arms are full."

"No, Massa Mike, yo' needs to come up first." Her face taught, her eyes leveled at the floor.

"Fanny, I insist." He stood aside and waited, and after a few seconds she did indeed come down first.

Mike's orientation to his new surroundings

also came from the stories he heard from other boarders. Mrs. Lee, for example, talked about her late husband, a major in World War I who had been stationed at Camp Gordon just outside of Augusta. His job had been to train and discipline colored troops. Mrs. Lee said that when they made mistakes, even relatively minor ones like not marching in a crisp line, Major Lee would tell them they couldn't wear their uniforms on weekends.

"And that was a big deal for them," Mike asked, "having to wear their civvies instead?"

"Oh yes," said Mrs. Lee. "Those darkies had such a sense of pride wearing those uniforms."

But the most intriguing stories were the ones about Mrs. Watkins herself. She had made Mike feel welcome from the moment he walked through the door. He guessed that she was in her mid-sixties, but it was really hard to tell. What he could see was the beauty that lay beneath her skin. She told stories from when she was a chorus girl in New York City, including how she met Joseph Watkins, how he swept her off her feet, out of the theaters, and into marriage. Mike noticed a sadness behind her eyes. Perhaps the rumors were true. Joseph Watkins,

a local attorney who loved to laugh, was apparently sitting in his office inside the ten-story Marion Building with his back to a large open window. Something set him off, and he began rolling and shaking with laughter. He laughed so hard that his chair tipped backwards, and Joseph fell right out the window to his death.

If the rumors were true, Mike thought, he could understand why Mrs. Watkins was running a boarding house. It was something many widows had to do to survive. Like Mike's landlady in Harrisburg, who had children to raise but no husband to bring home the pay. Mrs. Watkins clearly cared about her boarders, and in turn Mike's respect for her grew deep and abiding. She made him feel at home there, even if the other residents didn't.

Mrs. Watkins also respected Mike. One day as he arrived home, bone-tired and about to haul himself up the stairs, she stopped him on the landing.

"Mike, would it be easier for you to get to work if you had a car to drive?"

"It sure would. It would save a good deal of time, but you know I don't have a car," Mike said.

"But I do. I also have enough ration cards for gasoline. Would you like to use my car during the week?"

Mike said yes, of course, surprised at the generosity. Of course, Mrs. Watkins had conditions.

"You would have to drive me for groceries on Saturday, and I would need a ride to church on Sunday. Other than that, I don't use the car during the week. You might as well make use of it."

Mike was doing the math in his head. Having a car to take back and forth to Daniel Field would save him at least an hour each day and it would save him money on bus fare. This was a very good offer. "Yes, to the groceries. What church do you attend?"

"I go the Catholic Church called St. Mary's on the Hill. It's not far from here. I'd need you to pick me up afterwards."

"That makes it easy. I'm Catholic too. We could go together."

So began a new ritual. Mike drove himself to and from work during the week. On Saturdays, he took Mrs. Watkins grocery shopping. Together, they attended church on Sundays. He

marveled that a sense of family could occur any-
where and with people you'd least expect.

It was not a feeling that he got around some
of the other boarders. One couple, an old World
War I colonel and his wife, always made him
feel uncomfortable. If Mike said something at
dinner, they'd turn their heads and look away. If
he passed them in the hall they would move as
far away from him as they could. He never knew
what he had done to deserve this treatment,
until one day when he was walking past them as
they sat perched on rocking chairs on the front
porch.

"Damned Yankees," he heard the wife say
under her breath.

Mike stopped and looked directly at her.
"Ma'am, is that one word or two?" He kept his
voice calm and smooth with just the tip of his
tongue in his cheek.

She looked up, her eyes like shards of ice.
She didn't answer. But after that, Mike never
heard another word from her. It apparently mat-
tered a great deal that he was from the north.

When Mike first arrived at Daniel Field, he
had felt a similar chill from some others, but it
soon disappeared. He reasoned that his skills,

work ethic, and, as a foreman, how he treated others helped thaw the air. He tried to be fair and even-handed with everyone who worked for him.

Two sergeants appeared on the shop floor one day, escorting General Hap Arnold. Mike lifted his head from his repair work long enough to note that General Arnold was stopping to talk to workers on the floor. Then he got back down to the task at hand.

"General Arnold, this is Mike Caputo," said one of the sergeants, startling Mike into an upright position, knocking some tools to the floor in the process.

"General Arnold?" Mike's tone a statement and a question at the same time. He cleared his throat to cover his confusion. The five-star chief of the Army Air Force was standing before him. The man who had learned to fly from the Wright Brothers! There wasn't anyone higher in the Air Force command than Hap Arnold.

The general seemed to fit his nickname, Hap. Mike's heart thudded so loud in his chest he was sure the general could hear it from clear across the shop floor. "Young man, I've been told you ordered the Cincinnati Press Brake from the

Middletown Depot. What made you think you could do that?"

Now Mike's heart stopped. He'd been so focused on doing what he believed needed to be done, he hadn't for a moment suspected *this* would be a problem.

"With respect sir, I knew Middletown had it, and I needed it. So, I requisitioned it."

Mike thought Daniel Field should have a press brake because of the sheer volume of planes being repaired. A press brake is a large machine that holds pieces of sheet metal in place so they can be bent or punched. Mike was one of more than 23,000 workers repairing airplanes during the war who worked on more than 6,500 planes. Only one Cincinnati Press Brake was sold during the entire Second World War.

"Well son, that press brake was supposed to have gone to Cochran Field in Macon," the general said. Was that the slightest twinkle in his eye? "I'm afraid we have to send it there."

Mike got right back to work after General Arnold and his two sergeants left the hangar. He'd nearly forgotten about the exchange when a few days later he received new orders, signed by—General Hap Arnold.

Was this punishment, or reward? Mike fought a bitter taste in his mouth. He'd just been getting comfortable in Augusta, and it was going so well with Mrs. Watkins. But, an order was an order. Mike Caputo was on the move again.

THE MISSING WING

*M*ike arrived at the massive Cochran Field in March 1942. There were buildings and hangars everywhere. He couldn't see from one end to the other.

He passed brand new barracks on his way to the maintenance office. Once he reported in, he was free to go back into Macon to find a place to live. His civilian status was still such a boon. No Army Air Force lean-and-mean quarters for him. He was sure that he wouldn't be able to re-place the luxurious accommodations that he had left in Augusta. Nor could he ever replace Mrs. Watkins, but hopefully he'd snag a private room in a decent house.

He found a place across the street from Wesleyan College. He'd just have to manage with the sight of all of those lovely women attending the college. The campus was as elegant as its attendees. It sat on acres of wooded land interspersed with manicured green lawns. All of the buildings were red brick built in the Georgian style, and many had elegant white columns supporting porticos. College education for women? He'd just gotten used to the idea of working with them. He was surprised to learn that Wesleyan had been around since 1836, the first college in the world to grant degrees to women.

Cochran Field's history was much more recent. In 1940 the field didn't yet exist. The Chamber of Commerce, through its Aviation Committee, petitioned the Army to have the airfield built. The city obtained 1,010 acres for $103,247. The land required would be given to the federal government free of charge. The site eventually chosen southwest of the city meant that farm houses, barns, pecan and peach groves would have to be cleared. Ground was broken in March 1941, and the first class of pilots arrived in June 1941. In August, British cadets arrived for flight training. Barracks hadn't yet been

completed, so the airmen were housed and fed in tents. When finished, Cochran would have administration buildings, cadet barracks, enlisted barracks, mess halls, hangars, and a swimming pool.

By the time Mike arrived, all roads were paved. The stories he heard made him cringe. He didn't have to deal with the horrendous dust or mud depending on the weather. What he did have to deal with were the planes beaten up by the pilots in training. For much of the time, he worked on the Vultee BT-13 or the BT-15 Valiant. These were replaced with the North American AT-6, which was about to change his life.

The AT-6 had a reputation as the best-built plane for training fighter pilots. But it was notoriously difficult to fly. It was very poor at landing in a crosswind. "Don't do it unless there's no other choice and then be prepared for a rough ride!" It was no surprise when one came into the shop missing its entire right wing.

Mike called Middletown depot, but they didn't have a wing. Call after call to all of the third and fourth echelons netted the same answer: no wing. Walking around the shop, he for-

mulated a plan. He could build his own jig to hold the wing. Then all he needed were the blueprints for the AT-6.

The maintenance shop superintendent reluctantly handed over the blueprints, making it clear he didn't believe Mike could rebuild the wing, blueprints or not.

"Sir, a blueprint is a blueprint. I used to build models all of the time. Now, instead of using balsa wood, I'll use aluminum."

"Okay, smart guy," the superintendent challenged. "The root of the wing needs to be lower than the tip. How are you going to figure that out?"

"I'll use my high-school trigonometry," Mike said. "If I find one angle on the blueprint, I can figure out all of the others. And yes, I know that the leading edge of the wing has to be higher than the trailing edge. Otherwise the plane will stall out when making a hard turn."

Mike walked a little taller as he headed back to the shop. He had to hold himself in check and not bounce all the way back. In his head he sang, *I'm a whiz, I'm a whiz. Watch me do this, cause I'm a whiz.*

Piece by piece, Mike fashioned what he

needed for the spars, wing tips, ailerons, and the aluminum skin. When finished, the wing was over seventeen feet long, and it was attached and ready for a test flight. A tractor pulled the airplane out of the hangar and towed it over to the airfield. He really wanted to see the plane fly, so he accompanied it. The pilot walked around the plane doing his visual inspection. When he finished, he approached Mike and asked, "Are you the young hotshot that built the wing?"

"Yes sir," Mike said.

"So, am I to believe that this thing is going to fly?"

"Yes sir."

"You're absolutely sure it will fly? It's my life that's at risk."

"Yes sir."

"Good," the pilot said. "Climb in, because you're going with me."

This was Mike's very first plane ride. It was one thing to build a model, but this was the real thing. In truth, he wasn't as confident inside. But he wasn't about to pass up his first chance to fly, in a plane with his hand-built wing.

Mike climbed into the seat directly behind

the pilot. The engine started, and they began to taxi down the run way. His heart raced as the plane began to lift off and gain altitude. He saw the buildings below him become smaller the higher they climbed. Now, he could see the enormity of the air base. Otherwise, there was nothing but flat land dotted with farms and groves of trees for miles and miles.

The pilot then began to put the plane through its paces twisting and turning in the air. For Mike, this was heaven. *I don't want to fix 'em anymore. I want to fly 'em,* he thought.

By the time the plane touched down, he knew he was going to enlist so he could fly.

Mike hadn't been required to register for the draft in 1940, because he hadn't turned twenty-one. He was, however, required to register in 1942 while he was living in Augusta. The enlistment was a legality, but because he was considered part of war production, he had received a presidential deferment. His skill at repairing airplanes was more important than his becoming a soldier. It had kept him out of the war. If he was going to join the Army Air Force, he would have to get out of his deferment, and if he was going to get into flight

school, he would have to take an entrance exam.

The exam was easier than Mike had expected. He couldn't believe that he'd worried so much about it. The questions were common sense and logical. For example:

How far do you go into the woods?

Answer: *Halfway, at which point you start coming out.*

Another example: *It is 8:00 a.m. and you see enemy planes flying directly underneath. How do you approach to shoot them down?*

Answer: *From the east. The sun will be in the enemy's eyes and they won't see you coming.*

A prerequisite for pilot training was at least two years in college. When Mike reached that question on the form, he felt only a twinge of guilt when he wrote that he had been a student at East Stroudsburg State Teachers College. His application complete and having passed the exam with flying colors, Mike enlisted on December 19, 1942. He was going to fly.

He celebrated when his buddies received their orders for basic training, but month after month he kept waiting for his. When he asked the draft board about his orders, he was told he

was too good at his job. Not to be deterred, thinking the squeaky wheel gets the grease, he kept on pestering.

Finally, he was cleared of the deferment and he was to report for basic training. He was now a cadet in the Army Air Force, and his orders were to go to Miami Beach. Not a bad start on the road to his new dream.

LATRINE BEACH

Miami Beach. How had he been lucky enough to be assigned to basic training in Miami Beach? He was the only one of his buddies from Macon to get what was considered a plumb assignment. Not even the July heat and humidity could dampen his spirits as he and the other recruits marched to headquarters. At least there was a breeze.

Mike's group reported to headquarters and filled out more forms that he'd ever seen. An assembly line of recruits at the troop supply area stripped down to their underwear for inspection and size analysis before receiving new service uniforms: chino cotton khaki shirts with

matching trousers, olive drab mohair neckties, and reddish-brown leather belts and shoes. And a duffle bag for all personal belongings.

Mike expected his next stop would be to his hotel room so he could unpack. Instead he was ordered to march, with the heavy duffle on his back, through a series of other stops. Ah, this was Mike's first glimpse of the reality of camp personnel barking commands and the expectation of snapping to obey. It was just day one. His back and feet ached, and he was drenched in sweat. He tried to focus on why he was here: he wanted to fly.

Otherwise, Miami Beach was a slice of heaven, truly the most beautiful bootcamp in America. And it had been taken over by the Army Air Force. It was cheaper and more efficient for the Army Air Force to rent hotels and apartment houses than it was to build new barracks. Hotel dining rooms converted into mess halls, and one of the theaters became a testing center. The beaches served as physical training areas and rifle ranges. Golf courses were parade grounds. Life-saving techniques were taught in hotel pools and the ocean. More than a half a

million men were trained at Miami Beach, and while hotel owners weren't paid their normal seasonal rates, their rooms were filled year-round.

Mike cheered inwardly when he heard he was billeted in the Beach Plaza hotel. Two blocks from the beach and two blocks from Washington Avenue. Palm trees dotted the streetscapes. He could smell the ocean as he walked into the hotel. Still, the wind went out of his sails when he got to his room. Every luxury had been stripped away, except the carpet on the floor. It was a bare-bones room with nothing in it except two small beds.

The sergeant who marched Mike to the hotel noticed the perplexed look on his face. The sergeant barked, "Listen pal, consider yourself lucky. The other enlisted recruits are sleeping four or five to a room. You're only sharing with one. To get ready for daily inspection, you'll use

a vacuum cleaner instead of broom and dust pan."

The cadets went through physical and equipment training, had lessons on first aid, general and sexual hygiene (lots of information on sexual hygiene). They were immunized and their blood types recorded. They learned how to dress, how to pass inspection, details of the Army Air Force rule of law and how to avoid military court. They were tested and interviewed. And they drilled and marched, and then drilled and marched some more.

One of Mike's first lessons was to be careful what he volunteered for. When one officer asked his group if anyone could drive, one eager cadet spoke up.

"Good! See that wheelbarrow and that pile of sand?" the officer pointed. "Take the shovel, fill the wheelbarrow, and move the sand to the other side of that building," he said, pointing to a building 200 feet away. "Keep working until all of that sand has been moved. Understand?"

Mike was familiar with the heavy hand of discipline from his father, but this was a whole new level of regimentation. He was wakened at 4:00 a.m. He was on the beach for calisthenics at

6:00 a.m. doing a rigorous routine of jumping jacks, squats, pushups, and other exercises totally new to him. He was feeling muscles he never knew he had. Conditioning for the high school football team was a picnic compared to this. Exercise finished, he was marched back to his hotel for a shower, a uniform change, and room inspection.

Mike failed his first white-glove test. He'd heard the rumours. He and his roommate worked hard on their room and both thought they had it nailed. Alas, the white-glove test on the top of the door jamb revealed just a bit of dust. Mike and his mate were gigged. They'd be spending their weekend in their room, rather than exploring Miami Beach with the other recruits. Whatever it took, Mike vowed that he'd never miss the wonders of the Miami Beach night life again. The night clubs, movie theaters, and bars provided plenty of entertainment, and the Cadet Club provided a very cold beer.

From then on, Mike's room was spit-and-polish clean. Every corner, window sill, and door jamb were always whistle clean. The bed was made with smooth precision, the corners of the blanket and sheet tucked taut. A quarter

dropped onto the bed from three feet above bounced just as it should. There was not one speck of dirt on the carpet.

The same meticulous approach to hygiene and personal dress was required for lunch. Mike showered and changed into his Class A uniform, every crease exactly where it should be. Mike liked how the Class A made him look and feel — it gave him a sense of well-being and pride. His shoulders were square and there was a certain click in his heel as he entered the mess hall.

Mike's classification as a flight cadet rather than as infantry was a bonus where food was concerned. Real eggs, steak, and ice cream were frequently on the menu. Even with all the good food, Mike dropped from a flabby 195 pounds to a slim and trim 158 during his thirteen weeks of basic training.

It wasn't all due to the physical exercise. Mike had been up all night with the runs, but he didn't report his problem to anyone. He went to calisthenics as usual. Minutes into the exercise routine, his gut wrenched and he headed for the latrine. The latrine slit consisted of four chan-nels, each two-feet wide by four-feet deep, dug into the beach. Vertical poles sunk deep into the

ground around each trench held tarps that offered a little privacy. Horizontal poles set crossways near the edge of each trench gave men something to hang on to for stability.

Mike dropped his drawers and began to relieve himself. With the lack of sleep and dehydration from diarrhea, he was weak. He couldn't maintain his grip on the horizontal poles, and he fell into the bottom of the sewage trench with a slimy thwack. His yell brought a bunch of guys running, and they lifted Mike out of the trench. Mike gagged, his embarrassment almost as bad as the smell. The guys who'd lifted him out of the trench tossed him into the ocean for a welcome rinse before he was transported to the base hospital.

It seemed that some of that wonderful food had been contaminated, and Mike was diagnosed with amoebic dysentery. The treatment, standard at the time, included small doses of arsenic. Penicillin had been discovered but it wasn't yet readily available.

In spite of the illness, Mike did well on his exams and was officially assigned to college as an aircrew trainee. He loved being by the ocean in Miami and requested a California training as-

signment. When California wasn't listed in his transfer papers, he knew better than to complain. He was going to Allegheny College in Meadville, Pennsylvania. Even though he was from Pennsylvania, he'd never heard of either Allegheny or Meadville. He stuffed his disappointment to the bottom of his duffle bag and prepared to follow orders.

EIGHT GIGS

*H*e had been on a train for over twenty-four hours. He longed for a bed, any bed. His duffle bag felt like it was full of rocks as he lugged it down onto the platform. Mike and eighty others had just traveled over 1,300 miles, from Miami to Meadville, but there was no time to rest. He had just been assigned as cadet officer of the day. That meant he was to see that all of the men were marched from the train station to the college.

Shrugging his fatigue off like an old blanket, he stood up tall and called out, "Form *up*! Right, *face*!" There were now two lines of cadets ready

to march, and Mike's "Right, left, right, left," es-
tablished the rhythm.

The October air was cool, which helped ease
the burden of carrying his heavy duffle. Mike
didn't relax until they had marched several
blocks, and then he began to notice his sur-
roundings. The cars on the street were modern,
but the buildings seemed to have come straight
from the last century or two. He drank in the
scenery and kept marching through the
quaintest town he had ever seen.

In the business district, small stores, in-
cluding a men's clothing store that caught his
eye, were tucked into two-story buildings that
lined both sides of the two-lane street. He
marched past buildings of grey stone, sandstone,
and red and yellow brick. The Meadville Post
Office, with its red brick exterior punctuated by
four columns of white, the magnificent six-story
Crawford County Trust building in a similar
red-and-white brick-and-sandstone style.

He turned his marching column of GIs to the
left toward Allegheny College. He'd never seen
anything quite like it. To his right lay the mani-
cured lawn of a park surrounded on all sides by
churches, mansions, and the court house. In the

park's center were a fountain and an octagonal gazebo sitting adjacent to each other. The fountain was spewing water high into the cool autumn air. Majestic oak, cherry, and maple trees dangled vibrant colors of yellow, gold, rust, red, and brown. The benches in the park beckoned Mike to sit and rest, but he was in charge, and he needed to press on. The cadets marched up the small incline of the street that would take them to the college, past homes of painted clapboard, window shutters, and wide porches that ran the full length of the house. More of the same colorful trees lined the sidewalks creating a promenade that Mike would never forget.

After several blocks the gentle incline changed to a steep hill. Mike could feel the weariness of the men behind him, but he kept up the same marching rhythm and pushed them forward. When they reached the edge of the college, which would be their barracks, he saw more of the red brick structures with cream-colored stone cornices and pillars.

Allegheny College sat on a hill that sloped off to his left into a valley. Passing through the college gates, the cadets marched down the hill along a wide brick path to the front of Brooks

Hall, the most imposing building of all. At its center was a second-story porch tucked behind imposing white columns. On either side of the porch were symmetrical wings of red brick.

Mike's temporary leadership duty was complete when the commanding officer met the arriving cadets. His dorm room was in Cochran Hall, another imposing building. It sat at the crest of a small hill, at the top of three sets of wide steps emptying under carved columns and into the lobby. Mike's room, a spare but comfortable double, was on the second floor. He dropped his duffle and forced his lead feet to take him a few more steps to the window.

Gazing out at the vista, Mike realized with a jolt that he was in college. The Army Air Force had more cadets in flight school than it could handle, and so at the end of basic training men were sent to colleges around the country to continue their study of flight-related core subjects. Could he handle the academics? Or would he wash out?

His fear of inadequacy was pushed aside as he once again realized he'd never been to any place quite as beautiful. *When this is all over, this is where I want to hang my hat*, Mike said to himself.

By American standards, Meadville was old. Its first settlers arrived in 1788, making it the first permanent settlement in northwest Pennsylvania. Meadville sat on a large meadow that lay between two wide, deep creeks that joined together making it easy to transport goods both in and out of the settlement. In the 1830s canals were built which enhanced Meadville as a transportation center, and that continued with the arrival of the railroads in the mid to late 1800s. The architectural styles throughout town were a reflection of those periods of growth.

Allegheny College was founded in 1815. New settlers wanted to have the access to the educational opportunities that they had known in New England. They recruited a minister, Reverend Timothy Alden, a graduate of Harvard Divinity School, to start a college. Alden traveled throughout the eastern states seeking financial support. In 1820, the library was the first major building erected. As the college continued to thrive, dormitories and academic buildings were added through the 1800s and 1900s. Green space and trees were as important on the campus as the buildings, making it an idyllic place to study and learn.

Since Michael was sent to Allegheny through the Army Air Force, his days were somewhat different from those of the typical college student. After breakfast, weather permitting, he donned sneakers and a sweatsuit and ran a daily eight-mile loop out to the football field and back to campus. On wintry days, the clomp of his boots replaced the slap of his sneakers and he frequently had to tramp through deep snow. After every run there were mandatory calisthenics in the gym.

The rest of Mike's days were filled with classes on mathematics, physics, political science, history, geography, and English. Officers told him these classes would prepare him for flight school. Mike understood the connection between mathematics and physics and learning to fly, and the connection between political science, history, and geography and the current war. But English? The subject wasn't any easier for him now than it had been in high school, and he initially feared he wouldn't pass. As the weeks passed, his confidence grew.

The cadets were required to march from class to class. They sang Army Air Force marching songs or created lyrics of their own to

sing along with the cadence calls, which are the traditional call-and-response work songs sung by military personnel while running or marching.

Not marching in cadence would result in a report to a cadet's superiors, and this infraction of the rules would earn the cadet a "gig," which is a military term for demerit. Mike received several gigs one winter day. He was once again the cadet officer responsible for marching the group from class to class. He had his group form up, but he didn't make them march. His commander called Mike to his office and asked him to explain his behavior.

"Sir, the thaw and refreeze made all of the walks covered in ice," Mike said. "For the safety of the group, I didn't have them march."

"Caputo, that decision is going to cost you your weekend. You will remain on campus."

Eight gigs and a cadet couldn't leave campus for the weekend. It was worse for the non-commissioned men: eight gigs meant they walked around campus carrying their rifle and wearing a gas mask, one hour for every gig. Mike saw one poor soldier that had so many gigs he had to walk all Saturday and Sunday over an entire

weekend. Despite the gigs, Mike's admiration for the college and the city grew, and he was determined to come back here when the war was done.

The college sponsored recreational and social activities for the aviation students. It had even opened a center with games, magazines, and newspapers. Mike attended open houses, music listening hours, dinners for small groups, and Saturday night dances at Brooks Hall. All of these efforts made Mike feel welcomed and accepted as a part of the student body.

Social and recreational activities didn't just happen on campus. The whole city of Meadville became involved. The American Legion sponsored open houses, local churches provided services at Ford Memorial Chapel on campus, and the YWCA and the student nurses of both City and Spencer Hospital offered informal social affairs. Just one month after his arrival, a United Service Organization Club (USO) opened on Market Street about a mile from the college.

One day Mike was walking past the post office when he heard the voice of an older postman calling out to him.

"Hi! My wife and I live about six miles out

of town, and our children are grown. We like to say thanks to you Allegheny cadets for stepping up to help us all win this war," said the man who introduced himself as Joseph Harl. "Would you and your roommate like to come for Sunday dinner?"

The food served at the college was good, but a home-cooked Sunday meal? That was so much better. Mrs. Harl was as kind and welcoming as her husband, and they hosted Mike and his roommate for many more meals, picking them up and driving them home afterward. The couple's kindness even extended to offering the use of their car should they ever need it for a date.

One day, after classes were out, Mike and a group of other GIs walked into town, joined once again by Rusty the Irish Setter who seemed to have adopted the men. They were headed to the Lafayette Hotel for a beer. Except Mike, who wanted to pop into the men's clothing store he had spied on his first march through town. He loved to look sharp, neat, and pressed, and now that he was so fit and thin, his uniform, even the khakis, made him look dapper. He ended up buying all his GI trousers and shirts at Al's Clothes Shop and en-

joyed many conversations with the owner, Mr. Phillips.

"Mike, if you do decide to settle in Meadville after the war, know that you have a job waiting for you."

Mike let out a whistle. "Wow, that's certainly a surprise. Thank you, sir."

"You are always so well dressed, and you have a great sense of what looks good. You get along well with the others here. I think you'd be a great salesman and an asset to the store."

One morning, when the cadets formed up, Mike learned that he would be cadet officer for the night, which meant he'd be on constant parole. His thoughts went sour. "Damn, that means no sleep for me tonight." Starting at the allotted hour, his first check was the laundry room. When Mike arrived, Rusty was waiting outside the door, ready to get into the makeshift bed the GIs had made up for him there. Mike fluffed up the smelly blankets on the floor and gave Rusty the needed strokes to get him to settle.

GI bed check was Mike's next responsibility. He went from dorm to dorm, room to room making sure all of the cadets were where they

were supposed to be. Several of the dorm rooms were empty and ten men were missing. Mike needed to find them or report them. If he reported them, they'd be sent to the infantry and they'd never fly.

They weren't in the games room. They weren't in the library. They weren't in any of the usual spots. Getting angrier by the minute, Mike signed one of the Jeeps out from the garage and headed into town to check all of the bars. He tugged his jacket tighter around him. The Jeep had no canvas covering and the cold air seemed to penetrate his heavy clothing. He checked all of the bars, leaving the Lafayette until last. Much to his chagrin, they weren't there. It had started to drizzle by the time he left the Lafayette. His mood worsened. The last place to check was the USO Club, right down the street.

When he stepped through the door, his heart did several flips. There was the most beautiful girl he had ever seen, her blonde hair swept up and her face… dirty. She was playing ping pong with another woman. "Hey there," Mike said, his earlier anger forgotten. "It looks like there's more dirt on your face than there is on the floor."

"We're closed," the young woman said before looking up. She stood up straight and rubbed her hands across her face, which spread the dirt even more. "Thanks for noticing my face," she said sarcastically. "The person who was supposed to close up called off, so it's now my job to clean up."

"I'm on duty, and I have to find ten missing men," Mike said. "I guess both our noses are out of joint." He paused as if looking for the right words. "Why don't we end the evening on a bright note? Underneath all that dirt is someone I would like to ask out for dinner. What do you say? What's your name?"

She began to blush, the color starting on her shoulders, up her neck, and into her cheeks.

"Teddy," she said. If he was asking her out even though she was tired and filthy at the end of her shift, perhaps he was okay.

She wrote down her phone number and address, and they set a time for Sunday. Mike left the club with wings on his feet and a grin taking over his entire face. He couldn't help but feel like something important had just happened.

Now, Mike didn't notice the cold rain soaking through his uniform. He didn't notice

pulling into the garage, and he almost forgot to sign the Jeep back in. The beds in the dorm were still empty, and he left a note saying the same thing on each one: *The Honor System.* When the men finally returned to their rooms, they would know the meaning of the note. In the morning they would have to report to the commanding officer and tell him they were absent at lights out. The commanding officer would then decide their fate.

Mike went back to his dorm and changed his clothes. He reported to the desk where he would finish out his duties for the night, which meant continuing to do bed checks every hour. The rest of the night passed quickly, because he had this vision in his head of the woman he was sure would one day be his wife.

In the morning, Mike was relieved to hear that all ten men had reported to the commanding officer, which meant he wouldn't have to report them. They had been gigged, but none had washed out. If they kept their noses clean and did well otherwise, they would move on to flight school.

On Sunday, Mike and Teddy walked through town looking for an open restaurant.

The only one open was an Italian restaurant. When they walked in, Mike knew he was in trouble. He couldn't think of a good excuse to turn around and leave, and there was no other place to go. A man greeted them, grabbed menus, and took them to a table. Much to Mike's chagrin, they were seated in the section of a certain waitress he did not want to see just now.

As they placed their order, the waitress's tone was clipped and cold.

"What's bee in her bonnet?" Teddy said.

When the waitress brought the food, she slammed Teddy's plate down, and slid Mike's to the edge of the table, tipping the spaghetti into his lap. Her apology dripped with sarcasm, but she promised she'd bring another serving. After she left the table, Mike encouraged Teddy to eat quickly, and he would explain all when they were out of the restaurant.

Outside, Mike suppressed an embarrassed laugh.

"Well, I'll just have to tell you the truth." There was a long pause as he considered how to go on. He wanted to grab Teddy's hand but didn't. "She and I were supposed to go out later

tonight. I called and told her I couldn't make it. I had no idea she worked here! I guess I got what I deserved, but you shouldn't have been treated like that."

Teddy laughed.

They saw each other as often as they could. They would always meet at the Old Rustic Bridge which spanned a small ravine in the center of campus. From his room Mike could see the rhododendrons covering the hillsides to the base of the ravine. They wouldn't bloom until late spring into early summer, but their waxy green leaves splayed up along the logs that made up the bridge.

When the weather was warm enough, he and Teddy would sit on one of the many benches around the campus and talk. If the weather was snowy, they'd meet at the bridge and find an indoor space for warmth. When he was allowed off campus, they both loved the movies and going out to dinner. Mike especially liked the evenings when Teddy's mother Kate was off playing bingo. Then, he and his new-found love could spend time alone in the apartment that his girl shared with her mother.

The five months Mike spent at the college

and in Meadville seemed like they were over before they began. He thought about Teddy as he packed for San Antonio, Texas, and wondered how they would continue the romance that had so filled his heart.

He awakened early on his twenty-second birthday. As he swung the duffle bag packed with all his belongings, his mood was as deep as the pre-dawn outside. He was leaving this beautiful place and the beautiful girl he had come to love. They had agreed to write daily, but beyond that, they hadn't discussed the future.

Even the weather seemed to conspire against him. It had snowed for a day and a half, and the streets and the sidewalks had not been plowed or shoveled. Each step in the knee-deep snow seemed to suck at his feet, trying to get him to stay. He wrestled with his thoughts, trying to focus on the glow of having passed all his exams, but they kept sliding back to what he was leaving behind. Boarding the warm train and its shining interior lights did nothing to lift Mike's spirits. He still wanted to fly, but now he wanted more. And the future seemed more uncertain than it had ever been before.

THE ORANGE TICKET

As Mike's train pulled into the station at San Antonio, Texas, he looked up at the huge basket stored over his head. He could not leave it and what was left in it behind. He would have to find a way to carry it, along with his duffle bag, to his new barracks. He had left Teddy behind. He wasn't about to leave her parting gift behind as well.

He still felt a little of the pleasure of seeing her waiting at the train station in Meadville in those oh-so-early hours. He hadn't asked her to come and see him off, and he hadn't thought to ask her how she managed to get to the station in all that snow. Thankfully she was dressed for the

weather. She was all bundled up, sensible rubber boots wrapping around her slender ankles. She had put her hair up on top of her head. He loved it that way, and he understood that she had done it just for him.

At least the station platform had been shoveled, so the huge basket at her feet would remain somewhat dry. She opened the lid, and said, "Happy Birthday, Mike. I thought you might appreciate a little food for your trip. I packed enough for you and some of the guys, so feel free to share."

Mike's eyes popped as he saw the contents. Sandwiches, chicken legs, potato salad, cake. There was enough stuff in there to feed, well, an army. It was just another one of those things making him think that perhaps he loved this girl.

San Antonio Aviation Cadet Center was located on Kelly Field, part of army aviation going back to World War I. With the beginning of World War II, it was restructured as a preflight school and classification center. When Mike finally arrived at Kelly Field, he was kept Army-Air-Force busy.

When he finally had some free time he wrote to Teddy, apologizing and explaining why he

hadn't written before now. He told her about his new accommodations, or rather the lack thereof. One of the first things they were ordered to do was to spit and polish their new digs. His room was shiny and thank God he had a bunk, but that was it. He had to kneel on the floor and use the bed's surface as a writing table. He told Teddy that every time he opened the basket, he thought of her and her kindness. The food in it had lasted four days, even sharing it with his buddies.

What amazed him was that he could say on paper what he couldn't easily express out loud.

I seem to have lost all my confidence in myself.
Funny how leaving people and a city makes
you feel as though you're heading to some un-
known place of terror.

He knew the source of his terror: all the tests he would have to take in the coming days. His immediate future rested on how well he did on these tests. At the end of it all, he would either go on to fly, or he would wash out. He did not see himself in the infantry. These tests felt like do or die.

The Army Air Force kept him busy his first week with training films, retreat parade, kitchen patrol (KP), and physical training (PT), but that only heightened his anxiety. It was hard to take anything seriously knowing that so much lay ahead. It made him often wonder if there was a method to what seemed to be the USAAF's madness. Was his reaction to the waiting also a part of the assessment? Were they measuring his performance while totally exhausted? Mike's suspicions were confirmed when, in one lecture, the instructor revealed that the assessments, developed by the leading psychologists of the time, were indeed designed to reveal how well he performed in stressful situations.

The heat exacerbated the exhaustion. The barracks and classrooms were simple wooden structures. The inside walls were plywood-covered studs. Even in February, the temperatures could reach the low seventies and eighties, and without insulation to keep the heat out and the cool in, the barracks and classrooms would become ovens. Outside was more bearable, thanks to a light breeze. Why hadn't they been assigned the tropical khaki uniforms? Mike couldn't understand why they were still wearing the olive

drab wool. He sweated profusely and it became trapped under his skin. His chest, back, and upper arms were covered with blisters. He purchased every possible remedy at the Post Exchange, but nothing seemed to give relief for more than a few minutes. The nights were the worst. He badly needed to sleep, but hour after hour the intense itching kept him awake.

The days of testing finally arrived. The evaluations covered both physical and mental capabilities and would determine his aptitude for aircrew training. He read maps, remembered numerical series, and took written comprehension tests and the like. The mental exam consisted of some paper and pencil tests, and a psychiatrist asked him a series of questions. When one of the testing psychiatrists asked Mike what he wanted to do, Mike said he wanted to be a pursuit pilot. The psychiatrist laughed. "You're not crazy enough. You would have to fly ahead of the squadron looking for enemy planes, and then shoot them out of the sky. You gotta be real crazy to do that. But you do have the leadership ability to be pilot on a bomber and to command a bomb crew."

Mike's first exam day lasted ten hours, and

when he finished, he felt like he'd been marching the entire day. His brain felt like it was wrapped in dark gauze.

The second day was not quite as long, and he returned to his barracks energized. He had played all day in a penny arcade. His coordination was measured in a variety of ways, and he marveled at the engineers that had created the machines. One test had a lathe that turned counter-clockwise. It had a cutting disc that had to be held in place for a certain number of seconds. The more seconds, the better. Another machine looked like an audio turntable with a dot on the plate, and the task was to see how long an armature could be kept on that dot. His favorite was a mock airplane with foot pedals and a hand stick. He had to operate both at the same time, keeping the plane level. Mike was giddy when he finished that one. *So, this is what piloting might feel like. I can't wait to experience the real thing.*

The final exam was the physical. For two days he was tested for strength and endurance. He had to do as many squats, pushups, and sit-ups as possible in a certain amount of time. The ticking of the stop watch rang in his head for each one. His reaction time and steadiness were

assessed. His depth perception and color aware-
ness were evaluated. The most embarrassing
part was having to undress and stand in just his
undershorts. Every inch of his body was exam-
ined in detail. Thank God he didn't blush, his
discomfort assuaged because every other GI in
line was going through the same thing.

He was taken aback when the physician ex-
amining him said, "Mister, your next stop will be
the base hospital for a little surgery."

"What for?" Mike asked more quickly than
he meant. "With all due respect, sir."

"You are going to be circumcised."

This was a challenge Mike had not counted
on. "Why?"

"Sometimes as a soldier it's hard to maintain
good hygiene. It's for your health. The army
would rather have you in the air than in the hos-
pital because of an irritation or an infection."

When Mike received the results for all his
assessments and exams, he returned to the bar-
racks, stunned, and immediately wrote Teddy.

*Today, of all days, was rather rough on me. I
was a nervous wreck. I was worried like an ex-
pectant father. You could have knocked me over*

with a feather when the major said I made all three.

He had qualified to be a pilot, a bombardier, and a navigator.

Later that day, Mike saw a cadet sitting on the curb, crying. Mike's elation over his own results eroded as he asked, "We were together at Allegheny. What's happened?"

"I washed out," the soldier said, looking at Mike through red-rimmed eyes. "I passed my first eye test but failed the second. That's the vision color test. The instructor told me I wasn't fit to walk on the curb without a seeing-eye dog. He told me I was color blind and would never become a pilot." It was a scene and a story Mike heard many more times, as men were reduced to tears when they hadn't made it through.

Being classified for all three positions was a major accomplishment, but Mike knew there was a lot of training he had yet to master. More than 100,000 of the men before him had either washed out or, even worse, had died while training. The USAAF had an attrition rate of over forty percent, due primarily to physical problems or accidents, or cadets who were un-

able to master the rigorous academic requirements.

Mike had a decision to make. He wanted to be a pilot, but it was already 1944, and he wanted to be overseas. Of the three positions he'd qualified for, becoming a pilot would take the longest. So, when the commanding officer asked Mike which position he wanted, his response was clear. "Sir, I would like to be assigned to navigation. I like the work, I understand how important it is, and, it will get me overseas that much faster."

Mike's surgery and hospital stay caused a delay. Twice he passed out because of excruciating pain from the incision. Once when he went to the latrine, and a second time when he tried to change his dressings after a bath. Mike took it all in stride, understanding the operation was necessary in the grand scheme of things. He didn't say much in his letter to Teddy.

The surgery is genital in nature, and I must admit it's very painful.

There were a few upsides to this medical procedure. He hadn't had as much sleep since he

entered the service. He was finally able to finish reading *Gone with the Wind*. He didn't have to participate in PT and he was relieved of any KP duty for the short term.

The army had a system that determined what he could do and when. If he had a red ticket, he had to stay in bed. An orange ticket meant that he could attend classes, a blue ticket meant he could do light PT, and a green ticket meant he was discharged and could assume all assigned duties, even KP. Under cadet code, KP for white GIs only meant waiting on tables. That's because there were black members on permanent KP duty, doing all the so-called dirty work: washing, cooking, peeling, and prepping.

As soon as Mike started to recover and he received his orange ticket, he was taken to another airfield some twenty-five miles away from Kelly.

Teddy, I go to Randolph Field tomorrow to be used as a medical research guinea pig there. They are doing all kinds of experiments either trying to prove something or develop ideas which will help the future flyer. The medical officer said the experiments were to be used for

high altitude flying. Our newest dreadnought
[a battleship] the B-29 has an operating
ceiling of 50,000 to 60,000 feet. (Don't spread
this as it's confidential.)

German flak (anti-aircraft fire) was effective up to 45,000 feet, and the shrapnel from exploding shells could cripple an airplane, sending it and its crew spiraling out of the sky. The new B-29 was able to fly above that altitude because it had a pressurized cabin. It was sealed, and oxygen pumped throughout, leaving the crew able to move around to do their work without the aid of oxygen masks. On one test flight, the cabin sprang leaks. The B-29 couldn't dive fast enough to get to 39,000 feet where the men might have been able to recover or don portable oxygen masks. The crew was overcome, and the plane crashed. Autopsies of the crew members showed that they had all died of anoxia.

The research Mike participated in was to find a solution to the problem of loss of oxygen and blood circulation at high altitudes. He was first x-rayed for the size of his heart at sea level, and his blood pressure and heart rate were taken. Researchers put him into a chamber and

gradually decreased the pressure. At 18,000 feet, he was told to put on the mask. He was now breathing pure oxygen. The pressure continued to decrease until it simulated what it would be like at 50,000 feet. He stayed in the cabin for fifteen minutes, and when he came out the size of his heart, his blood pressure, and heart rate were monitored again.

All went well. I felt fine. Nothing went wrong with my physical features. They said they got very good information. Just think, darling, perhaps it will be because of me that our future runs over enemy territory will be successful. I hope so. It makes you proud to know you did something in the line of Medical Research (sic), even though you were the guinea pig.

Mike's orange ticket meant he could also start classes. They were technical and complicated, and some days he ended class at ten o'clock in the evening. He was conscious of his grades and what they might mean in the long term. Math and physics pertained to bombing, aerodynamics, energy, power, velocity, and the pressures of flight. He had to learn to read

maps, charts, and aerial photography with precision. He had to study chemical warfare and incendiary bombs. He quickly mastered the identification of both allied and enemy airplanes. He needed to recognize the difference between allied and enemy airplanes, which was easy. He also needed to instantly recognize the difference between allied and enemy marine vessels, which he found difficult. The end of every class meant an exam, and all of his scores were recorded.

Mike enjoyed Morse code, the dots and dashes used to send messages. He liked the feel of the key under his finger as he tapped out the words. He quickly reached ten words a minute, but he wouldn't pass the code class until he mastered fourteen words a minute.

Most of his grades were in the nineties, but he received an eighty-three in physics. Even so, Mike worried about washing out.

I could have done much better, Teddy, provided that the classes were held in the day. I was too exhausted in the late evening to even remember my own name.

On another physics exam, he kicked himself up one side and down the other.

I would have had a perfect score, but I made a moronic mathematical error in the computation.

He needn't have worried. Mike passed all of his courses. There would be a graduation ceremony and a dance, but where Mike's next assignment would take him was still unclear. He'd either be assigned to gunnery school or to advanced navigation. All he knew was that either way, he'd be staying in Texas.

By now, May 6, 1944, Mike knew he wanted Teddy to be his wife.

I have wanted to say this for a very long time, but it's not very romantic through the mail. Honey, would you marry me? Or is it foolish to marry at times like these? Then there is my religion. You know I can't marry out of the church. It's a bit complicated, isn't it dear. Well what am I going on for; I don't even know if you'd have me. I hope anyway. I wish I could be with you to say these things. Unfortunately, I

was just beginning to know you while in Meadville. Now, I have had the time to think. Here's wishing for good news.

Mail service between San Antonio and Meadville could take time. Mail call was a GI's favorite time of the day, and there were days when Mike was despondent because nothing had come through from Teddy. Other days, he was high as a kite when two or three letters would come at a time.

It had been a week since graduation, and still there was no news, gunnery or advanced, or where.

NO LUCK AT ALL

The Harlingen Army Airfield was alive with the news when Mike arrived from San Antonio at 4:30 a.m. The invasion of Europe had begun. The Allies had landed on the beaches in Normandy, France. June 6th, 1944 was a date Mike and the rest of the world would never forget.

He was doubly excited because he'd heard from Teddy. She said yes! As soon as she could reserve train tickets, she would be on her way. She had completed her classes on how to be a good Catholic wife and have a good Catholic marriage at the Roman Catholic Church in Meadville. Teddy didn't even think about the

fact that the priest leading the classes had never been married. Although she had no plans to convert, she did agree to raise their children Catholic. That meant that they could be married by a priest, which satisfied a deep part of Mike's soul. His faith was a primary part of who he was and how he viewed the world.

However, his elation only lasted a couple of days. As he went through the processing that was routine every time he changed bases, he learned of his upcoming schedule. He would be stuck in classes the first three weeks. He would then move to the gun range on the coast for the subsequent two weeks, and on his final week he would be back on the base. It was there he would finally be on a B-24 bomber practicing gunnery under simulated combat conditions. It was the only week of this part of the training he looked forward to, as it was the only portion that satisfied his drive for action.

On his first night, his group had scrubbed the barracks and had made it the neatest on the base, which gave all of them an open post. It meant they all had a free night in town, but he found that Harlingen, thirty miles north of the Mexican border and the Gulf Coast, was

nowhere near what San Antonio had been. It was small, only 13,000 inhabitants, and it was dead. There wasn't even a bar, but at least it had a USO Club.

Bringing Teddy to Texas was going to be more difficult than he thought. Mike spent most of his free evening looking for housing for Teddy. Unsuccessfully.

I tried finding some place in which you might stay but to no avail. The hotels are very good, but it would be quite expensive for a long period of time.

He only hoped that something might open up when the next graduating class left on their way to another assignment.

Classes were nothing like he expected, and he chided himself for again letting his impatience get in the way. The manual reminded him of the instructions for building model airplanes. They were clear and concise, and the illustrations and photographs guided him through everything he needed to know. He learned about gun sites and sighting. He learned how to use these to aim in front of a moving target, which if

done right would have the target run into the bullets and not the other way around. Hands-on meant that he learned each gun's parts and how to strip, assemble, clean, and operate. He had to be able to do much of this by feel. In order to pass the course, he had to put a gun back together blindfolded. Then he learned to operate turrets and machine guns.

On his very first week, Mike stood on the range with a twelve-gauge shotgun in his hands. A clay pigeon, or skeet, was mechanically flung into the air from a variety of angles. He anchored his feet on the hard-packed ground and rested the gun against his right shoulder. At first the recoil of the gun surprised him, but he adjusted. Shooting skeet out of the air was fun.

The next phase of training was somewhat more challenging. He had to learn to shoot from a moving open truck. Men would stand on the bed of the truck while a driver went around an oblong mile-long dirt track. GIs would take turns jettisoning the clay pigeon from inside a wooden slat hut at the edge of the track. Standing firm on the truck, sighting the target, and firing was no easy feat. Hitting the skeet was harder still.

On one sweltering day, it was Mike's turn inside the hut. He was operating the trap that jettisoned the pigeon, but it wasn't firing correctly. The clay disc would get to the end of the arm and break apart. Mike put out a white flag as a way to indicate that things weren't going well. He finally got the machine operating properly, and he pushed out a bird. He felt a peppering sensation on his chest and face, which he ignored. He just kept pushing out birds.

Outside, the tropical Texas air was oppressive with heat and humidity. Inside the hut it was even worse. Mike's T-shirt was soaked with sweat, and he realized the dastardly prickly heat would be back. He looked down at his wet shirt to discover it was not just sweat. It was covered in blood. He put out a red flag to let the others know that he was in trouble.

Trucks continued around the track several times until his warning flag was noticed. At the base hospital, the attending doctor pulled forty-nine pellets from Mike's face and chest.

The doctor put his instruments on a tray, looked at Mike with a semi-smile and said, "There is a pellet in your chin. It is buried too deep for me to get it without doing more damage

than is necessary. It won't hurt anything to stay right where it is, but I want you to know that it will travel. One day you'll be taking a shower or a bath, and you will feel it, and months later you may feel it somewhere else. Just remember not to worry."

The doctor then cleared Mike to report back to the firing range. When Mike got back to the track, the instructing officer in charge told Mike to get up on the truck. It was time for him to do some shooting. Mike made it around the track several times with no incidents. However, the third time around one of the clay pigeons was coming straight at him. He fired and hit it, but it broke up in his face.

Off he went to the hospital again to be treated by the very same doctor. "What's up with you?"

"If it weren't for bad luck, sir, I'd have no luck at all."

The weather was more bad luck as far as Mike was concerned. The Harlingen base was new, built in 1941. The ground beneath and adjacent to the runways and practice ranges, flat and bare as far as the eye could see, was perfect for a gunnery school. The base had been hastily

built but designed with precision, making it pic-turesque. Row upon row of white wooden struc-tures lay in straight lines at angles facing the airplane hangars and the runways further out. The layout was clean, neat, and tidy. Live oaks and palm trees had been planted all over the base, which gave it a welcoming feel. They were placed in neat exact rows, but they weren't close enough to provide any shade to the buildings. Once again, his barracks was like an oven, and he sweated profusely while on the field. His prickly heat had come back with a vengeance. Adding insult to injury were the mosquitoes.

I'm at the point where they can't bite me any-more, Teddy. Just last night I was awakened only to find them turning my dog tags over in order that they might discover what type of blood I had.

On the upside, every evening and weekend Mike was free. There was a beer garden right around the corner from his barracks. It was there, while sitting around a picnic table under the shade of a palm tree, that he met John An-dersen and his fiancé, Mary Spiridigliozzi. The

two men became fast friends, and John asked Mike to stand up for him at his upcoming marriage.

There was only one problem with the wedding. Mary had yet to find a dress. John and Mary thought they might have some luck shopping across the border in Mexico. They asked Mike to accompany them the very next weekend. All went well, and Mary purchased a lovely gown. John wasn't allowed to see it, but Mike gave his approval and they headed back to the border. Mary was Italian with dark hair and deep olive skin. The US border guards could not be convinced, even with all of her paperwork in order, that she was an American and not a Mexican trying to sneak into the country. Six hours later, and with much wrangling, a phone call from the base convinced the guards to let her through.

Mike's own wedding plans were also coming together. The base Catholic chaplain was on leave, but the priest from Harlingen was filling in. He came out every Sunday to say Mass and he was available for all of the upcoming Saturdays. He would perform the ceremony at the base chapel.

Mary had agreed to help with Teddy's arrival. She would also help Teddy find more permanent housing.

"Mary can pick you up at the train station. She is a very sweet girl, and she is also Catholic. She may give you all the advice you need. She will be a witness if it's all right with you."

Michael approached the colonel on two occasions asking permission to be married on an upcoming weekend. Each of those times the plans fell through as Teddy had trouble reserving a seat on the train. When Mike asked for the third time the colonel said, "I really don't believe you are getting married."

"Sir, I know I have asked you twice before, but I just got a telegram. My fiancée will definitely be here this coming weekend."

"She'd better, because I will be in attendance," the colonel said. "And I will announce the ceremony to the entire base. It'll give these guys something to look forward to on the weekend."

The colonel was true to his word, and the chapel was filled with about 200 airmen. At the end of the ceremony, Mike hailed a taxi and waited for Teddy to get through the receiving

line. Each man considered it his duty to give her a kiss. She was the most beautiful woman he had ever seen, and she glowed with the attention from all of those men. He was so pleased and proud that this lovely blonde was now his wife. But his irritation and impatience mounted as he waited and waited for her to get through that line.

Later Mike thought about the date: June 27, 1944. He and Teddy had only spent six weeks together in Meadville. Now, less than six months later they were married. Her family was not pleased. His family wasn't either. She was neither Italian nor Roman Catholic. What had he done? Where would this go? He let these questions slip away with a shake of his head as quickly as they came. What he knew for sure was that he loved her, and that was more than enough. They snatched a long weekend away in San Antonio for their honeymoon.

Life at Harlingen took on a brightness which colored Mike's remaining days at the base. Teddy and he lived together in a rented room in San Benito, which was only five miles away. She was able to join him some evenings at the base. Sometimes they'd go see a movie, but often they

would simply sit at the picnic table outside the beer garden with the other guys and their wives. Now instead of writing letters, he was able to share his daily experiences directly with her.

He couldn't believe how the weeks had flown by, and Teddy was here for his most anticipated training week. Gunnery practice in the air was mandatory for the entire air crew. Should a gunner become disabled, one of the other crew members would have to take over. Mike was excited because he was finally getting to fly. He'd be practicing on a B-24, the very heavy bomber on which he'd be a navigator in the near future.

There were two different exercises. The first was out over the water on the Gulf Coast. Motorboats pulled targets through the water. The other involved a lead plane towing a large black banner. For safety reasons, the targets and banners were towed quite far behind both the boat and plane. Each gunner fired differently-colored bullets, so that at the end of both exercises it could be determined how many hits each man made.

Mike did well. He was so pleased to have passed all of the requirements for accuracy. His

scores were good, and he knew he would move on.

It was different for some of the others. Some of them were being trained specifically as gunners, and once again he watched as many washed out. The USAAF was exacting on the proficiency of the gunners. It had to be, but the anguish he witnessed once again shook him, and he wondered whether he might be shedding some tears at the end of his next assignment. The toughest part of getting overseas was before him: he was assigned to San Marcos Army Airfield for navigation school.

The pleasure of being with Teddy as his wife was about to end as well. San Marcos was small, housing was limited, and he was going to be in school for a long eighteen weeks. Teddy wanted to work, so they decided she would go to Austin. They'd only have weekends together, and the mail. His heart ached at the thought.

A CELESTIAL RHYTHM

Mike's loneliness and isolation surprised him. The time he'd spent with Teddy since they married resulted in a profound connection that, now that he was away from her again, pained him deeply. He shook his head, reminding himself he'd see her on the weekend. Ah, young love.

Remember honey, to have a wife and a home, anything like a home, is new. I've just begun to live. Thanks to you. Then I'm all worked up and strained because of this schooling.

The classwork made his head spin. What was written on the page often just didn't make sense, and the lectures from the instructors didn't always clear up his confusion. He questioned his own intelligence, especially when the others sitting around him seemed at ease with the material. What in the world had he been thinking when he chose navigation? Astro compasses? Gyro compasses? Six hours of lectures was all Mike could take. He worried that having come so far it would be the navigation classwork and tests that would do him in.

Thank God he'd made good friends. John Anderson came with him from Harlingen, and they hooked up with Cal Carlini and Joe Cardillo. Caputo, Carlini, and Cardillo: inexplicably they became known by the other cadets as the Three Irishmen, despite being Italian. They'd complain that Texas and the USAAF knew nothing about how to make good pizza. Where were the anchovies?

When John returned from leave, he brought a gift from New York he was sure his paisan (Italian) friends were going to love. Mike, Carlini, and Cardillo roared when they opened the

box to find a case of sardines: not anchovies at all. John would never live that one down!

Once Mike got his fingers on aeronautical charts and could physically manipulate the navigational tools and instruments, his anxiety about failing diminished. Pointing to landmarks, laying the instruments on charts and drawing lines, rotating the dial on his dead-reckoning "computer," a navigational slide rule, the complicated theories and computations come to life.

All of the pieces started to fit. Pilotage was easy to understand, especially when he could locate land features and cities on the charts and maps. When Mike finally got up in the air, he'd have to learn how to calculate the route using visual landmarks on the ground, but that seemed easy compared to the theoretical mumbo jumbo he'd first started wrestling with in class.

Dead reckoning was complicated. Mike learned to calculate the plane's current position by using a previously fixed position, and then estimating using direction, speed, time, and distance traveled.

Radio navigation meant listening for and logging one radio signal, then a second signal,

and using the time difference to determine his position. The enemy could bend or jam these signals, though, so radio navigation always needed to be accompanied by other tools.

Celestial navigation was a different kettle of fish. Once he got more comfortable with the sextant, an instrument with a sighting mechanism and graduated 60° arc that measured the angular distances between objects, he quickly became adept at determining latitude and longitude. He'd look through the lens, find the moon, or sun, or a star, or any other object outside the Earth's atmosphere. Combined with charts, tables, and the exact time, Mike was thrilled when the first time he nailed their position. As a kid, Mike had loved looking at the stars and being able to name to constellations. Now he loved using the ancient practice of relying on the stars to navigate the plane and crew in the deep of the night.

Mike's confidence on the ground evaporated once he started navigating in the air. On the first mission Mike's crew encountered heavy turbulence. Bouncing around made it tough to do his calculations. His stomach made it impossible. Mike blamed the drift meter.

The drift meter was a tool that measured how far the wind was pushing the airplane off course. Looking through the eye piece, Mike saw the internal gauge rotating counter clockwise while the plane was moving forward. He felt like he was going backward and forward at the same time, and he threw up his lunch. From then on, Mike was the only navigator he knew who always flew with a large empty coffee can tied to his belt: if he was going to be sick he was at least going to be prepared.

Why in the world is it so simple on the ground, then in the air everything leaves my mind? Perhaps I was rattled because it was the first mission, and I didn't expect the adverse conditions in the weather.

After losing his cookies during the morning flight, Mike decided to lie down and forgo lunch. He felt just as queasy on the afternoon flight, but his stomach was empty and there was nothing to come up. Dry heaves and all, he turned in a 0-0 mission. His calculations were right on the money. They arrived at the exact

time his calculations said they would, and at the exact location.

Overall, his grades were good, sometimes at the top of his class, and otherwise in the average range.,

His confidence mounted, and he wrote again to Teddy.

For the first time I have visualized the tremendous amount of work a navigator has. As I said before, doing it is simple. It's remembering all you are supposed to do that's hard.

Underneath the blustering confidence in his letters was the fear that his ongoing stomach issues would mean he'd wash out. After all of this time and effort, he couldn't conceive of not getting his wings.

Meantime, there was another responsibility looming on the horizon.

They'd been using contraceptives because Mike couldn't fathom leaving a pregnant wife behind as he headed overseas. But then he learned, or perhaps he'd always known and subconsciously turned a blind eye, that in the

Catholic Church using contraception was forbidden.

> *Honey, if this is to continue, I shall not be able to receive communion. However that only concerns the fact that if I want to receive communion, we cannot do this. I wish you would discuss this with Father. You and I were ignorant of that fact so get some light on the subject.*

Teddy had been taking classes with a priest at St. Mary's Church in Austin. By the end of her classes, Teddy decided to convert. She'd been searching for a church, looking denomination to denomination, but none seemed to resonate deep inside. In the Catholicism classes she began to understand her husband's deep faith and she found her own spiritual longing quenched. She was baptized, received her first Holy Communion, and was confirmed all in the same day.

Teddy confirmed that Mike would not be able to receive Communion if they continued to give in to their physical desires while using any-

thing other than the rhythm method or abstinence to prevent pregnancy. She told Mike that going to Mass and not being able to receive was like not going to church at all. She also said that one of the things that had made her fall in love with him in the first place was his active faith. He didn't miss Mass unless the circumstance was extreme, and he always received communion. Teddy did not want to take that away from him. They committed to practicing abstinence when her cycle dictated.

They had made the decision together not to use contraceptives. They had not decided they'd always abstain. Soon, Teddy brought home news from her doctor. She was pregnant.

Saturday was the happiest day I've ever experi-

*enced. You just don't know how happy that
news had made me. I'm walking around camp
proud as a peacock. I just keep telling all the
married men what a man I am. To think only
one night and we rung the bell. Of course, you
get a lot of the credit. We are a good pair.*

Now that Mike was going to be a father, his
fear of washing out was stronger than ever. His
grades were good, and he was becoming more
accurate each practice mission, but he was still
getting sick on flights. With a growing family, he
not only wanted his wings, he needed them.

*A commission at one time darling was a thing
of great pride to achieve. Yes, it still is, but to
me it's differently attached. Now I need it to
have the best for you and the coming baby.*

Mike spoke with his instructor, Colonel Bob
Teague, about his fear of washing out. Teague
offered to go to bat for him, asking the board to
look at every single log Mike had completed. He
challenged them to find a mistake in any of
Mike's logs. They couldn't.

Mike learned he had successfully completed

navigation school, and that he was immediately shipping out to Charleston, South Carolina, on the same day. He went looking for Colonel Teague to thank him for going to bat for him, but he couldn't find him.

*M*ike and Teddy headed back to Meadville for his short leave. He originally thought he'd have to say goodbye to her there, but then he learned there was housing available for married couples in Charleston. This trip's purpose changed then: to share the big news with Kate, Teddy's mother, and to invite her to come stay with them in Charleston. He might only be there for twelve weeks, but they were family. Mike wanted them together.

"Kate, we will have two bedrooms. Would you consider coming down and spending some time with Teddy and me? I don't want her to work, and there probably aren't jobs for her

anyway." Mike saw confusion on Kate's face, because Kate knew that Teddy liked to work. She was wondering why Mike didn't want her to work now.

"I would feel so much better with you there now that Teddy's pregnant," Mike watched the dawning awareness in Kate's eyes turn to delight. "I will often be away overnight and for days on training missions, and it will give my mind ease knowing she isn't alone."

With his new and growing family sharing the Charleston home, the USAAF was busy trying to create another sense of family with the crews training together stateside, which had been proven more effective than throwing them together once they arrived overseas. Each crew was becoming a band of brothers.

A sergeant picked Mike up at the train station in the deep of the night. The ride to the location of the extended training exercise in the open Jeep in the damp mid-forties had him hugging himself against the chill. The sergeant stopped the Jeep right in front of Mike's assigned Quonset hut, and it looked like a haven of warmth with smoke pouring out of the chimney.

Inside, despite the late hour, a man was adding more wood to the potbellied stove.

"I'm Jerry Paikan, and I've been assigned as the bombardier on your new crew. I waited up because at night the fire will go out, and this place is like a fridge. And, there's something I really need to say to you."

Mike wondered what could be so urgent. Had something happened to Teddy in the short time he'd been traveling? Was the war over and his service no longer required?

Jerry's face was tense as he continued. "I am a Jew, and I want to know if that is going to be a problem for you. Are you going to want a Jew on your crew?"

Mike laughed out loud as relief flooded his veins. Then he saw Jerry's face and realized this was a pivotal moment. "I was laughing at the rhyme, 'Jew on a crew.' I just really have one question for you. Can you hit a target? Can you get those bombs to go where they are supposed to go?"

"So far, I have done very well," Jerry responded.

"Well, all I care about is you hitting the target. As far as the other thing is concerned, look

at this mug of mine. I have frequently been mistaken for being Jewish. Italian, Jewish, we just need to be able to do our jobs."

Mike turned toward the empty cot, paused and turned back around. "Thanks for keeping the hut so warm. All my sorry ass wants is to be horizontal on that thing." All the tension had dissipated, and both men smiled.

The following morning as Mike was on his way to his first meeting at headquarters, he passed a man running out of the shower, buck naked, holding a towel in front of him. He was yelling at the top of his voice, "Hey, you can't start without me! You can't start without me!"

Mike shook his head and laughed. A few minutes later the same man showed up to the meeting crisply dressed in uniform. The two crosses on his lapels identified him as the base chaplain. Mike couldn't shake the image of the naked screaming man from his head and he worked to suppress the laugh. When the chaplain stood to speak, Mike had to work even harder. If he had heard this "sermon" once he had heard it a thousand times.

"Men, the best defense against contracting venereal disease is abstinence."

Mike allowed himself a broad smile. Abstinence might very well be a good defense against VD, but it would also prevent fatherhood. And, Mike thought happily, *That cow's out of the barn!*

After he'd returned to base from the training exercise, Mike brought Teddy with him one day to the mess hall, where again he met the chaplain. When the chaplain saw Teddy in line, he pointed to the very visible bump on Teddy's belly and signaled for the German POWs who were dishing out the food to load up her plate. It was more than Teddy could eat, so Mike happily finished the plate for her.

Mike frequently saw the POWs around the base. They were put to work in maintenance and the motor pool. They were transported out to the local farms to provide much-needed labor with husbands and sons being off at the war. Mike sensed that they were treated well, and in return the POWs introduced to the mess hall the Black Forest Cake. Saliva filled Mike's mouth the minute he spied it on the dessert table. Layers of moist chocolate cake sandwiching bright red cherry filling, all coated with a frothy layer of whipped cream.

When Teddy was with him, she usually got a

larger piece. He loved seeing the POWs smile at her, whether it was just because she was so pretty or because she was pregnant, he didn't know. In those moments, his beloved beside him, glowing and growing with their child inside her, other men admiring her, he felt he had never been happier. *Wasn't this the sweet life?*

He wished that those thoughts and feelings would stay with him, but they were fleeting against the reality of his experiences on the base. A war room had been created in an empty building, equipped with large maps on the walls and sliding stands with more maps. A projector whirred as images from the front were splashed on a big screen at one end of the room. Intelligence officers outlined the progress of the war twice a day, six days a week. Mike started to feel the enormity of the responsibility he was training for. Responsibility for his wife, his child, his life, the lives of his crewmates, for all the other American servicemen currently fighting, for the very outcome of the war itself. That responsibility lay like a rock in his stomach. When practicing his navigation skills with his new crewmates, the rock became heavier. The consequences of making even the slightest error in

calculation threatened to distract him from the task.

He had to focus on the business at hand. There were exercises with other navigators and evening celestial navigation flights. There were classes and practice in gunnery with his entire crew. Once a crew member had reached a certain level of proficiency they were allowed to opt out of practice. They met and worked with the maintenance and ground crews that would follow them overseas, transported by ship, meeting the flight crew at their assigned base.

Altitude training with the crew was where the magnitude of their responsibility to one another really took hold for Mike. He learned the correct way to put on his own oxygen mask, and how to determine if it was operating properly. He learned how to put a mask on a crew member, and how to tell if it wasn't working for them. Flying at high altitudes meant less oxygen. If a crew member's oxygen mask malfunctioned, he wouldn't sense anything to let him know he was in trouble. His thinking would become confused and his reaction times slowed. He would appear drunk, and within six minutes he would be dead.

The crew went on practice missions together in the cramped quarters of their B-24. Being so close in the tight space, all working on the same objective, had exactly the effect the USAAF wanted. It created the camaraderie that was necessary for the success of every mission. Each crew member was well-trained in their individual roles, now they needed to train as a crew —putting it all together, flying a mission, finding and getting to the target, and bombing—with as much accuracy as possible.

The winter weather in Charleston sometimes prevented the crew from flying. The skies would often have dense cloud coverage making flight impossible, or at least unsafe. The war wasn't waiting for good weather, however, and the USAAF found clear skies and a practice range in Cuba: Batista Field near Havana. The barren flat fields surrounding the airport provided the perfect place for bomb practice.

As the B-24 carrying Mike and his crew approached the practice target, white circles on the ground got bigger and bigger. Mike knew they were about 100 feet across. In the center of each was a bullseye. Over and over, they'd approach the target, trying from different directions. Over

and over, the bombardier would release his load of fake bombs, made of sand or flour, Mike didn't know and didn't care. He was navigator, but the accuracy of the drop depended on all of them. Mike plotted the course that gave the pilots the direction they needed, and the gunners were ready to protect the plane should they find themselves under attack.

Mike and his crew were also trained on how to bail out if the plane was going down. There wasn't much room to maneuver inside the B-24, even stripped down as it was for training. With his heavy flight suit and his parachute, Mike wondered, *How in the hell am I supposed to get out when this plane is loaded for bear?*

QUITE THE GAME

The flight from Charleston to Mitchel Field on Long Island, New York was uneventful. Mike felt at home with his crew. The team was excited about deployment, if a bit nervous beneath the surface. The back slaps, the camaraderie, the jokes… all masked the subsurface tension.

The Army Air Force had preached the importance of their training together as a crew. Mike and his mates had worked together for twelve long weeks, and they had become close in unexpected ways. Which was why the USAAF's move made no sense. Jerry Paikan was ordered to the South Pacific. Whatever the crew's final

destination across the Atlantic, they'd be a crew of nine instead of ten.

Mike was angry. This felt personal. From that first night in Charleston, Mike and Jerry had built a strong bond. They could sit together in silence or spar in mock fisticuffs. It was a rare sort of friendship for Mike. And now? Would he ever see him again?

The only thing that soothed his anger and disappointment was that he was going to see Teddy before he got his orders and left New York. Teddy was settled in their apartment in Meadville with her mother, and she was at the hotel in Garden City now waiting for him. They'd have three glorious days together, and Mike planned to make each day with her last a lifetime.

At the end of the three days, Mike told his wife to take care of herself and their baby. He said he'd miss her. His feelings for her were so big they threatened to swallow him whole. He wanted to tell her but couldn't. The thoughts were in his head, but the words stuck deep in his throat. *What in hell is wrong with me?*

He wanted to tell her where he was going

next, too. But he couldn't—because he didn't know.

"We've been given heavy winter gear, so I guess we're not going to the Pacific," Mike said, standing with Teddy before she got on the train back to Meadville, rubbing her arms against the damp February chill. "We'll have an envelope with us, and we're under strict orders not to open it until we've passed over the St. Lawrence River at Lake Ontario." Mike watched Teddy climb the steps of the train, wondering when— or if—he would see her again.

In the air over the St. Lawrence, the contents of the opened envelope told the crew that their final destination was to Valley, Wales. But they wouldn't be flying straight there. They'd be doing shorter puddle jumps, base to base, along the coast and island to island.

The North Atlantic was an important sea lane getting men and supplies from the United States, Canada, and Iceland to England. Germany had invaded Norway, and there was fear that the same could happen in each of those countries. In the last four years, these bases had been built to protect against a land invasion.

Crews stationed there patrolled the coast for enemy-vessel-escorted convoys.

The crew's first stop was Goose Bay, Labrador, where the terrain was flat and the weather conditions were good for flying. Supposedly. When they landed, the snow was so deep the streets were hollowed out of it. Mike saw a moose trapped in it. He was thankful the stay would be short.

Soon after leaving Goose Bay, the crew began to have difficulty with the radio, which forced them to land at Bluie West One, the base in Narsarsuaq, Greenland. If Newfoundland was cold and snow-bound, Greenland was treacherous. As they approached, the hair bristled on the back of Mike's neck. The airstrip was at the end of a fjord, high mountains on both sides offering no room to turn around should that be necessary. They had to fly in low, which had its own risks. In his head, Mike kept repeating, *A wing and a prayer, a wing and a prayer.*

The pilot, Bob Hipps, safely brought the plane in with precision. But the landing was jarring. The runway was made of pierced metal planking, and the thundering sound of the tires rolling across it sent shivers up Mike's spine.

Like a thousand fingernails raked across a chalk board.

Their stay on Bluie West One was also short. They couldn't fix the radio there and so they headed to Iceland. The takeoff was a breeze, comparatively speaking, the runway slanted toward the sea, the view of the horizon stunning as they gained altitude and turned eastward.

The weather turned ugly soon after their landing at the Keflavik Army Air base, thirty miles from Reykjavik. Mike laid on his bunk listening to the icy wind howl around the Nissen hut. The oil stove in the center was as hot as it could be, but it never seemed to heat the air. Huddling under a pile of blankets, Mike took advantage of the down time and wrote to Teddy.

Since 1942, letters between servicemen and their families were sent using V-mail, short for Victory Mail. Letters were reviewed by censors, then photographed and transferred to microfilm. There were two benefits to this approach: it rendered espionage tools like invisible ink and microprinting ineffective; and it was far more cost-efficient. A single roll of film the size of a pack of cigarettes could carry 1,600 letters. One twenty-pound mail bag of V-mail replaced thirty-seven

mail bags weighing 2,000 pounds. Back in the US, the letters would be blown back up and printed before being delivered.

Mike told Teddy this forsaken outpost was overcrowded because the weather had grounded all airplanes. He told her his hut was the movie theater, so if he'd already seen the film playing, he'd head to the officer's club to write. He was limited in what he could say, every letter passing through the censors.

You should see these GIs during the romance scenes, honey. Back home they'd make fun of the lad and lass or pucker their lips and make smooching noises. Here, in these scenes, they quiet right down. They are quiet and intense, making believe it's them and their girl or wife back home. And I was right with them. I didn't see the hero or heroine, but you and I holding each other close, saying "I love you darling." I felt like crying many times because my heart was breaking from loneliness.

Mike explained to Teddy where some of the money he was sending home came from. He hoped some of his poker winnings would cover

the cost of the hospital when she gave birth, and they wouldn't have to use any of the money from his allotment.

Poker was a big deal. It was a way to handle the boredom and tedium of being grounded. Most games were light hearted and fun. Most, but not all.

One of the guys at the table was a navigator nobody liked. He was an arrogant know-it-all. He'd come into the service from a college Reserve Officers Training Corp (ROTC), which meant this lieutenant hadn't been subject to the hazing that was a part of basic training.

The airmen were playing five-card stud. Mike had two aces facing down. The dealer dealt the lieutenant a face-up king and the lieutenant kept raising, but Mike knew he had the guy beat. After the call, Mike showed his winning cards. Mike's smile froze as the lieutenant pulled a .45 and aimed it squarely at Mike's face. As the other players wrestled the lieutenant to the floor, Mike got up and left. When he was finally alone, he began to shake, tears of fear and relief seeping from the corners of his eyes, past the image emblazoned on the retina of his mind:

the muzzle of the gun and the twitching trigger finger behind it.

He had already sent Teddy eight-hundred dollars from his winnings. He would send what he won that night, but that was it. If he ever played poker again it would have to be penny ante.

Next morning's cooler heads were accompanied by a break in the weather. Mike's crew once again took off, headed to Valley, Wales. The flight took them over more than 600 hundred miles of open ocean.

Hipps thumbed the mic switch on his headset. "Mike, when should we see Stornoway?"

"Looks like it will be a minute and a half," Mike said. Ninety seconds later land, and Stornoway came into view.

In Wales, final destination orders were posted on a bulletin board in the hallway at base headquarters. When Mike read them, his palms turned sweaty and his stomach did somersaults. They were being sent to Thorpes Abbot, a small village twenty-five miles southwest of Norwich, England. It was the home of the 100th Bomb Group. Its reputation was well known throughout the USAAF, and it wasn't good.

ADMINISTRATIVE ERROR

The Bloody 100th—the nickname of the 100th Bomb Group—was legendary stateside.

The legend was that a B-17 from the 100th had been hit and was flying with one of its engines out. The plane, Picklepuss, was surrounded by the Luftwaffe when the landing gear was lowered. This was a signal to the Germans that the plane was surrendering and to cease the attack. As the Luftwaffe began to retreat, the B-17 then opened fire. Furious, the Germans shot the plane down. From that time, so says the legend, the 100th became a special target of the Germans.

The casualty rate of the Bloody 100th was high for two reasons. First, because the gap between each plane flying in formation was too large, making for easier targets. And second, because the 100th was often the "tail in Charlie," the last group in formation, they were easy for enemy fighters to pick off. Only four of the original thirty-eight copilots in the group completed their combat tour of twenty-five missions. The Bloody 100th lost 229 planes, 768 men were killed or missing in action, and 939 men captured as prisoners of war. Mike didn't care where he was posted, except he didn't want to go to the Bloody 100th. But an order was an order.

It turned out to have been an administrative error. Thorpes Abbott was a B-17 base. Mike and his crew flew B-24s. He blew out a long breath of air and the tension in his neck disappeared. His orders had changed! He and his crew were *not* assigned to the Bloody 100th. They were going to someplace called Rackheath, near Norwich, twenty miles northwest of Thorps Abbott. He knew nothing about the

base, but anything had to be better than going to the 100th.

Mike wrote to Teddy as soon as he was settled in his Nissen hut at Rackheath. War rules permitted him to tell her that he was in England, but not precisely where. He thought carefully about each sentence as he wrote, being as truthful as he could without breaking the rules or burdening her with worry. He was happy to report that the conditions were good.

I have everything I could possibly wish for. We have a rather nice club, and quite a bit to do here.

What he didn't have was a bicycle. The base was large and sprawling. Buildings were scattered, strategically spread out over acres to make it more difficult for enemy bombers to cause widespread damage. German fighter pilots had more area to cover if they dropped low and strafed, which would cover sections of the base with machine gun fire.

Mike's hut was blocked from enemy view under a dense canopy of trees. He had long walks

to the shower or the mess hall. Many GIs had bicycles to get around, and Mike planned to get one from the next GI who had finished his missions and was going home.

With his new bicycle, Mike began exploring more of the surrounding area. The roads he traveled were flat and the pedaling easy. Bordered by newly planted fields or lush forest. The smell of spring and loamy earth reminded him of Teddy. Everything reminded him of her.

When he returned to his empty Nissen hut after chow, his eyes lingered on her picture on the shelf. The hut was damp and cold. The oil stove hadn't yet been lit, and the canopy of trees over the hut prevented the sun's rays from warming it up. He sat on his bunk chilled to the bone. His fingers were so stiff; it was hard to write.

Gee darling, I'll smear this whole page if my tears don't stop. But, don't worry too much, honey. I'm all right. Guess I'm very lonesome

tonight. At least when I'm in the sack, I have your picture to watch over me.

Often the English weather was overcast and bleak, but he felt lucky in spite of it.

When the sun is shining (which is rare), it's beautiful. But it sure is terrible while it continually rains... You know the usual dreary type so common of England. The little potbellied stove is just throwing enough heat to take the dampness out of these Nissen huts. I am not complaining though for it is very restful and cheerful considering that I am in a combat area. I only wish that thousands of boys have quarters and food half as good as I am receiving. Sometimes I forget that I am in combat and think it's just another peaceful countryside to enjoy a vacation.

Rackheath was beautiful, and Mike was fascinated by its history. He thought his hometown of Scranton, established in 1840, was old. This little place was established in 1422 when two smaller and even older villages combined. That was seventy years before Columbus attempted

his ocean voyage, and 300 years before the American Revolution.

The village of Rackheath was about five miles northeast of Norwich, its economy based on agriculture. Even now, the villagers still relied on what they grew in their own gardens or purchased from local shops. They rarely, if ever, visited Norwich since transportation services were limited.

The villagers had become accustomed to the war, fighter aircraft often circling overhead or lined up between missions at the base airfield nearby. Construction of the air base began in the autumn of 1942, on land belonging to Sir Edward Stacey. Most of the airfield was completed in mid-1943. Hundreds of Irish labored to complete the base, and hard-core rubble from bombed-out homes and factories in Norwich and London provided the raw material for the runways.

The main runway ran north to south, 6,000 feet long and 150 feet wide. There were two other runways, each 4,500 feet long. Crews tried to lengthen at least one of the shorter two. But the path traversed a bog, and no matter how much debris they put into it, the runway kept

sinking. Circling the runways were hardstands with parking space for two planes each.

Once completed, the base was handed over to the Royal Air Force. Much to the villagers' surprise, trains loaded with Americans began to arrive. It soon became clear this was to be an American base. Locals were horrified, having heard the American men had "loose morals," and they feared for the safety of the ladies in the village.

Mike had heard the reputation American men had here: they were "oversexed, overpaid, and over here." A British pound was equal to four American dollars at that time, so Mike understood the overpaid part. He howled when he heard the often-given retort by the Americans that the Brits were, "undersexed, underpaid, and under Eisenhower."

STANDING in the chow line waiting for his supper, Mike found himself looking at a familiar face.

"Joe Fantino, what the hell are you doing here?" Ready for a fight, Fantino turned to see

who the gruff voice belonged to. A huge grin soon broke out on his face. Both men put down their trays, cutlery rattling, and pulled each other into a back-slapping hug.

They hadn't seen each other for two years. Mike and Joe had worked together at Cochran Army Airfield in Macon, Georgia. Both had repaired airplanes. Both had petitioned to be released from their jobs. Both had taken the entrance exam at the same time and had passed. Both had lied about having spent time in college. Both had signed up for the Army Air Corp to become cadets. Joe was released from his deferment two months before Mike. They hadn't seen each other since.

When their trays were full, they headed to the nearest table. At first neither was able to speak. Mike asked again, "What are you doing here?"

Joe looked back with a how-stupid-can-you-be expression on his face. "I'm stationed here, you idiot. I'm a navigator."

It was the same old Joe. Mock attacks were his specialty. Mike fired back, "So smart ass, how long have you been here? And, by the way I am a navigator too."

Joe chuckled as he swallowed another mouthful of his A-rations, consisting of canned meat, powdered potatoes, and locally-sourced vegetables. A-rations were the best military meals of all, served at bases behind the front lines where kitchens were equipped with both refrigeration and cooking facilities.

"Twelve missions in. You're still doing practice missions?"

"Yup. Ready for the real thing, though."

"Come and find me when you do. We can compare notes."

Mike couldn't wait to get back to his hut and write to Teddy. He could tell her he now had a buddy on the base (which relieved some of his homesickness), and that Joe's experience from his missions told him the war was going well for the Allies. Today Mike was full of hope about the future.

You were talking of my sending you plans of any home that I saw and liked. Well, darling, there's a very cute house plan in a magazine... and I'll have to save it. I'm very much in favor of the fire place in the living room. I should like one in our bedroom, too. I have great visions of

*you and I before the fireplace after we've put the
kids in bed and heard their prayers. We won't
be saying much—just sitting close together
with your arm around me and our hearts full
of peace and happiness.*

As Mike penned those words, change was in the works. The practice missions were finished, and base commanders were slating Mike's crew in for their first combat mission.

SHORT CIRCUIT

Mike sat through so many ground school lectures he felt like he could stand up at the front of the class and teach the crews himself. The repetitive lectures under Colonel Shower's command became tedious. The colonel was also responsible for the hours of flight practice, and when exhausted from a long training mission, Mike was none too fond of the colonel. Once he was rested and had a clearer head, he couldn't argue with the 467th's record or reputation.

Colonel Shower's superiors commended him for the performance of 467th bomb group. They led in the percentage of aircraft fully operational

and came in first or second for many months with the lowest loss rates. They set a record, flying 100 missions in 140 days, dropped 13,353 tons of bombs, and flew 35,537 operational flying hours. The men who drove the base vehicles also set records for low motor-pool accident rates. There were also records set for the best-kept aircraft, a thirty-hour engine change being done in just over eight hours, and the highest number of war bonds sold.

Colonel Shower's nickname was "Black Al." He fired bombardiers, demoted pilots, and transferred anyone who didn't perform up to his standards. He insisted on flying tight formations, peeling off with precision, and assembling with speed. He made sure that pre-mission briefings included the locations where flak was most likely so that squadrons could avoid it where possible.

Colonel Shower told his men that the tighter the formation, the less vulnerable the squadron of B-24s would be to fighter plane attacks. The colonel would fly in Big Pete, a stripped-down, war-weary B-24 painted in garish colors. He circled around gaining altitude, lights fully on. The other planes would latch on to these lights and

circle as well, until the last plane was off the ground. Sometimes the Colonel would fly Little Pete, a P-47. If any aircraft lagged behind, he'd use hand signals or flares to direct them back into formation. When all planes reached the pre-determined altitude and Shower was satisfied, he would peel off and head back to the base.

Mike felt as prepared as he could be for his first live mission. His wake-up call was early, he dressed and headed to the mess hall for break-fast, where real eggs were served, not the pow-dered kind. The pre-mission briefing was clear and precise, a subtle electric tension in the air. The war was going well. General Patton and his troops were in the area of the proposed bomb-ing. If they got too close to Patton, they'd be given a secondary target or a place to release their load. A plane fully loaded with bombs was too heavy and would run out of fuel before making the return to base.

After a special meeting for all of the naviga-tors, Mike dressed in his flight gear, picked up his parachute, and climbed onto the truck that would take him and the rest of his crew to the plane. Nobody said a word on that ride, which gave Mike the time and space to pray.

The instructors at ground school had repeatedly stressed the dangers the crew might encounter. Temperature, for example. The B-24 did not have a pressurized cabin, and flying between 18,000 and 28,000 meant the temperature dropped to -40°F. Those altitudes also brought physical changes: sluggish minds and muscles affected response times; ears plugged; stomachs and intestines expanded.

Like all the airmen fighting in World War II, Mike and his crew all wore the F-2 electrically-heated flying suits, gloves, and boots. When plugged into a twenty-four-volt receptacle, the rheostat controls would heat the lining, thus helping to keep the men warm. Strict training instructions warned airmen to avoid perspiration and wipe their bodies dry before dressing in the flight suit, and then to avoid anything that would trigger perspiration while flying wearing the suit. Moisture and electricity are not happy bedfellows.

These heated suits caused some issues for navigators like Mike. The electric current affected the magnetic compasses, and before taking any readings, Mike had to turn off his rheostat control or unplug his suit. His stubby

fingers on their own made tricky work of the instrument calculations he needed to make to keep the plane in formation and on course. Add the insulated gloves and he needed to exercise tight focus and special care. If he removed his gloves, his fingers would freeze in minutes. If he began to breathe heavily for any reason, his goggles would freeze over, making it impossible to see.

Mike checked his oxygen mask before the flight, and he was extra careful putting it on as they reached 10,000 feet. If the mask failed, he would pass out in thirty seconds and be dead in two minutes. As navigator, it was his job to monitor the other crew members. He'd call on the interphone, and if there was no response another crew member would be assigned to do an in-person check.

There were medics on the ground crew, but none on the air crew. It was also Mike's job to assist with casualties and administer fairly basic first aid, the only treatment available to an injured crew member, who could otherwise lie for hours until the plane could get back to base. But on this first mission, they flew to the target, released their bombs, and flew back. They encountered no flak on the way in or out.

Back at the base, mission completed, Mike wrote to Teddy.

Well hon, it finally came. Your beloved has put in mission number one. I can't say anything about it, but it was too easy to suit me.

Too easy, but not totally easy. For once Mike was glad for the censors because he didn't have to own up to the fact that, this time, he didn't *want* to tell it all in his letter to Teddy. He didn't tell her that Patton's army had indeed been close, so the squadron dropped low over the countryside looking for a place to release the bombs. He didn't tell her he'd never forget the name of the place: Unterschlauersbach, Germany. He wrote that he missed her, visions of what he saw out the nearest window as the pilot banked for a turn swirling in his head.

They flew low enough that Mike could clearly see it was civilians working in the field. Some had turned terrified faces skyward, wondering if the payload would drop on their heads. Most were already on their knees. Mike saw hands pressed together in prayer, and his heart lurched with the realization that he was the in-

strument of death these people feared. Not exactly his first enemy sighting, but the first glimpse of the fact that to those people below, *he* was the enemy.

The ground reconnaissance complete, the pilot pulled back on the yolk, climbed to a safer altitude, circled back, and released the bombs. Mike would not look out the window, but he would never forget the images of the defenseless German peasants as they contemplated the end of their lives at the hands of Allied bombers.

Mike and his crew were listed for another mission the following morning. The target was Lechfeld Air Base in Germany, home to many of the new Messerschmitt Me 262 fighter jets. The USAAF did not want these planes able to get off the ground. The Me 262 was the first German operational jet-powered fighter aircraft. These planes were fast, flexible, and deadly.

Bad weather kept the group from flying at the intended hour. The pea-soup weather around England and the English Channel could roll in fast and thick. Planes already in the air risked crashing into each other mid-air or on landing. When missions were delayed or cancelled due to weather, they wouldn't count to-

wards the threshold needed before an airman was eligible to be sent home. The three-hour weather delay added to Mike's tension, growing like a balloon in his gut. Yesterday had been too easy, Unterschlauersbach aside. Mike was certain flying so close to an enemy air base was going to be different.

He was right. The flight out was uneventful, and they dropped their bombs right on target. As they turned for home, the flak started. The explosions bounced the plane, wings shuddering, the sound inside the aircraft deafening.

The Germans used radar to estimate the altitude of the Allied planes and fire eighty-eight-caliber guns into the air. The shells exploded, sending sharp pieces of steel in all directions — above, around, and below the aircraft. The explosions were so intense that they could throw the pilot and copilot out of their seats and through the roof had they not been strapped in. Flak pierced metal, fuel lines, oxygen lines, and bodies.

When Mike saw one of the planes in his squadron hit and go down, he swallowed his fear and forced himself to focus on his navigation tasks.

Then came the Me 262s. Mike craned his neck and watched helplessly as an Me 262 approach an Allied bomber, dropped under and behind it, then gained speed as it climbed to the level of the target. The B-24 was a sitting duck before the murderous Messerschmitt shooting its 30mm cannon at close range. The B-24's turret guns couldn't turn quickly enough to knock them out of the sky. By some miracle, Mike's B-24 approached the English Channel, the flak and the Me 262s receding.

Realizing they'd survived the worst of the mission, Mike's bladder let loose, which short-circuited his heated flying suit. At this altitude and temperature, without his heated suit, he'd only have a few minutes. He used the interphone. "If one of you ever says anything about this, I will have your heads. I just peed myself. Get this damn plane down to an altitude so I don't freeze to death."

When he wrote to Teddy that night, Mike told her what he was allowed and what he could. When he finished, he laughed to himself. It was funny how you could explain a thing and keep things hidden at the same time. He recalled a conversation that he'd had with a psychiatrist

who bunked for a time in the same hut. "What is it with you Catholic boys? You seem so calm and relaxed before missions," said the psychiatrist.

"If we come back, it's His will. And if we don't, it's His will." Mike believed that with all his heart. His faith soothed him in a way nothing else could. Even his solid, unshakeable faith didn't erase the terror of the afternoon and the dodge-and-weave game of chase with the Messerschmidt. It was a terror so deep he had no words to describe it, nowhere to put the massive feeling. Stuffing it all away into the deep recesses of his psyche was the only way he could keep going, return to the plane for mission number three the next morning, and all the missions that followed.

Flak brought down many Allied planes, and German fighter pilots brought down many more.

Mike loved the idea of taking out German fighter planes. Every one they brought down helped ensure the safety of the American crews going in.

After mission number three, Mike's crew had a day off. He stood in the air control tower counting the returning planes, mentally com-

paring to the number that had taken off that morning. The loss statistics had been hard enough to fathom. Now the losses were names and faces and empty bunks.

Training was over.

THE LIBERATOR

Mike had climbed in and out of B-24s more times than he could count. Mostly during training and practice flights, but he had spent hundreds of hours in her. He'd flown in variants H, M, and J. The J was his most frequent. He knew every nook and cranny from having repaired them, and he was as familiar with her as any model airplane he'd ever built from scratch.

Unlike models, the B-24 was a huge work-horse. When she worked well, she was beautiful. The strong and steady hum of her engines was unmistakable. The passing ground below and the sky above on clear days was a sight to be-

hold. Using his navigation skills to get the plane and crew safely to and from their destinations gave Mike a deep sense of satisfaction. In calm weather, the '24 felt solid and Mike felt safe.

But the weather wasn't always calm, nor were the battle conditions always conducive to a comfortable ride. In fact, when crawling up through the nose wheel to get into the navigator's station, he often felt claustrophobic. Secretly, he found flying four to five miles above the earth unsettling. When they encountered turbulence or, even worse, flak, the shuddering of the plane matched his shuddering nerves.

The '24 had dropped more bomb tonnage than any other bomber in the war, earning her the name "The Liberator." She didn't feel liberating to Mike.

There were two nicknames for the B-24. One was "Flying Boxcar." Its spacious slab-sided fuselage allowed the aircraft to carry up to 8,000 pounds of bombs. The other nickname was "Flying Coffin." That's because it was difficult for some of the crew to get to an exit in an emergency. There was only one exit and the openings were such a tight fit it was virtually impossible to bail out.

Over its lifetime, there were fourteen variations of the B-24. Mike flew three of them, but most of his training and combat missions had been on the J, of which 6,678 had been built. With a top speed of 290mph, it boasted a cruising speed of 215mph and a landing speed of 95mph. It had a 110-foot wingspan and its fuselage was over sixty-seven feet. Empty, the B-24J weighed 36,500 pounds. Maximum weight fully loaded was 56,000 pounds. It had a flying range of 3,700 miles.

The B-24J had thinner metal skin than other models. That brought an advantage in terms flight-distance capacity. But it wasn't helpful when surrounded by flak. Shrapnel easily pierced the skin, cutting the hydraulic and electrical lines that were attached to the inner wall. The J had a reputation for easily catching fire because the fuel tanks, placed throughout the upper fuselage, were often hit by flak.

The B-24J was also more difficult to fly. Even though lighter than other models, it was 8,000 pounds heavier than its predecessor, thanks to additional defensive armor. But there was no corresponding increase in engine power. It's climb rate was slower than the B-24D, and

there were more take-off accidents with the J. With a sluggish response time, tight-formation flying was more difficult. Heavier weight meant higher fuel consumption, which reduced its maximum flying distance.

General Hap Arnold approved the plans for the B-24 in 1938. The first prototype flew in December 1939. Britain and France both placed orders for the plane as they built up their airpower. When France fell to the Germans, the airplanes they'd ordered were instead shipped to England. One B-24, called the Commando, was modified for very long range and outfitted with more comfortable interior seating, even a bed, and was used a couple of times as a personal transport plane for Winston Churchill. The Royal Canadian Air Force, the United States Navy, and the United States Army Air Force all had B-24s in service as more and more were produced.

One of the five construction sites for the B-24 was the Henry Ford Plant at Willow Run, Michigan, outside of Detroit. The plant had more than three million square feet under a single roof and a mile-long assembly line. At peak efficiency, one B-24 rolled off the produc-

tion line every sixty-three minutes, twenty-four hours a day, seven days a week. That was 650 planes a month. By September 1945, over 18,000 B-24 bombers had been built.

The Willow Run plant played a key role in a shift in the American workforce. At first, a cantankerous, rigid Henry Ford refused to hire women at the plant. When the draft started to make a dent in the pool of potential male workers, he was forced to relent. An ad campaign encouraging women to work in defence-related factories featured Rosie the Riveter, flexing her biceps and wearing blue coveralls and a red polka dot bandana. Thus began the shift in how women saw themselves—and how the world saw women. Mike had seen that shift himself when he was a supervisor at the repair depot in Macon. And he had seen for himself the work that women could do.

The Willow Run plant was also responsible for building the most celebrated B-24 in the entire Eighth Army Air Force in Britain: Witchcraft. She rolled off the plant floor in December 1943, and after test flights she was delivered to the 790th Bomb group in Wendover, Utah. Her original crew flew her the southern air ferry

route to Kansas; Palm Beach, Florida; Trinidad; Brazil; Morocco; Cornwall, England; and finally to Rackheath.

The Witchcraft's first mission was in April 1944. She flew for a year, completing 130 missions without a single abort for mechanical failures. She was peppered by flak, changed engines thirteen times, and visited sub-depots twice for major repairs. Her ground crew was credited for her stellar record. Sergeant Joe Rameriz and his crew of four were nicknamed "League of Nations" because they were descendants of Mexican, Chinese, German, and Irish immigrants. They built a shack out of salvaged wood next to the Witchcraft's hardstand. They equipped it with a kerosene stove so that they could cook and make coffee. This saved them time and they didn't have to keep bicycling to and from their huts to deliver the constant care the plane required.

Mike had seen the Witchcraft and her distinctive nose markings on the hardstand, and her record was well known all over the base. One of her most appreciated contributions to the base was during the 467th bomb group's celebration of the 200th mission. To mark the occa-

sion, the Red Cross had made a large batch of homemade ice cream, but there was no way to freeze it. The "Witch" did the job by flying the liquid ice cream in the bomb bay at 18,000 feet for an hour. It seemed fitting that the plane that had ferried so many GIs, dropped so many bombs over enemy territory, and returned her crew so many times safely to base should now contribute to the war effort by delivering ice cream for a party.

PERFECT BOMB SCORE

He awoke to the news and it was like a blow to the gut. Franklin Roosevelt: dead of a massive stroke. The base was rife with talk and sorrow. Missions were grounded, and Mike shared with Teddy what so many others had talked about.

I only hope now that the men put in charge of the US use the power to keep world peace, do the utmost, or our cause in which we are fighting will be in vain. I certainly would hate to see our child grow up and go away from home to another war. It is the one thing I long for so passionately.

Mike's fourth mission was called two days later. He had gone to bed at 10:00 p.m. only to be awakened at 01:30 a.m. It was April 14, 1945. The targets were the German encampments and coastal guns at Pointe de Grave, France. Thankfully Mike and his crew saw neither flak nor enemy aircraft. Flight in, bombs dropped on target, flight out. Return to base without incident.

At the post-mission debrief, the room erupted. The mission was a so-called "perfect drop." The bombs hit the targets with precision: 100 percent accuracy within 1,000 feet of the assigned main point of impact for all squadrons. There were no casualties and no planes lost. The exhaustion of navigating for ten straight hours vanished, and Mike felt suddenly charged with electricity with the realization he was part of a history-making perfect drop. Hearing later that there were no Germans at the targets, as they'd gone into town to fraternize with the French, didn't diminish Mike's pride or sense of accomplishment.

The next day was mission five for Mike. At the morning briefing he learned their bombing target was Royan, France, where there was a

pocket with thousands of German troops. Thirty of the B-24s on this mission were loaded with napalm bombs.

A Harvard scientist developed Napalm in 1942 after discovering that gasoline, mixed with an aluminum salt or soap, produced a material that was thick, slow burning, and could be propelled more accurately and to greater distances than gasoline alone. The napalm was encased in heavy cardboard wrapped with iron rings. The bombs tumbled to the ground, and when they hit, they burned everything in sight.

Mike was relieved his squadron would carry the normal incendiary bombs. Their mission was to arrive at the target exactly at noon and bomb any sections of the German encampment that weren't already in flames.

It just seems like a bad dream coming to an end. When I returned awaiting interrogation, the Red Cross had sandwiches and hot coffee for all the combat men. Naturally I was starved. I'd forgotten it was Sunday. I'd still like to go to Holy Communion, but I'm going on missions just the same as though I had gone to confession — namely in the state of grace. It's

*the best feeling to know regardless of what you
meet you are prepared to meet your maker. I
shall always go living that way. I always say it
is much easier to live a good life rather than
lead a bad one.*

Mike didn't like missing communion, but he went to church anyway to pray. He needed the church. Was the church the source of the courage Mike heard so much about but didn't really feel? There was a new book out that many were talking about on the base: *The Anatomy of Courage*, by Lord Moran. Was Moran right, that courage was in limited supply, and when it was used up it was all gone? Was willpower the source of courage? Or hatred of Hitler? Did courage come from the bond developed between men who shared an often-unspoken fear of combat?

Mike and his crew were slated for training to become the lead crew, and that meant many more practice missions working on tight formation flying.

From his navigator's seat in the lead plane, Mike keyed the mic on the interphone. "Damn guys, I wish you could see what I see. A sea of

planes behind us and a sea of planes under us. They're so close it looks like you could jump from wing tip to wing tip."

The trick was to fly tight enough, but not too tight. Prop wash could be a real problem: the propellers of the plane in front created a turbulent air current that could wreak havoc if another plane was following too close.

On the morning of April 27, 1945, Mike's crew was assigned two hours of flight instrument training in the Wabbit, a B-24H. The pilot was in the copilot's spot on the right and the copilot occupied the pilot's seat on the left, to gain additional hours toward becoming a pilot. At least that was the plan. But the weather wasn't cooperating. The ceiling was too low, and once in the air the pilot wasn't comfortable with the safety risks of the training configuration. Instead, he secured permission to practice touch-and-go landings.

Once the plane touched down, instead of slowing down to stop, it would speed up to take off again. Mike's crew managed two of the maneuvers successfully. On the third landing, which was to be a full stop, the left tire blew about 200 yards from the end of the runway.

With fifty yards to go, the right tire blew. The plane slid and skidded off the runway, the main and nose gear collapsing in the soft ground. The pilot cut the main line and battery switches and ordered the crew to evacuate. The plane was now on its belly in Sir Edward Stacey's alfalfa field.

They began to exit the plane quickly, as they'd been trained to do after any non-standard landing. Mike unstrapped his seat belt, crawled into the cockpit, and boosted himself out the emergency exit on the top of the plane. He slid down to the wing, walked a few feet out, and jumped to the ground. He heard a crack when he landed, and he cried out in pain. Base medics had already been running toward the aircraft. They lifted Mike onto a stretcher and took him to the base hospital where doctors put him in a cast from his waist to his ankle. Mike's leg would heal, but the damage to the Wabbit's fuselage and the number four propeller was so extensive that the plane was sent to salvage.

Heat crawled up Mike's neck and into his face when he learned that Colonel Shower had fined Mike and each member of his crew seventy-five dollars: a substantial portion of his

monthly pay. The Wabbit had previously been recommended for salvage, so that didn't explain the fine. It didn't seem that their slide off the runway had destroyed seventy-five dollars worth of alfalfa. Mike hadn't been privy to the mistakes made in the cockpit, and as far as he was aware it was a mechanical malfunction. The fine made no sense at all.

LONG ROAD HOME

Mike still flew practice missions even with the cast on his leg. He needed to keep his navigation skills up, and he assumed he'd soon be transferred to the Pacific theater.

Germany surrendered on May 8, 1945. On May 16, Mike flew a mission over Cologne, Germany. Mike was used to the high-altitude bomb drops and appreciated not seeing the resulting devastation below. But on this trip, they dropped to 500 feet for a little post-bomb-drop sightseeing.

God, honey you should see how that place has

been left. We saw the old cathedral still standing and hardly a shell hole anywhere near it. Yet all around it for many square blocks nothing has been left standing. All the bridges crossing the Rhine from one end of town to the other have been completely wiped out. It was good to see our handiwork.

Through the remaining days of May and into June, the rumors flew. While the US military grappled to implement Operation Magic Carpet, the code-name for the plans to bring nearly twelve million service men and women scattered around Europe, Asia, and the Pacific home. At Rackheath, they heard they were going home tomorrow. No, it was next week. Some would stay on much longer. There were no official answers and Mike was irritated. He knew he would going home, but when? Doctors pegged Teddy's due date sometime between June 4 or June 12.

We are coming home — it's definite. The date hasn't been set, but it's between the 28th of May and June 10th. I hope it's the 28th, so I can be with you when dear baby comes into the world.

Mike's temper, however, interfered with this departure window. One of Colonel Shower's aides approached him, saying the colonel wanted Mike to navigate his plane home.

Colonel Shower? The guy who had "stolen" seventy-five dollars in fines from each of the crew members involved whether or not they had anything to do with the incident? The hair stood up on the back of his neck. "Is this a request or an order?"

"It's a request, and you'd be guaranteed a spot leaving June 10th," said the aide.

"Then you can tell the colonel my answer is no."

Mike fumed all the way back to the hut. "Black Al had a hell of a lot of nerve asking me for a favor," he thought. "That fine was uncalled for."

He stepped into his hut and immediately saw the photo of Teddy on the shelf above his cot. He swore under his breath. He'd just screwed up big time. He had a child on the way, and he had let the hair up his ass, as he called it, his stubbornness, and his pride get in the way of a firm date for his trip home.

Would he miss the birth of his first child?

He knew he wouldn't be able to keep in touch with Teddy once he was on his way back home, and the trip could take up to a week. On May 28, 1945, he sent a V-mail to Teddy telling her not to write any more letters, and that he was going to stop writing as well. But May 31, he wrote again.

I know I said I was going to stop writing, but I was worried that my delay would be greater than I mentioned before. I am writing so that you will still get a letter or two.

Meantime, Mike continued with nighttime practice flights where he honed his celestial navigation skills. He knew there was a possibility he'd be flying non-stop over the Atlantic for his flight home, much of it during the night. He kept his sextant calibrated, and with each flight he became more confident navigating via the sun and stars.

June 3, 1945, Mike wrote Teddy another letter.

If the baby is born on the seventh, I should be

home when it's about ten days old. I only wish I could be home when it is born.

Now even the practice runs had ceased. The waiting was killing him. He'd learned celestial navigation, now if he could only make the stars align so he could go home. He had to wait because his bombardier, stationed outside of London at North Pickenham, hadn't yet been released. He had to wait because the plane he was scheduled to fly home was still in Liege, Belgium being repaired. When the Rosalyn arrived at Rackheath, Mike learned that there would be ten additional passengers—from the Bloody 100th.

It was June 21. Mike's telegram to Teddy was clear and concise.

FINALLY ON WAY =
FLYING HOME
LOVE = MICHAEL CAPUTO

They first flew to North Pickenham to pick up the bombardier, and from there they flew to Valley, Wales, a Royal Air Force base on an island just off the coast. It was their last stop be-

fore crossing the Atlantic, and they'd need every ounce of fuel they could carry.

Pilot Robert Hipps invited Mike to join him for a walk on the beach.

"I ran into an old buddy of mine back at the base," said Hipps, looking out at the ocean, his voice trailing off in the stiff breeze.

"Well, knock me over with a feather," Mike said, intending to be funny.

"Sometimes, Caputo, you can just be such an ass."

"Yeah, I know. Carry on."

"We were in flight school together, and I can't tell you when we last saw each other. We didn't have a lot of time to catch up because he was just shipping out. He's the one who suggested I head to the beach."

Mike turned toward Hipps, more serious now. "I know how great it can be to meet up with friends. The same thing happened to me at Rackheath."

"My buddy's flying a B-17," Hipps said. "He said I'd be able to see him tip his wings to say goodbye if I was on the beach."

Just then, they saw a B-17 gaining altitude, the roar of the engines reaching them a couple of

seconds later. Sure enough, the B-17 tipped its wings.

Hipps laughed aloud. "Well I'll be, that's him."

Robert and Mike stood silently watching the plane recede in the distance. The war was over and they were all heading home.

Then the plane exploded in a ball of fire.

Mike screamed.

For a long time, Hipps said nothing, watching the flames and falling debris. Mike turned away to give his friend space.

The magical feeling Mike was enjoying as he thought about heading home dissipated. The bloody horrors of war were far from over. As he stared at the wisps of smoke where the plane used to be, he saw again in his mind's eye the Messerschmitt Me 262 chasing, dipping, and firing. He saw the faces of the German peasants looking up seconds before they dropped their bomb. He squeezed his eyes tightly to try to erase those images, along with the one of the fiery ball that had just taken the life of Hipps's friend as he watched from the sand. Mike wondered, not for the first time, if he'd ever see

Teddy again or meet the new baby she'd deliver any day now.

The crew and passengers were wakened in the deep of the night. They ate a full breakfast, which they'd need for energy on the non-stop cross-Atlantic flight. No hopping from Iceland to Greenland to Canada this time. They'd be in the air for fourteen hours before landing at Westover Field in Massachusetts.

Once in the air, Mike pulled the camera out from the top of his duffle and set it on the navigator's table. The camera was a gift from his sister and he wanted to take snaps to help him remember the trip.

They were flying into the dawn when ahead of Mike, from one end of the curved horizon to the other, was an expansive orange half ball. He was so mesmerized he forgot about the camera. It was glorious, a welcome omen for the new day, the new phase of life waiting at the end of the flight.

When Mike spotted Greenland, he remembered to pick up his camera. He snapped pictures of the white beauty of the glaciers on Greenland.

The plane touched down at Westover Field

on the morning of June 25, 1945. Mike's feet hit the tarmac and he felt instantly energized, not exhausted as he'd expected. He just needed to be patient through the tedious processing, and then he could put in a call to the apartment in Meadville. He was desperate for news of Teddy.

The hours seemed to drag until he could finally get to the phone. It rang several times before Teddy's mom, Kate, picked up. When she heard his voice, she couldn't hold back. Her words tumbled over each other.

"Mike, you have a son. He was born this morning. Teddy is fine, and she's resting comfortably."

Mike's hand gripped the receiver so tightly his fingers turned white. He opened his mouth to speak but no sound would come out. Kate continued into the silence.

"I will go back to the hospital and tell Teddy that you called. She will be so relieved. What time did you land?"

Mike found his voice and told Kate he'd landed at nine, unsure why it mattered. "Tell Teddy I'll be there as quickly as I can. And that I have a thirty-day leave."

Mike stepped off the train in Meadville and

headed straight to the hospital. When he walked into the room, Teddy was sitting up in bed holding the baby. Her face was radiant.

"Meet your namesake, Michael Caputo," Teddy said, looking down at the cherub face. "His middle name is Joseph, like we agreed." Joseph was the first name of Father McAllister, the priest that had brought Teddy into the Catholic church.

When all of the catching up was done, and Mike had held his newborn son, Teddy turned serious.

"So, you landed at nine?" Teddy asked. Mike nodded, curious at the tears gathering in the corners of her eyes.

"I have been going to Mass and Communion as often as I can. I prayed for nine days straight that the baby wouldn't come before you were back on US soil. Baby Michael was born at 9:40 a.m."

Prayers answered. In more ways than one.

THE OLD SHOP

*M*ike's furlough turned out to be a mixed blessing. He treasured the month he spent with Teddy and the baby, and delighted in this new sense of family. He proudly stood at the altar next to Teddy during the baptism of his son, Michael Joseph Caputo. He roared with laughter when baby Mickey peed on his own face during a diaper change. From then on, Teddy placed a diaper in the appropriate place whenever changing the baby.

There were difficulties tempering the joy. Teddy wasn't able to breastfeed and she took it as a personal failure. Living in the small apart-

ment together with Teddy's mother, was hard. Mother and daughter often didn't get along, and Mike didn't understand the ongoing tension.

But he knew this was temporary and he clung to their plans of buying a house of their own. He and Teddy talked about it all the time. His poker winnings were safely in the bank, Teddy had added a little to them, and Aunt Ada offered to lend them whatever else they might need for a down payment.

Plans, however, were just plans. His furlough would soon end and he'd have to leave again. He began to miss Teddy and baby Mickey even before his new orders arrived. As he wondered whether he'd be sent next to Okinawa, which had fallen, or somewhere else in the South Pacific, he was acutely aware that he wanted to be home to see whether Mickey would be blonde and green-eyed, like Teddy, or dark like him. Mike didn't

want to miss the baby beginning to crawl or taking his first step.

His orders arrived at the end of July. He was to take a troop train from Newark, New Jersey to the air base in Sioux Falls, South Dakota, a temporary reception center for GIs returning from Europe. There he'd wait for his assignment to the next training base.

The train trip was rough. The shortage of rail cars, because of the war, meant the troops had to cram into old wooden passenger cars. Packed in like sardines, the odor of sweaty bodies hung like a suffocating cloak in the summer heat.

Civilians were riding in the more upscale Pullman cars. It was frustrating for the soldiers to be treated like second-class citizens: had they not been fighting in the war for the very freedoms the citizenry could now enjoy?

During a stop in the rail yards at Leavenworth, Kansas, some servicemen set fire to one of the wooden cars. They'd angered the management of the railroad, but in the end the GIs got what they wanted. They rode in the comfort of the Pullmans the rest of the journey.

At the Sioux Falls Army Air Base, Mike couldn't believe the chaos. It was crowded, disorganized, lacking in the usual military discipline. There were no formal briefings to either dispel or confirm the rumors about who would be sent where, when, or why.

Before he left, he and Teddy had decided that as much as possible, the family would stick together. But there was no point in moving her and Mickey to Sioux Falls, as it was even more temporary than usual for a military posting. It was hard. In his letters, Mike described the waiting as being worse than being in combat.

The good thing about being at Sioux Falls was running into old friends. He met some of his airplane-repair buddies from Macon, and Hipps and White, his pilot and copilot from Rackheath. It felt like old home week. Mike didn't understand why the brass wouldn't keep crews together, but it wasn't going to happen.

Having friends around was helpful, but life on the base was weird. Decision making and normal army routines were stalled. There wasn't much to do, but Mike couldn't just lie around and wait.

When he learned there was a model shop in

Sioux Falls, Mike's problem was solved. His first purchase was a P-38, and when he'd finished building that model, he bought another. He set out to build models of the planes that had flown in the war.

August 6, 1945, the US dropped a nuclear bomb on Hiroshima, Japan. Russia declared war on Japan on August 8, and the US dropped another atom bomb on Nagasaki August 9. Mike wrote to Teddy.

If the atomic bomb is what they say it is, I can't see how Japan can be spared the complete devastation connected with it. Honestly, it is almost unbelievable as to its power.

On August 15, 1945, Japan surrendered. The war was over. Mike was off the base in town when the news arrived. He was elated, but disappointed with how some of the GIs chose to celebrate.

I decided to come back to camp before the town got too rough. Believe me the GIs certainly wrecked the town. They overturned cars and

even set one old Ford on fire right in the middle of the street.

Mike needed prayer, not violence. He went to Mass. It was the feast of the Assumption, a celebration of Mary, the mother of Jesus, going to heaven. It seemed fitting.

A week later, with four airplane models ready to be shipped home, the Brigadier General called a meeting. Even though the war was ending, troop strength was still necessary. Men were assigned points, based on their overseas service, and these points dictated where they'd be assigned—first for training and then on to their next post. Some were volunteering to serve in the Pacific theater, and those would ship out almost immediately. Next, apparently, were the GIs who hadn't yet been overseas. Mike was in the third group: GIs who had already seen action.

Mike learned he'd be trained on the B-29, but he still didn't know where. He'd requested to be assigned to the First USAAF, because all their bases were on the east coast. That would make it easier for his wife and son to join him. Meantime, there was more waiting. Day after

day, the only thing that kept his head on straight was building models. Mike started something: he looked around the barracks and saw GIs hunched over every available table, working on models of cars, planes, ships.

It was the last week of August when Mike finally heard he was being assigned to Colorado Springs. He assumed, but didn't know yet for sure, that after that he'd be sent to the Pacific.

Teddy, Washington doesn't trust Joseph Stalin, and we must keep him in hand. This little information is confidential, so please do not discuss it with anyone.

But one week after Mike arrived in Colorado, September 5, 1945, he was told that he was being discharged and sent home. A letter would not do, and he called Teddy to let her know the good news. Except, of course, he didn't know when he would be home. For that, he'd have to wait. Again.

Meantime, Mike checked the assignment board. One day he was scheduled for a practice flight, which meant an additional seventy-five dollars in his pay. However, he wasn't going up

in a B-29 but a B-17. Oh, the irony. The ribbing from the other guys would never end. He could hear the taunts and jibes: *"Well, Mike, smart ass, see you're finally going to fly in something decent."* It was because Mike had been vocal about comparing the '17 to the '24 in unflattering terms. The '24 was faster, it could go further, and it could carry a heavier bomb load. His friends would shoot back that the B-17 was safer, it took flak better, it was easier to fly. Mike enjoyed the banter, but he wasn't good at eating humble pie.

It was the only flight Mike had while at the Colorado base. His discharge came through and he was being sent back to Newark, New Jersey to be processed out. He had his baby son to thank. Being a father gave Mike the points he needed for a discharge. He was going home, permanently.

He was back in Meadville for three days when he received new orders to report back to Newark. Mike was baffled. Was the USAAF so disorganized they didn't know he'd already mustered out? Then he was told to report directly to the base hospital and the chief physician.

"The news isn't good," the doctor said once Mike was in his office. "You have diabetes."

"Is that bad?" Mike asked.

"Not as bad as it used to be. Until the 1920s, it wasn't treatable. Then we discovered insulin and we can now keep people alive much longer. You'll have to give yourself daily injections."

Mike's head was reeling. Daily shots? Diabetes? He felt so healthy, and he was still so young. He asked the doctor about the implications long term.

"Not so good. There are long-term complications with the eyes and the kidneys. We need you to stay in hospital for a few days so we can run more tests."

The next day the doctor came into Mike's room with a smile on his face. "We did some double checking, and we mixed up your test results with someone else. You don't have diabetes. We're sending you home, and since it was our mistake you will be given a week's wage for your troubles."

A week's wage for the medical mistake, and he got $500 as part of the process for mustering out. This would all go toward the money he and

Teddy were saving for a downpayment on a house.

When Mike returned to Meadville, he and Teddy talked about what was next. Mike loved Meadville, but the hands-on work with models made him think of going back to Georgia. He had loved repairing real airplanes. He and Teddy both agreed that he should return to Macon to see about getting his old job back.

Mike's old job was indeed available, should he want it. However, walking into the old shop, with its jigs and ailerons and rivets and tools, Mike experienced a claustrophobia so intense it shocked him. Sweat broke out in bubbles on his forehead and his hands turned clammy. His breath became shallow, and he felt a knot in his chest the size of a football. He got out of the shop as quickly as he could.

He had no idea what was going on. He just wanted to get back to Meadville. On the return trip, Mike rationalized. Teddy loved Meadville. Being close to her mother was important to her. His sister Josephine was still in Scranton, and Meadville was closer to her than Macon. He also knew there was a job for him in Meadville. The man he'd first met during training had told

him he could start work anytime at the men's clothing store he owned.

Mike prepared the story he'd tell Teddy and everyone else. He was good with people, he had a sense of style, and he knew he could help others look good. Working with airplanes was going to be a part of Mike's past, not his future.

PRETENSE OF NORMALCY

Mike and his crew were returning from a mission under heavy flak. The plane had been hit and it was in a nose dive. Mike had his parachute on, and he was desperately trying to get to the bomb bay where he could bail out. He was on his hands and knees trying to crawl through a companionway that was lined with smooth stainless steel. There was nothing to grab onto and he kept slipping, slipping, slipping backward. If he didn't manage to get to the bomb bay, he would crash with the plane. He could see the bomb bay just ahead, but no matter how hard he tried, he couldn't get there. He was going to die.

"Mike, you're screaming again. What's happening?" Teddy shook his shoulder and woke him up.

"It's just a nightmare. Go back to sleep. I'm fine."

Meadville *should* have felt safe. It's where he met and fell in love with Teddy. It's where he watched his son's face light up with laughter or at peace while sleeping in the crib. He went to work every day wearing normal clothes instead of his uniform. He collected a regular pay check. Life was good. Why, then, was he tortured with the same recurring nightmare?

Every day he kept up the pretense of normalcy. Every night before bed Mike became apprehensive. Would the nightmare come tonight? Would he wake up screaming? He was ashamed, embarrassed, and had no idea what was wrong. He refused to talk about the dream or its terrorizing effects.

Soon Teddy stopped asking what the dream was about or whether he was okay. It was a relief for them both on the mornings they awoke after sleeping through the night.

Mike was convinced that talking about the

nightmares would only make matters worse. Maybe it was because of the tension between Teddy and Kate in the small apartment. Maybe once they were living in their own home, the nightmare would go away.

Seven months after his discharge, in July 1946, Mike, Teddy, and baby Mickey moved into a house at the edge of town. It was an un-adorned, white clapboard Victorian home, built in the 1890s, that sat up on a hill far from the road. The entrance off the small front porch led into the dining room. There was a living room, a kitchen, and a long hallway off the kitchen that Teddy used as a pantry. At the end of that hallway was a bedroom. There were three more bedrooms on the second floor. They were going to need one of those extra bedrooms. Teddy was pregnant again. Another healthy child was all they wanted but they'd be pleased with a little girl.

It wasn't the dream house they had naïvely described in their letters. It wasn't new. There was no fireplace in the living room. But both front and back boasted a large yard. There was plenty of space for children to play. Teddy had a

plot with plenty of sun for a vegetable garden. Mike and Teddy had a chicken coop, chickens that produced eggs, and that meant from time to time dinner included a stewing chicken.

In the basement Mike had space for his hobbies. Model planes had temporarily lost their allure, replaced by model railroads. He filled one large room in the basement with a track layout. He hoped moving the focus from planes onto trains might help keep the nightmare at bay.

Mike and Teddy settled into a peacetime routine. On Sundays, they attended church together. During the week, Mike went to work, and Teddy stayed home tending to Mickey and chores. They ate their meals together in the evening. They had a son they both adored. Baby number two was due in December. Life was good.

If life was good, then what explained the awful recurring dream? Mike was confounded. He was blessed to have survived the war and come home to a loving wife and growing family. It didn't make sense. He had only flown five missions. There were plenty of others who flew twenty-five or thirty-five missions. What was wrong with him?

He had seen others break, like the young man who screamed, "I can't go out again, I won't go out again." Mike was among those who watched as the guy ran full speed into the rotating propellers of the plane he should have been on. He was decapitated.

At the time, Mike couldn't relate. He'd felt terror, sure, but he'd never experienced the depths of despair that pushed that man to take his own life.

Mike hadn't broken. He prided himself on his level head, crediting his faith for helping him come through the fear. If he had died on a mission it would have been God's will. The fact he was alive also had to be God's will. Where was God's will in the recurring nightmare?

He would wake with Teddy pushing on his shoulder. He knew he'd been screaming. He was covered in sweat, and his fingernails ached from scratching at the smooth stainless steel in his dream. He tore the sheets beneath him and ripped holes in the mattress. Teddy had tried to repair them, stuffing old socks in the holes in the bed, patching the surface, and patching the sheets. The day soon came when the mattress

was in such bad shape, they had to purchase a new one.

It was crazy. Mike felt crazy. The dream made absolutely no sense. He wouldn't have been trying to get to the bomb bay. B-24 crews were trained to bail out through the nearest exit. Mike's navigator station was in the nose, so his exit was through the nose-wheel opening. Why did his dream have him trying to get to the bomb bay?

From time to time, other GIs in Meadville would come into the shop for clothes. They'd chat about where they had been and how good it was to be home. They might even rag each other about whether the army, the air corps, the marines, or the navy had won the war, but none ever mentioned having nightmares.

Mike's nightmare was something he carried alone. Teddy knew, of course, but he simply couldn't discuss it with her. He was sure that neither she nor anyone else would understand. How could they, when he didn't understand?

As time passed, the nightmares came less frequently, stopping altogether after three years. But the questions remained. Why did it happen? Why to him? What did it mean? What was the

matter with him? Was he insane? Flawed? He'd heard the terms "shell shock" and "battle fatigue," but those terms described other, weaker men. He couldn't be the sort of man that those terms would apply to.

THE CHRISTMAS GIFT

The box was huge and heavy, too big to fit under the tree. It was a generous and loving gift from Teddy for the Christmas of 1994: not just because of the size and trouble getting it into the house and close to the Christmas tree, but because of what it represented. It meant Mike would be spending countless hours at his workbench building another model airplane.

This time it was a B-24. In the box were the blueprints and sheets of balsa wood. There were forty pages of step-by-step instructions in tiny print. There were fifty-three steps to follow for the fuselage. Fifty-one steps for each wing. For

the entire model aircraft, 331 steps. There were photos and drawings to illustrate what each part should look like and intricate designs for the interior of the plane: the cockpit's instrument panel, the floor plan, cross section of the cockpit, nose section and the navigator's section, which Mike knew intimately, the turret, the bomb bay. When complete, the model would be four-and-a-half feet long with a wing span of seven-and-a-half feet. It would be the largest and most intricate model he'd ever built.

The model B-24 kit under the tree was the Strawberry Bitch, a plane that flew in North Africa during the war but had never flown in the 467th, Mike's bomb group. He wanted to build something that would have meaning for the 467th, and he chose to complete the model with the markings of the most famous plane flown at Rackheath, in fact the most famous B-24 in the European theater: Witchcraft.

The B-24 Witchcraft was produced by Ford Motor Company's aircraft plant in Willow Run, Michigan. She rolled off the assembly line on December 15, 1943, with the serial number B-24H-15 FO 42-52534. The name Witchcraft wouldn't be ascribed until much later.

B-24H-15 FO 42-52534 and her crew departed from Wendover, Utah, and flew the southern route to England. In Brazil, one of the crew members became sick and was hospitalized for six days. It was during this layover that the healthy crew decided to name her Witchcraft and paint nose art with a witch riding a .50-caliber gun and holding a bomb.

The crew and plane arrived twenty days later at Rackheath, Norfolk on March 19, 1944. Before Witchcraft returned to the United States on July 10, 1945, twice she suffered battle damage and needed major repairs, but no one aboard her during any of her 130 missions was killed or wounded. Three times, she dropped bombs while flying with only three engines. Mike was well aware of the reasons that her air crew gave credit for this superlative record to her ground crew.

All this Mike thought about as he scoured the blueprints, which were huge on their own: thirty-six by eighty-eight inches. He used transparent paper to trace parts of the plane. He then laid the transfer on the balsa, pinned it in place, traced around it, used a band saw to cut out the pieces, and then he sanded them. He had a

knack for taking two-dimensional drawings and creating something three-dimensional without needing to follow the instructions too closely. He could see in his head what needed to be done.

When he'd finished building the model, Mike started researching the markings and painting of the Witchcraft. He placed a help-wanted ad in a newsletter for the 467th called *Poop from the Group* and asked for pictures of the Witchcraft. Robert McEwen, a tail gunner from the original crew, replied and sent pictures along with the name and address of the Witchcraft's crew chief, Joe Ramirez. With pictures in hand, it took six coats of paint until Mike was satisfied with the color.

"I'm having trouble getting the rivets right," Mike said to Teddy. "I want the indentations to be perfect. At first, I couldn't figure it out. Then I spied your tracing wheel and pulled it out of your sewing kit. It's perfect."

Teddy's tracing wheel had a five-inch plastic handle attached to a metal wheel with serrated tips. Mike applied just enough pressure on the wheel as he ran it along the body of the plane and the wings to produce the appearance of the rivets.

He took McEwen's color photographs of the Witchcraft to a local computer store to blow them up to the size of the finished model. He cut out key pieces of this large photo to make decals and glued them to the model.

He sent pictures of his completed model B-24 to Joe Ramirez. Joe phoned Mike as soon as he received them. "Where did you find her? I thought she'd been scrapped."

"Joe, this isn't the real thing. It's a model I just finished."

"That model needs to be in a museum," Joe replied.

And that was Mike's idea all along.

UNTERSCHLAUERSBACH

Mike answered the phone as quickly as he could get to it. His kids knew to let it ring a long time. He had slowed down considerably, and he had to be careful not to fall. He'd fallen a few times already. He hadn't hurt himself, yet, but getting back up was a real problem. He'd have to roll over and crawl on hands and knees to reach one of the over-stuffed chairs. Putting his hands on the seat and then on the arms, he'd use his upper body strength to stand.

He made it into the kitchen to the phone on the wall near the oven. It was Yvonne. "Hon, let

me sit down first." He reached over and pulled the rolling chair underneath him, the doughnut cushion absorbing his weight as he plopped into the seat.

"Dad, I got a call from Tommy," Yvonne said. "He's in Meadville and he'd like to come for a visit. But he won't come if he isn't welcome."

Tommy was Mike's nephew. He'd had drug problems, money problems, and most of the Caputo family had pretty much given up on him. Yvonne had stayed in touch, but it had been years since Tommy had reached out to anyone else.

"I'd like to see him," Mike said.

"Ok, I'll let him know. He doesn't go by 'Tommy' anymore. He's back to Claude."

Claude was Tommy's birth name. Allegheny College had invited Claude to speak to students about his book and being ordained as a Buddhist monk.

Claude called Mike later the same day and arranged a time for the visit. "Uncle Mike, I'll be wearing my robes, not street clothes."

Mike sat in the living room, transfixed by the

view out the front window. It was October, and the trees were aflame with color. The maple he had planted thirty years ago at the edge of the driveway was alive with scarlet. The golds and oranges of the other trees reminded him of why he fell in love with Meadville those long years ago.

Mike was standing at the top of the stairs when Claude arrived with a woman. They were dressed in black robes, their shaved heads shiny and smooth. It took just a second for Mike to see that it was his nephew, and he broke out in a grin. Instead of grabbing Claude's outstretched hand for a shake, Mike pulled him into a hug.

Seated in the living room, Claude introduced Veepkah, explaining that her ordained name was KenShin. They talked about their health and Claude's journey to becoming a monk. Mike listened intently. If that was Claude's path, it seemed okay. Better, much better, than when Tommy was caught in the grips of addiction.

It was a frank and open conversation, more comfortable than it should have been given the circumstances and the years they'd been out of touch.

"Uncle Mike, what was it like for you coming home from the war?" Somehow Mike wasn't surprised by Claude's question.

"It was awful. I felt like a fish out of water. A stranger in my own land. I'd see people in church and on the streets and I knew they had no idea what I'd been through." Claude and KenShin were focused on Mike, their expressions full of compassion. Mike wasn't sure why he felt safe sharing these details, but he did, and he plowed ahead.

"The nightmare was the same, sometimes night after night. I'd come home at the end of the day, exhausted, and all I wanted was to be able to sleep through the night. Poor Teddy, she would wake me and tell me I was screaming again. I could never tell her what the dream was about. I just didn't know how. Mainly I think I was afraid that there was something really wrong with me and I couldn't face it. Thank God, after three years they just went away."

"It was the same for me when I came back from Vietnam."

Mike suddenly remembered his own harsh words to Claude and was ashamed. "We weren't very nice to the GIs who

came home from Vietnam. You guys didn't get a hell of a lot of support. It wasn't the same for us at the end of World War II."

Mike looked up from his lap and into Claude's eyes. "I'm sorry I told you to 'quit your whining' and get on with it."

"I did need to 'get on with it,' but it took me a long, long time," said Claude. "First there was rehab. Being drug and alcohol free didn't bring me the peace I needed. So that's when I went to live with the monks in France and joined the pilgrimages.

"Even then, I had to learn that it really isn't something you ever get over. I had to learn how to live at peace with the un-peacefulness of my service."

The conversation meandered and then Mike turned to KenShin. "I hear your accent. Where are you from?"

"I was born in Germany," KenShin said. "I too had to process what happened in my country during the war." She talked a bit more about what happened to her family and how she came to Buddhism.

Mike sat up a little straighter. "I have a story to tell. My first mission was to Unterschlauersbach. We'd been told that Patton was on the move and if he was anywhere near our targets, we were to drop our bombs wherever we could before returning to England. We were flying so low I could see people's faces. Some were waving, some were on their knees praying. We dropped our bombs." Mike paused, the memory forming images behind his eyes like a movie reel.

"When I was selling insurance, I used to have to collect the monthly payments. At one house a young woman answered the door. She invited me inside where her husband was writing a check. As we chatted, I noticed her accent and asked where she was from. She was from Germany, and she had met her husband when he was stationed there." Mike stopped to sip his coffee, clearing his throat before continuing. "She was from Unterschlauersbach, but she'd been sent to live with her grandparents. Her parents had been killed near the end of the war when the Americans had flown in real low and dropped their bombs.

"I don't remember leaving that house, but I was shaking like a leaf when I got back to my

car. It was that white VW bug with the red interior. The memory of what I'd seen and what we'd done in Unterschlauersbach haunted me for years after the war. Her story took me right back. It wasn't just the nightmares that were hard to live with. It was the guilt I felt about that raid."

The air in the living room shifted at the end of Mike's story. He felt strangely relieved, lighter somehow. Claude and KenShin seemed to know when enough was enough, and they exchanged a few more pleasantries until Claude stood up, explaining that he needed to get back to the college to prepare for his talk that evening.

As they said their goodbyes, Mike turned to KenShin. "I'm so sorry for what we did to civilians during the war. I hope someday I can be forgiven."

Mike sat back in his chair after they'd pulled out of the driveway. For the first time, Mike understood that the value of Confession extended far beyond the confessional, where he'd unburden himself of his sins in front of a priest. Today, he had unburdened himself to two Buddhist monks and healed a rift with his

estranged nephew. An odd thing to have happened.

"*I had to learn how to live at peace with the unpeacefulness of my service,*" Claude had said. Mike thought he'd like to give that a try.

FLOOD OF PURPOSE

\mathcal{M}ike lay back in his hospital bed, mindlessly watching his favorite football team on the TV that hung from the wall at the end of his bed. In his mind he didn't feel eighty-one. His diabetic body told him otherwise. Years ago, he'd ignored his doctor's advice to become more active. He'd gained weight and earned a serious diagnosis.

Back in 1972, he told Mickey, now holding a PhD in clinical pathology, that he'd walked out of the Erie hospital without getting a cardiac catheterization. Mickey was furious. "Listen, Dad, pack your bags, get in the car, and come to

Wisconsin. I have a heart specialist friend here, and you're going to get that procedure. Got it?"

Mickey's cardiologist friend told Mike he had arteriosclerotic heart disease. "One of your arteries is completely blocked. With only one blocked, it doesn't warrant splitting open your chest to try to fix it. But, given your condition, you need to reduce your stress. Would you be less stressed working, or not working?"

So Mike began his retirement. He was fifty. It seemed a long time ago now, more than thirty years living off his disability pension.

Yvonne had just left his hospital room, coming to say goodbye before she drove back to her home on the other side of the state. She'd asked him all kinds of questions the night before. Questions about how he wanted to be treated at the end of his life. He'd never have spoken aloud about those things, to anyone, if Yvonne hadn't raised them.

With his head against the pillow, his eyes slid between the Steelers game and the view out the big window to the right. Now was as good a time as any to examine the life he'd led. Who was he? What had driven him to do the things he'd done? What did it all mean? Tommy

Maddox was back-peddling after the snap, the quarterback effortlessly passing the football before he was tackled to the ground. If his life had been a football game—oh yes, he'd have been Steelers' number eight Tommy Maddox—when had he thrown the ball for a completion? When had he been sacked? When had he run the ball the entire length of the field, scoring a touchdown in front of a roaring crowd? When had he thrown an intercepted pass or dropped the ball? Where had he lost yardage? And what was central to how he played the game?

Maddox and the rest of the offensive line were trotting over to the sidelines, the Steelers having exhausted three of their four downs. Todd Peterson took his characteristic three-step advance and punted the ball. Love, faith, and duty had always been central to Mike's life, certainly after the war. Life after the war wasn't what he and Teddy dreamed. There was no cuddling at the end of the day in front of the fireplace when the children were asleep. He knew he'd been distant, but he could neither explain nor change it. With all those mouths to feed—four children, plus whichever family member was living with them at the time—money had

been tight. As good as he was selling men's clothes, then jewelry, and finally insurance, none had lined his pockets with gold. When he came home in the evening, exhausted, he found solace in his hobbies. But was there a deeper meaning in his models and shortwave radio? Had he been avoiding a deeper connection with Teddy?

Mike left the jobs selling clothing, then jewelry, because the pay was lousy. He'd always felt his sales skills were under-appreciated by the store owners, but not by his customers. People knew him around town. When he started to sell insurance, he had contacts that he could tap, and he was selling a product that he really believed in. He was often the highest-selling salesman in his region. It meant there was more money, but meaning?

The Steelers defense intercepted the ball and Maddox, in his black jersey and gold pants, bounced back onto the field. What about the twenty-five years he'd spent in the Air Force Reserves? He'd joined in 1946, at first thinking the extra money would be helpful. But there was more to it than that. He missed the camaraderie of his crew. He'd volunteered to go to Korea, but they apparently didn't need navigators.

When the country was embroiled in the Cold War, he asked to be assigned to an intelligence unit. The Reserves sent him back to college and he learned to speak Russian. He enjoyed the classes and his active duty requirement. When he finally resigned, he was proud to have reached the rank of captain. The Reserves had given him a much-needed sense of belonging and purpose, but had it been enough?

Last night Yvonne had asked him how he wanted to be remembered. His answer came in a flash, and to his surprise he hadn't said it was his work as a navigator, or a salesman, or the Reserves. What made him say what he did?

In 1959, Meadville experienced the worst flood in its history. The city lay along the banks of French Creek, and flooding began when the waters rose to over twelve feet. Ice and debris collected in the twists and turns in the creek, causing the meltwater to spill over the banks and into the low-lying areas of the town. At one point, a two-mile-long ice jam pushed the water level to seventeen feet, which covered much of the Fifth Ward of the city. Fifteen hundred people were forced out of their homes, schools and businesses were closed.

Mike volunteered for the Red Cross during those two weeks. He wouldn't see his family, safe and dry in their home up on the hill on the outskirts of the city, for days. He remembered the first break he had. He'd walked into the house at dinner time. The family was around the kitchen table having supper. He stood in the doorway; their faces turned to him eager for news.

"You can't imagine the devastation. I know you've seen the pictures in the newspaper, but they don't even begin to tell the story," he remembered saying. "I'm not going to come in. Even at this distance, I think you can tell how much I smell. I'm just here to shower and change. Then I need to get back."

He'd returned to the kitchen feeling much fresher, and some of the deep exhaustion had lifted. "I don't know when I'll be home again. Don't worry, because I'm safe."

Thinking about it now, some forty-plus years later, the flood had been the great turning point. He was once again part of a team. It had filled a spot in his soul he hadn't known needed filling. He was connected to other people around a purpose, and the work had been so gratifying he

had continued to volunteer until his health had declined to a point that he had to resign just a few years ago.

The year after the flood, he'd started dabbling with shortwave radio. All because he hated this new rock and roll music his kids loved. Someone told him that if he had a shortwave radio, he'd be able to listen to swing music on European stations. With tiny turns of the dial, he began to hear people from all over the world. He'd purchased or built what he needed and studied for his shortwave license.

Soon, he had his own call sign. "This is K3YAK, does anybody copy?" The stack of postcards on his desk reflected the connections he'd made over the years: Japan, Sri Lanka, Russia. As much fun as it was, he realized quickly that his shortwave radio hobby was most helpful during times of crisis, like the Meadville flood. So, Mike adopted a philosophy: public service first, hobby second. Again, he wondered what it meant that he was more comfortable seeking human connection through his shortwave radio than he was

having heart-to-heart talks with his wife upstairs.

On the TV, the cheering crowd brought the game back into focus. The Steelers had scored a touchdown, but they were still behind in the game. Perhaps winning wasn't always about coming out on top.

He'd connected families to their sons in Vietnam, by radio. He'd located the parents of a college student after a hurricane had hit his island home in the Caribbean. He happened across an emergency request from South America. A cardiologist needed a specific medicine for a critically-ill patient. Mike located the drug at a Cleveland Clinic. Thanks to his connection with the Air Force, he even arranged the flight to deliver the medicine.

He'd been the disaster chair of the Meadville chapter of the Red Cross, as well as serving as chair of its board. He'd led the group that built the 150-foot repeater tower to enhance emergency communications for Meadville, and of course he'd built a repeater in his own back yard.

While Amos Zereoue, the Steelers' star running back, was spinning and weaving, the ball

safely tucked in the crook of his arm, Mike's head kept spinning from memory to memory, landing on an image of the Public Service Award he'd received from the American Radio Relay League in January, 1978, for outstanding emergency communications. That simple brown piece of paper was one of his most precious treasures.

His eyes filled with tears. Yvonne had asked, "Dad, what do you want to be remembered for?"

The Red Cross. He wanted to be remembered for his work with the Red Cross. He wiped his eyes with the back of his hand and turned his focus back to the TV to watch the rest of the game.

PART III
DAD AND ME

G3JPZ AND K3YAK

The dining room table was strewn with paper and newspaper clippings and photos, a large white envelope to one side. Dad's smile lit up the room, like a ten-year-old kid who had just gotten his first model airplane. He was almost giggling. "You've got to see this, Yvonne." He plucked the white envelope from its perch and pointed to the return address. Great Britain.

Who was sending Dad stuff from Great Britain? I loved the UK. When I was a teacher, I would save as much money as possible during the school year in the hopes I'd be able to swing

a month abroad. Great Britain was always my choice. I loved it, at least in part because I didn't have to struggle with the language. Twice I even took students to England on an exchange. Alan and Heather Morton, the host teacher and his wife, became dear friends. Whenever they visited the US, they would spend a week with me and a day with Mom and Dad.

The story of the envelope started to spill out. "I talked to this guy with an English accent on the radio not long ago," Dad said, referring to his ham radio. "He sent me all this stuff..." He swept his arm across the table top, the movement of the air rippling the corners of the yellowed newspaper clippings and photos and other bits of paper. "The articles are about the library in Norwich and the photos are from places around Rackheath. Boy, does all this bring back memories."

One by one, Dad lovingly picked up the items on the table. An article from the Guardian newspaper talked about the proposal for a new library to replace the old one destroyed by fire. The reporter mentions that the plans include dedicating a section of the library to the Second Air Division. Dad beamed. "When I left Eng-

land in '45, I gave twenty-five dollars to the trust fund for this library. I never knew whether the library was ever built. Now I know."

He showed me photographs of the places he remembered from his time stationed at Rackheath air base. There were pictures of the air tower, the crumbling remains of the runways, and the Green Man pub where Dad admitted to enjoying a gin and lemon or two. He told me he loved the UK but hated the warm beer.

"How on earth did you get this stuff? Was it through Alan and Heather?" I asked, unaware he knew anyone else in the UK.

"Nope. It's because of my ham radio," and Dad set about explaining how he had conversations with men and women in this country or from around the world. Some were old buddies, but many were new acquaintances.

Every connection Dad made with someone new started the same way. Dad sat at his radio, twisting the dials this way and that as he searched through the squelch for a strong frequency. When he'd hear a clear voice reciting their call letters, he knew an adventure and a conversation was about to begin.

"One evening I even spoke with Tex

Beneke," Dad explained. Tex sang vocals on the hit song "Chattanooga Choo Choo" and went on to be the leader of Glenn Miller's band, Mom and Dad's all-time favorite musical group. Miller, incidentally, disappeared during an Allied bombing run over the English Channel in December, 1944.

One night, Dad caught a distinctive British accent through the squelching. Dad slowed the turning of his dials, backing up a bit to where he thought he'd heard the voice. "This is G3JPZ. Is anyone out there? Over."

"This is K3YAK," Dad replied with his call sign. "You're coming in loud and clear. Over." The Brit, as Dad called him, responded back, and they began sharing details of their identities. Dad got excited when the Brit said he lived in a little village outside of Norwich.

"I was stationed outside of Norwich during the war! Perhaps you know my air base, Rackheath? Over."

"I do," the Brit responded from across the Atlantic. "I grew up close to Rackheath and I saw servicemen all the time. Over."

The man was Ian Denny. In a blossoming

friendship, Ian and Dad spoke by ham radio nearly every week. Once they both got computers, they would also connect via Skype. It was Ian that sent Dad the white envelope full of clippings.

VE 50

ad finally met Ian in person during the 50[th] Anniversary of the Victory in Europe, or VE Day, in 1995. The Second Air Division Association coordinated the trip for American veterans of World War II.

Dad wanted to show Mom the places he spent time during the war, and he wanted to meet Ian. My husband Kirk and I joined them for part of the trip. We wanted to spend a couple of days with Heather and Alan Morton, who were on the VE Day planning committee

for their village, which was several hours' drive west of Norwich.

Ian Denny and his wife Sue drove in from their little village of Harleston, and Heather and Alan drove Kirk and I to meet my parents at their hotel in Norwich. We made our plans for the trip to Rackheath, and Ian offered to drive the lead car.

At Rackheath Airfield, we stood on remnants of what had been the east runway while Dad told story after story. He pointed to where the west runway would have been and recounted his crash landing. Brush and weeds climbed halfway up the walls of the former control tower, now serving as a storage shed.

"There's a fundraising campaign underway to buy the old control tower building and restore it to its original condition," Ian told us. He bent over, picked up a chunk of what had once been the runway, and put it in my hand. With a furtive wink he said, "Now you will always have a piece of your Dad's history."

We completed the afternoon in typical English fashion with a visit to the Green Man pub. Dad told us that many airmen would ride their bicycles to the Green Man. "After several

drinks," Dad said, "the return trip was a challenge. Not everyone made it back with their bikes."

Pub employees all dressed in period costume. The inn was decorated with memorabilia and lots of red, white, and blue bunting. Employees and pub patrons alike responded to our American accents with enthusiasm. Dad, a smile pasted to his face, was surrounded by a group paying rapt attention as he regaled them with his memories of Rackheath.

Even the music over the pub speakers was from the war period, including Glenn Miller tunes. I was weaned on Glenn Miller, raised on Glenn Miller, and Mom taught me to dance to Glenn Miller. When "In the Mood" came on, Mom and I nodded to each other and in an instant we were out of our seats doing the jitterbug. Mom led and I followed, twisting, turning, each step the product of a visceral memory of the sequence she taught me long ago. Dad's memories, Mom's memories, my memories, the music, the pub, the friends from opposite sides of the Atlantic, all wove a time-transcendent tapestry indelibly stamped on my brain.

The following day, we joined the crowds in

front of Norwich City Hall to watch the VE Day celebration parade. At exactly 10:00 a.m., all the city's church bells started to peel. A squadron of jets seemed to appear out of nowhere and flew in formation over City Hall. The 1995 parade was comprised of the same groups, in the same order, that had marched in 1945. Boy Scouts, then Girl Scouts, followed by young British service men and women. British World War II veterans were next, and finally the veterans from the US Army and Air Force. The crowd roared for the Americans. I was perched on top of a stone wall and nearly burst with pride when my father came into view. Unable to contain myself, I screamed, "That's my dad! That's my dad!"

At the end of the parade, we kissed our friends goodbye and fell into line, following the parade to Norwich Cathedral for the Service of Thanksgiving, Reconciliation, and Hope. Mom went off to join Dad, while Kirk and I gratefully accepted invitations from some young British servicemen and women to sit with them. We would have been out of luck otherwise, the tickets to the standing-room-only event having long ago sold out.

As the service began, with a composition by a local musician incorporating the "American National Anthem", "God Bless America", and "God Save the Queen," I gazed around the cathedral, feeling small and insignificant in comparison with its history. Construction began nearly a thousand years before, in 1096. Two hundred years later, in 1298, Norwich Cathedral was consecrated. Here I was, participating with thousands of British and Americans in the liturgy marking another historic event. My breath caught in my throat.

The music producer had incorporated recordings of a B-24 taking off, then another and another, until the entire cathedral was reverberating with the sound of hundreds of planes climbing into formation to start their run across the English Channel those long years ago. I leaned forward to catch a glimpse of Dad, a glint of light reflecting off his cheek. Were those tears?

Behold how good and joyful a thing it is, brethren, to dwell together in unity.

— PSALM 133.1

At the end of the service the congregation joined together and sang both the American and British national anthems.

All across England, services were held with the same theme. In London, the Queen, Prince Charles, and the Queen Mother attended a commemoration service at the Cathedral of St. Paul in London, where the American Memorial Chapel sits, beyond the High Altar at the east end of the cathedral, as a monument to the deep friendship between England and the United States and the sacrifice so many Americans made during the Second World War.

That evening, we attended a production at the Theatre Royal in Norwich, *We'll Meet Again.* Old photos flashed on screens behind the actors as the audience sang along to war-era songs.

Mom and Dad's tour group took other side trips as a part of their week in England. They visited the beautifully-kept Cambridge American Cemetery at Madingley. "You never had the full scope of what you were doing, getting there and getting back, until you saw how many kids were killed," Dad told me later. "Pretty sad, all those crosses and all those names on the wall."

At the RAF air base at Coltishall, the base

commander led them on a tour of the airfield and the museum. There was a display of the interior of a control tower as it would have been during World War II and it included a table surrounded by seated mannequins. And one empty chair.

"We're looking for another dummy to sit in this empty base commander's chair," said the base commander.

"I have one," my mother cried out. "My husband, he could be the dummy."

There was a cruise on the Norfolk Broads, home to 125 miles of waterways and a wetland and wildlife preserve. During medieval times, people dug up peat to dry and use in their hearth fires. During Victorian times, the area was flooded to create waterways for the transportation of goods. On this cruise, Dad saw Lt. Colonel Shower out on deck, where, just as in Dad's gritty memories of Rackheath, the commanding officer was smoking a cigar.

Dad introduced himself. "Colonel, do you remember the crash landing in the middle of Sir Edwin Stacey's alfalfa field?" Colonel Shower said he remembered the event, the plane, and Dad.

"Why were we fined?" Dad asked. "It was an engine malfunction that caused the crash, not something that was in our control."

"Another plane ditched on the opposite runway," Colonel Shower explained. "And your pilot and copilot messed up. I was taking heat from my superiors, who were ordering me to scrap the whole Rackheath mission. I had to do something to satisfy them. The fines I levied against you and the other guys were the result."

"I appreciate knowing the real reason," Dad said to me later. "But I lost seventy-five bucks that day, and that was a hell of a lot of money just to satisfy the guys above Colonel Shower."

Another tour took them to the Second Air Division Memorial Library.

The Second Air Division was one of three in the Eighth Air Force. With 3,000 airplanes, 20,000 men, and control over fourteen airfields including the one at Rackheath, it was the largest air strike force ever committed to battle. During World War II, nearly 7,000 Second Air Division men lost their lives in the line of duty. Once the war ended, the division chose to honor those men with a memorial library. The men of the division, including Dad, wanted something

different, not a plaque or a statue or a monument. They wanted a living memorial and created the Memorial Trust. Servicemen and women provided donations, including Dad's twenty-five dollars that, at the time, was a good chunk of his weekly wage.

The Memorial Library was a part of the larger Norwich Library, and both were in a temporary home, an old furniture business called Glaswells. The relocation was necessary because of a 1994 fire the year before Dad's visit that destroyed its 1960s-era building and all of the display sets of books and artifacts. Books and memorabilia in the basement were saved, but suffered from water damage.

When Dad walked into the room dedicated to the Second Air Division in 1995 and saw the small plastic model of the B-24, he knew where he wanted his larger-scale model to hang.

Back home, the local paper interviewed Dad about his trip.

There were lighter moments. During the parade, Caputo said he heard a voice yell out of the crowd, "That's my dad!" "I was glad she had an American accent," he joked. The voice belonged to Caputo's

daughter, Yvonne, who made the trip with her parents and her husband.

— MEADVILLE TRIBUNE, MAY 28, 1995

Mom bought several copies of the newspaper and cut the article out. She sent a copy to each of her children. When I received mine, I called to say thank you.

"Yvonne, can you imagine? Your dad was eighteen when he learned to repair airplanes. He was nineteen when he made the replacement wing for the AT-6. He was twenty-one when he entered the Air Force and twenty-two when he married me. When he went overseas, he was considered old. He celebrated his birthday at Rackheath, and he was just twenty-three when the war ended. Incredibly young shoulders for all that responsibility."

"It was one of the best times of my life," Dad told me later about the '95 trip. He'd kept his name tag and other memorabilia, all of which sported the quote:

We came as friends; we stayed as friends; we left as friends; we've remained friends.

It was a soul-cleansing experience for my father. He finally rid himself of fifty years of guilt for having survived the war in which so many others had died.

PITCHING THE LIBRARY

*P*lans for the library hadn't yet been announced, and Dad figured that meant there was still a chance he could get them to agree to hang his model B-24 there. He wrote a letter to Phyllis DuBois, the trust librarian for the Second Air Division Memorial Library and a Fulbright scholar.

"This would be my gift to the library in commemoration of the war dead of the Second Air Division."

"My own opinion is (and I do not mean to offend you) that this model would be too large for us," DuBois wrote back. "Perhaps something smaller might be better."

Dad had no intention of altering the design or building something smaller. He knew this model, radio-controlled and all, would be perfect for the library.

"Even though the model has a seven-and-a-half-foot wingspan, it is only twelve inches high. Hanging from the ceiling it could readily be seen by all, but beyond the reach of hands."

Dad's pitch worked. By 1997, Dad was receiving letters from the chairman and vice chairman as well as DuBois. They were eagerly awaiting the model plane's arrival in England.

All the governors agree that your superb model of "Witchcraft" would be a stunning exhibit in the new Second Air Division Memorial Library and a fitting tribute to the Second Air Division.

— VICE CHAIRMAN DAVID
HASTINGS

My governors and I do wish to thank you so sincerely for this incredible act of kindness. The B-24 epitomizes the Second Air Division and to have a model of such a size and accuracy is just fantastic.

— CHAIRMAN PAUL KING

It took Dad seven years to complete the model, which is when he faced the next dilemma. How would he ship the model overseas?

He took it to a local wood shop and the owner built a box that looked somewhat like a coffin, complete with stanchions that Dad used to attach the bulkhead and wings to with rubber bands.

I heard some days ago from our Trust Librarian, Derek Hills, that your marvelous model aircraft has had a safe Atlantic crossing and "landed" at the home of my fellow governor, David Gurney, pending its installation in the magnificent memorial library in August. . . I cannot adequately express the gratitude of my board and myself for the incredible gift, which will take pride of place in our new library. . . The library will be the only memorial of its kind in the world and a fitting tribute to the members of the Second Air Division and to over 6,700 young Americans who died flying from bases in Norfolk and north Suffolk. ...I hope to welcome

you to Norwich in November and to thank you personally for generosity on such a large scale. All of us are much indebted to you.

— LETTER TO DAD FROM PAUL
KING, DATED MAY 25, 2001

Dad, Kirk, and I made a return visit to England in 2002, and we were joined by my brother Michael (Mickey) and his wife Linda. Once again, Dad's friend Ian drove us to all of the places that Dad would have known in 1945. We went to the Second Air Division Memorial Library, and we got our first glimpse of Dad's model B-24 hanging from the ceiling. On the wall was a plaque thanking builder Michael Caputo for his contribution to the library and to history.

Visitors, especially children, look up in awe at the plane that hangs above them. Dad's B-24 is helping people learn and understand more about the war and the people who fought for our freedom in it.

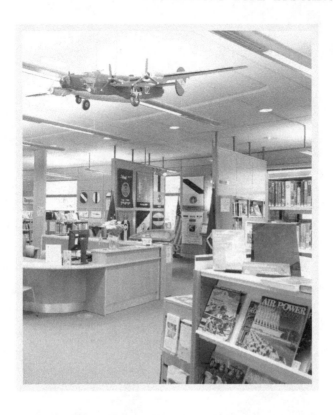

*Photo courtesy Second Air Division Memorial
Library*

THE PHONE CALL

I often heard my mother's admonition, the one she issued after that terrible Thanksgiving argument when I was in my late twenties. *"Yvonne, if you want to know your father, you will have to go to him."* Had I known how to follow her advice I might have gotten to know my father much sooner.

After Mom passed away, I kept up regular weekly phone calls to Dad. Dad was living alone at home. Still, I had to call at the right time. I couldn't interrupt a meal or a football game. I know he appreciated the calls and the connection with family. But we often struggled to find

something to say to one another once we'd talked about his health. We could discuss its decline, his doctor's appointments, and his dialysis treatments. He would sometimes criticize the in-home care he was receiving.

"Just remember that this in-home care is the reason you can stay living at home," I'd respond, twirling the phone cord around my index finder. "If we didn't have that for you, we'd have to move you into a facility like we did with Mom."

I didn't think my brother or sister had the same awkward phone experience with Dad. They shared with Dad a love of sports. All it took was a mention of the Pittsburgh Pirates or the Steelers for their conversations to take off. I knew that one team played baseball and the other football. That was it.

I was in my early sixties when I made the phone call to Dad that changed everything. It was a Sunday night. Winter. I remember looking out the window of my study, the lawn and split-rail fence obliterated from view by the darkness. My beloved birch tree was the only thing in view, because of the light at its base, shining upward and reflecting off the peeling bark and the patches of snow remaining after the thaw. I

knew that Dad would have finished his supper, and that the Sunday night football game was still hours away. It was our time to catch up.

On this particular night, we did the usual review of his latest health news. And then, for some reason, he broke into telling me an intriguing story from the time he was stationed in England near the end of the war.

"We had flown our mission and were heading back to Rackheath when our third engine stalled," Dad said, his voice still deep and resonant despite his age and declining health. The same voice that would reverberate off the back walls of the church whenever he read the scriptures. The same voice that, as a girl, often had me cowering. "I told the radio operator we needed to land, and we were instructed to land in Brussels. But we knew the plane wouldn't make it as far as Brussels and we needed to land right away."

There was an airfield and adjoining depot, and the 76[th] General Hospital nearby in Liege, Belgium, Dad said. It was late in the war and Belgium had already been liberated.

"Dad, hold on, I want to go and get a notepad and a pencil."

"What the hell for?" His brusque tone would have stopped a younger me in my tracks, but today I had no fear.

"This is really interesting and I want to remember it," I said.

THERE WAS VERY little housing available for the crew around the depot at Liege, Belgium. So, Dad and the rest of the Witchcraft crew were whisked from the airfield in the back of a canvas-covered army truck, bumping along muddy roads until they reached the city. The broad gray brick-paved streets provided a smoother ride, and the driver turned the truck down one narrow street after another until reaching its destination. The crew hopped out of the back of the truck to find themselves in front of a bistro. Inside, the bar was filled with Belgians, Allied soldiers, and the crew members were introduced to the bar owner. They were taken to an empty apartment above his restaurant. He welcomed them, and the American cash with which he would be paid. This would be the crew's home while they waited for the third engine to be repaired or replaced.

One evening the bistro owner approached Dad and asked if the crew had cigarettes they'd be willing to part with. He explained that what he had to offer, in trade, would be well worth it. All Dad would need to do was commandeer a truck to bring the bartered goods back to the plane.

"Of course, we had cigarettes," Dad explained. "They were a part of our C-rations, and we were always given extra. If we ever had to bail out, or if we were in some kind of trouble, we could use them to buy ourselves out of a jam."

Still not knowing what the trade was for, Dad and several of the crew climbed into the truck. In the deep of night, they drove far out into the countryside. When they reached a field covered with hay bales, the owner motioned for them to stop. They moved the hay bales until there was a big patch of clear ground and then started to dig. Soon the spades were hitting something solid, each with a "thud." They unearthed wooden cases of champagne and loaded them onto the truck. Dad and the crew handed over the cigarettes and drove back to the airfield and the repaired B-24, which was now ready for

flight. Dad and another flight crew member stayed and guarded the plane with its precious cargo all that night. They were scheduled to fly back to the base the following morning.

When they were safely landed back at Rackheath, Dad directed the military police to guard the plane carefully. "Don't let anyone on board. And I mean anyone. We are carrying top-secret cargo."

Dad and his crewmates managed to commandeer another truck, and the MPs were dismissed. The cases of champagne were distributed to the enlisted men's and officer's clubs, where it was readily and heartily enjoyed.

When Colonel Shower called the crews together the next morning to brief for a mission, he was none too pleased at the condition of the men. "The colonel never found out about the champagne," Dad said. "But he was livid over the obvious hungover state of the men. Many a hungover crewman found himself a canister of oxygen that morning. Breathing it cleared the fog from his head so that he could fly."

THAT STORY HAD ME. Was there more?

We spent every week over the next two years talking about his experiences during the war. I relished the change in Dad's voice when he answered the phone. The gruff "hello" revealed his impatience at being interrupted, but when he heard my voice, his would soften.

During those calls, I was usually sitting at my desk in my home office with a lovely view of our front yard and the birch tree to the right of the window. In the spring and summer, I'd gaze out at the sea of green, as the yard was filled with shag bark hickory trees, a flowering plum, redbud, a pin oak, and a red oak. In the fall the lawn was dotted with yellow, gold, and deep russet. When Dad and I spoke during the gray winter months and the trees were bare, I could see across the road to the neighbor's house, the distance between us covered with a blanket of white snow.

Dad would sit at one of two places. If he answered the phone and there was a faint echo, his voice would be bouncing off the walls of the kitchen. He'd be sitting at the small Formica table attached to the wall. On that table, spread out in front of him, were all of his medications. The pharmacy delivered them in tiny containers

with instructions on which medications to take at what time. He tested his own blood sugar morning and night and gave himself regular insulin injections. Above the table, there was a cut out in the wall with a small shelf. On it was the tiny TV that kept him company throughout the day. When he answered the phone and heard my voice, he'd reach up and turn the sound down.

If Dad's voice didn't echo as he answered the phone, I knew he was in the family room in the basement. His phone sat on his desk to the right of his computer. I'd picture him sitting there, the room generally quite dark due to the two very small windows, curtains drawn, at the edge of the ceiling. Table lamps were his only significant source of light. Behind him was his huge work table, filled with the tools and bits and pieces necessary to build the next model airplane or to repair one of his amateur ham radios.

There was an undeniable shift happening between us, and as much as I enjoyed the process there was something still missing for me.

I was getting to know the man, not just the father. As we became more comfortable with one another, Dad would show me a vulnerable side I'd not known existed. I'd pause, let him breathe

into the spaces of each story, afraid if I jumped in too soon or pushed him for more the magic would be lost.

"So, Dad, last week we talked about your time at San Marcos and navigation school. Where did you go next?"

He would name the air base, and the story would flow. I listened as much to his tone as to the words. It was in his tone that I discovered his feelings. He was amused by quirky, little things. He was doubtful of his own abilities. He was anxious when he was being tested, or when learning a new task. He was ticked at what he saw as the lack of foresight and planning by the army. He was annoyed by what he saw as interminable waiting. He was anxious but resolute prior to and during missions. Always his tone carried the young man he had been.

As a little girl, I hadn't known how to comfort him when his dog Fritz was killed. If his face registered sadness, I didn't know the right question to ask to get him to talk. If he was angry, I shut down. I didn't know what to say to make his irritation dissipate, or better yet, go away altogether. He was my dad, and I wanted to be able to help. I wanted to soothe.

It was the hesitance and confusion in his tone that took us where I wanted to go, that gave me an opportunity to soothe.

When he told me of the horrible recurring nightmare he had when he came home from the war, I waited until I knew he was finished describing it.

"Dad, did you know that given your experience during the war, having nightmares is normal?"

Before I could explain what I meant, he shouted, "Since when are nightmares normal?"

In an instant, I pulled back and found a calm from somewhere deep inside, my tone even and measured. "Give me a chance and I'll explain."

"Okay," he said, softer now. "Go for it."

I told him I was sad that no one really knew until well after the war that having nightmares was a normal reaction to the abnormal, awful events witnessed by the GIs. I told him that other things are normal too, like strong emotional and physical aftershocks. I told him that knowing what they are makes it easier for people not to think they are losing it or going crazy.

"How do you know this stuff?" he interrupted.

I continued to explain that treating post-traumatic stress disorder, or PTSD, was part of the work I do. I shared that there are coping mechanisms that can help, and sometimes people need medications and therapy.

"The biggest thing though, Dad, is just to understand that nightmares are a normal response to a traumatic event. Had you had some help back then, perhaps your bad dreams might have ended sooner than they did."

I ended with sarcasm, which is something Dad really understood. "Sorry pal, hate to tell you this, but you were then, and you are now, normal."

Near the end of our two-year weekly call period, Dad was telling me about a trip to Dayton, Ohio for the annual air show. As a part of the trip, he and a buddy went to the National Museum of the United States Air Force at Wright Patterson Air Force Base. Dad headed straight for the World War II gallery so that he could show his friend the B-24. He located it immediately and as he walked around it, pointing out its

features, he saw a Messerschmitt Me 262 parked alongside.

"Yvonne, I saw that plane and my heart seized like a rock, my legs went out from under me, and I dropped like a shot," Dad said. "It was the scariest thing and it came out of nowhere. I lost consciousness for a couple of seconds. I shook my head trying to clear it while my friend helped me to my feet. It was embarrassing. When my friend asked me what happened, I just said I didn't know."

I let Dad finish. Once he was quiet, I asked, "Dad tell me about the Messerschmitt. I remember you said a little about it when you were at Rackheath."

"I don't remember which mission. I was at my navigator's table when, BOOM, a Messerschmitt shot right past our plane, real close. It was so damned fast. My heart seized when watching it bob and weave at incredible speed." Dad's voice still shook fifty-odd years later as he retold the story. "There was no way our gunners could pick it off. We were sitting ducks with absolutely no protection whatsoever. Any minute we were surely going to be hit and we'd all die."

"Dad, do you remember me telling you that your nightmares were normal?"

"Yeah, so what does that have to do with this?"

"What happened to you when you saw the Messerschmitt in Dayton was a normal reaction to that experience all those years ago. It's called a flashback. That incident was so scary your brain latched onto it. You didn't expect to see that plane when you walked around the B-24, but your brain pulled that memory right back and down you went."

"Normal, huh?"

If I'd paid attention, Dad would have been willing to share stories with me long before the phone call in 2008. It was perhaps a year after Mom died. Reading between the lines I knew he was lonely. There was an emptiness in the house that got to him. He felt her presence, but it wasn't the same as having her physically there. Frequently, he'd tell me he would wake in the middle of the night and look at the end of his bed, certain Mom had pulled on his big toe, the way she did the last few years she was at home.

Loneliness and testosterone, diminished as it was at his age, prompted Dad to want to start

dating. He began going grocery shopping at Tops Grocery Store whether or not he needed anything: what he needed was to see the lovely smiling face at the checkout counter.

It was strange for me to hear him share his delight at having met someone new. I recognized the tone from the adolescents in my classroom when they started noticing and liking members of the opposite sex. Over the phone, Dad described his new friend as younger than he (she was actually my age), very pretty, and a devout Roman Catholic. It seemed to him to be a good match.

"She'll never replace your mother," he said. I understood. I was okay with the fact that he needed to have someone in his life.

I met her on one of my next visits home. We all went out to dinner, and she was lovely. I could understand Dad's attraction to her and I tried my very best to make her feel comfortable with me.

After I'd returned home, Dad raised a new, somewhat more surprising topic on our next phone call.

"I sure wish she'd be interested in sex," he said.

I was dumbstruck. What could I say to that? My abilities as a therapist didn't extend to pretending this wasn't my *father*. I was prepared to talk about his loneliness and need for friendship. Having a toe-to-toe conversation with my Dad about his sex life was something else entirely. I was like most children: as far as I was concerned, I was another virgin birth.

I changed the subject, rather abruptly, I fear, after I recovered my tongue. It never came up again. If Dad caught my dis-ease, he never said, but we never returned to the subject again. Did I disappoint him? Had he thought we'd become close enough that any territory was safe?

MUCH OF THE time when we talked, I felt like a kid at Christmas. Each topic covered, each area explored and researched, each new piece of information was like another gift, wrapped in sparkling paper. Each time I opened a present, I discovered another piece of the father that I had always wanted to know. I learned just how terrified he was during combat. I learned about the depression that commonly accompanied insulin reliance. I learned how he hated his declining

independence, just as my mother had, and I learned how he wished to join my mother. My mother's words from thirty years before came ringing back, once again, in my ears.

"Yvonne, if you want to know your father, you will have to go to him. He isn't going to change. If there is ever to be the relationship you want to have with him, you will have to make it happen."

FLYING WITCHCRAFT

As Dad aged and his hair became thinner, he wore a ball cap to protect his head from the sun. Often his cap would have an image of a B-24 emblazoned on it. He'd wear it everywhere except to church.

"I didn't know you flew B-24s," said a former B-17 flight trainer, breaking into a smile. "Too bad the B-17s were much better at taking flak."

"It might have been better at flak, but only because the '17 was always lagging behind the faster '24."

Dad loved to get into these friendly ribbing

sessions with other veterans, defending his beloved B-24s.

One day Dad was out at the flying field with his buddies and their radio-controlled model airplanes. He heard a plane overhead and exclaimed, "That's a B-24!"

"No way can you recognize a plane by the sound of an engine," scoffed one of Dad's friends.

"Like hell I can't. I'll never forget the sound of those engines."

Sure enough, when the plane came into view it was one of a few surviving B-24s in the United States. It had been restored by the Collings Foundation, painted as the Witchcraft, and was on its way to an air show.

I had no idea that I would ever get to see a real B-24, but one day on a whim, I checked the Collings Foundation website. The Witchcraft was being flown to York, Pennsylvania, a mere two hours away from my home. My husband and I scheduled a vacation day, and I was so excited I felt like a kid going to the circus. So excited that I neglected to write down the address of the exhibit. We made it with just an hour left before the exhibit closed. We paid our

entrance fee and headed straight for the Witchcraft.

Standing beside her, she was smaller than I'd expected. Somehow, I had assumed she'd be big, maybe even as big as a commercial passenger plane, Dad's big stories puffing up the size of the Witchcraft in my imagination.

I jumped at the chance to climb inside, wanting to see and feel the spot Dad had spent so many hours during the war. I climbed up three portable steps to get inside and found myself standing on a very narrow catwalk that led to the front of the plane. How in the world could ten men perform their essential, life-and-death duties in such a cramped space?

What I really wanted to do was sit in the navigator's seat. There at the front of the plane, on the wall behind the copilot's seat, was a chair in front of a small table. That must be it, I thought! But I couldn't get to it. There was a net barrier over the space. I was suddenly afraid I'd come all this way and wouldn't get to sit in that spot.

I was about to resign myself to the fact that I can't always get what I want. Maybe it was okay that I'd come this far, to see the plane up close

and personal, and to stand inside. Maybe that was enough.

Maybe not.

Mom and Dad taught me to speak up if there was something I wanted badly enough. Courage in hand, I went back to the exhibit entrance and asked a woman if there was anyone who could get me to that seat.

"Sure! I'm one of the pilots. I'd be happy to take you." She introduced herself as Janeen Kochan. I later found her described in an article in Forbes Magazine as an instructor, examiner, mechanic, bomber pilot, and role model. She explained that she loved old planes, and she loved flying the '24.

I thought I was small. Ms. Kochan smaller. How did she muster up the strength to fly the '24? She entered the Witchcraft bent over and went up through the bomb bay. She released the net barrier and invited me to climb up and sit in the chair I'd been asking about, just where I had wanted to go.

I was giddy sitting in that seat with a view out the tiny window off of my right shoulder. I thought sitting there would sate my curiosity. However, five years later

I discovered that the Witchcraft would once again be coming close to where we live. I called the Collings Foundation to reserve two seats: one for me and one for Kirk.

The night before the flight I didn't sleep well.

Flying isn't one of my favorite things to do. All night and all the way to the airport in the morning my chest was tight and my breathing shallow. I thought many times of cancelling.

The loudspeaker announced the flight, and we were urged to gather near the plane. A Witchcraft crew member delivered our safety instructions and told us where we'd find our seats. Kirk and another man were seated across from me on the floor in the front of the plane, and seven others were seated in the tail. I had made it clear I wanted the seat behind the copilot, and a crew member helped me to climb up to it. Seeing the straps hanging from the chair, I belted myself in.

I was thrilled and terrified at the same time.

I was about to fly in what looked like a bucket of bolts that for all I knew was held together with rubber bands and chewing gum. Climbing into the plane wasn't especially reassuring either. From my seat I could look up to the right into the cockpit, and to the left I could see the cat walk leading to the tail. Had I stood on that nine-inch cat walk and stretched my arms out to either side, it seemed like I could've touched the walls of the fuselage. Even sitting, if I wasn't careful, I would bang my head on the metal above me.

The B-24 has four engines. One engine started at a time, the first engine sounding like a string of tin cans trailing behind the car decorated with *Just Married*, then, one by one, all four engines were running, settling into a low, loud mechanical purr. Now I knew what my dad meant when he said the plane had a truly recognizable hum. Talking was out of the question when those engines were running, unless we wanted to shout directly into someone's ear.

We taxied and turned, picked up speed, and I felt the unmistakable buoyancy as we left the ground. For the next thirty minutes, the rumble of the engines washed over and through me as

the green Pennsylvania countryside rolled away underneath me.

Once we were in the air, we were free to move about, which meant crawling on hands and knees. I felt absolutely no need to get up and explore. Seated with my seatbelt secure was enough for me. I could imagine Dad here seventy years earlier.

I had two views: one out the cockpit window and one through the crack beside the bomb bay doors. As I sat and watched, I remembered that Dad would have been busy working. Calculating the route, location, entering logs. He'd look up at some point and say to the pilot over the interphone, "We'll be there in a minute and a half."

During my flight there was no turbulence and no flak. We weren't flying at extremely high or low altitudes and all four engines were humming away. The bomb bay was empty and we weren't on a mission. I may have been in the so-called "Flying Coffin," but I wasn't in combat. I was, however, really scared. I had gained a new appreciation for what Dad experienced and why he said combat was terrifying.

Several years after that flight, I discovered

the real location of the navigator's position. It was up in the nose against a wall in front of and almost under the copilot. I had never truly seen it. The disappointment was profound.

Still years later, when Kirk and I were in Seattle celebrating our thirtieth wedding anniversary, I wanted to see the B-17 at the Wings of Flight Museum. We made the museum one of our stops.

Our taxi dropped us off at the entrance and I heard the unmistakable sound of a particular engine. Turning to my right and glancing through the chain link fence, I saw the Witchcraft taxiing to a stop. I couldn't believe my eyes. We had no idea that on that weekend she'd be there for the Wings of Freedom tour. I paced up and down in front of the fence waiting for the Collings staff to set up. Money in hand, I paid our entrance fee. I had to hold myself back from running across the tarmac.

I explained my story to the two young engineers standing under the Witchcraft's wing. One of them showed me how to climb in under the bomb bay, along a passageway on my hands and knees, and into the nose. I was finally able to sit

in the navigator's seat. Somewhere, far above me, I sensed Dad smiling.

I SAW a photograph on the Second Air Division Memorial's Facebook page. I recognized it instantly, and I shared that on the 467th Bomb Group's Facebook page, along with a note that my Dad had been on that plane, on that day, as the navigator. You could have pushed me over with a feather when another comment appeared. "My father was sitting in the copilot's seat. Same plane, same day, along with your dad." Susan and I connected via email.

"Dad and I were going home from a shopping trip," Susan explained in her email. "A car passed us and (literally) written on the back of that car was *God is My Copilot*. Knowing that dad had flown big bombers in the war, I asked him if God had been his copilot. A few seconds of silence. Then dad said, 'No.'

"I sat in stunned silence. Not easy for an eight-year-old. This was the man who took me to church every Sunday, read the Bible with me, etcetera. Then he said this, and I remember it verbatim, '*Susan, God is able to work through all who*

believe, no matter what seat they are sitting in. However, when the Earth is five miles below you, and you're flying on flak-happy nerves, you pray for God to work through your navigator. And He did.' I asked, 'Who was your navigator, Dad?' And he said, *'Mr. Caputo.'* It would be years before I understood just how profound that statement was, and the navigator's role in bringing the boys back to the base, alive, from a successful mission."

THE FIVE WISHES

On my way to Meadville from Pennsburg for a weekend visit, I stopped at the dialysis center to pick up Dad and take him home. His late-onset diabetes meant he no longer had functioning kidneys.

Dr. Zelen approached, holding in his hand a sheaf of Dad's monthly bloodwork reports. I was keen to hear this conversation, because Dad had taken to passing out. Frequently. Dr. Zelen asked Dad a few questions about how he was feeling, what he was doing when he passed out, and whether he had any sensation or indication before he passed out. Dad said no, it came on

suddenly and he had no control. Oh boy, I thought.

"Mike, given your history, the state of your health, and in particular this problem of passing out, you should no longer drive," Dr. Zelen said. It was as if all the air got sucked out of the room for a moment, then came whooshing back in, all hot and moist with Dad's anger.

"Ridiculous," Dad said, furious. "I'm just as safe on the road as the drunks and potheads behind the wheel." Dad raged on, I sat frozen to my seat, and Dr. Zelen listened patiently.

"I understand how you feel. But, if I find out you've been driving, I will call the state and have your license removed."

Dad grumbled awhile more. Grumbling was a refined skill for him, but the conversation ended with Dad saying, "Okay, I won't drive." I wasn't convinced, and Dad's tone told me I hadn't heard the end of this.

The day before I planned to head home, I went for a long bicycle ride on a lovely trail along French Creek. For the hour of the ride and then the entire car ride back to Dad's house, I stewed. Should I just leave and take the risk that Dad would get behind the wheel? Should I

quietly remove the two sets of car keys from the house? How would I, or could I, confront Dad about not driving?

I arrived back at Dad's house to find him sitting in the kitchen, in the midst of his daily regimen of taking medicines and measuring his blood sugar. I offered to make his breakfast. He turned his chair around to face me but his head was down. He started to grumble again about not driving.

Oh here we go, I thought.

Dad repeated what he'd said at the dialysis center. He was safer than folks who were drunk or on drugs. He was still a capable driver. He'd been driving for more than sixty years! I readied myself for a battle, turning from the stove to face Dad. As I opened my mouth to say that I'd remove the keys, or disable the car, or something else I hadn't quite figured out yet, Dad looked up.

"But I won't drive, Yvonne. I gave my word."

HOW DID Dad want to face death? As hard as it

was to accept and deal with, as his health continued to decline, it was important for me to know. What treatments would he find acceptable? What exactly did quality of life mean to him? What was his tolerance for pain? How conscious or aware did he want to be at the end?

It was my own work in a retirement community that gave me the guts and the tools to talk with Dad and get answers to these questions. The retirement facility where I worked delivered all levels of care. We had seniors who lived independently, and those who needed assistance. We also had a nursing facility for those who needed care twenty-four hours a day, seven days a week.

I had watched families grapple for answers to questions like mine, often when it was too late, and their loved ones were unable to respond. The questions are tough to ask. Many of the seniors had never completed the legal paperwork that would guide the decision-making, and no family member had been selected to make decisions when the loved one was no longer able to do so. Often this was all complicated by the fact

that spouses and siblings had different views on what would be appropriate.

Dad did have a will and two power of attorney documents. He had given my brother legal authority to make financial decisions and he had given me authority to make health care decisions on his behalf. I thought we were in good shape, except for these additional questions around quality of life and care.

The Five Wishes, created by the non-profit organization Aging with Dignity, is a directive that combines a living will and medical power of attorney. It covers the personal, medical, spiritual, and emotional needs and wishes of the dying person. We recommended this tool to families at our retirement community.

Wish 1: The Person I Want to Make Care Decisions for Me When I Can't
Wish 2: The Kind of Medical Treatment I Want or Don't Want
Wish 3: How Comfortable I Want to Be
Wish 4: How I Want People to Treat Me
Wish 5: What I Want My Loved Ones to Know

I decided to use the Five Wishes to explain

to Dad how he could choose someone to speak on his behalf, and to clarify specifically what decisions that person could make, and what to do if he changed his mind about that person. It would clarify what medical treatment he wanted, what treatments he didn't want, and under what conditions. It would let me talk to Dad about the meaning of life support under specific conditions: close to death, permanent and severe brain damage, and coma. It would help Dad tell us if there were any conditions under which he might want to be kept alive.

The Five Wishes would also help Dad articulate any specific ways in which he wanted, or didn't want, to be treated. It provided a list of options and all Dad would have to do was cross out anything he didn't want. And it would also help Dad describe what he wanted his family to know, and what he didn't want them to know. It opened the door for him to talk about how he wanted to be remembered and what he wanted at his funeral service.

As a family we had some of the bases covered, but thinking about what was still unclear made me feel sick. We simply hadn't asked Dad some very important questions. If I took the

Five Wishes to Dad, would I be brave enough to go through it with him?

With the Five Wishes document in hand, I drove home to Meadville to see him, tension mounting with each passing mile. It was Christmas, and once again he was spending it in the hospital. His diabetes often led to complications. He'd spend several days as an inpatient getting things sorted out. The physical problems were real, but I think they were nudged along because Dad hated to spend Christmas alone. He no longer had the energy to decorate his home, and his children were states and hours away with their own children. At least in the hospital he could be surrounded by people who doted on him.

I walked into his hospital room to see him alert and laughing with his nurse. Whatever had been the health crisis seemed to have diminished, and he was delighted to see me. We chatted about his test results and news from the family, and when the time seemed right, I handed him the Five Wishes.

"Dad, I'd like you to take a look at this, and I would like to go over it with you."

"What the hell is this?" This was Dad, characteristically abrupt.

"It's sorta like the legal paperwork we did a while ago, but more thorough. Some of the questions will be hard for me to ask, and some of the questions might be hard for you to answer, but I want to make sure that at the end of your life, you get exactly what you want."

"What do you mean?"

"Well, what kind of treatment do you want? How do you want to be remembered? What kind of funeral do you want? Those kinds of things."

He swung his legs over the side of the bed and patted the space beside him. The bed was warm when I sat down. We were shoulder to shoulder, and his back was facing the door to his room. He didn't seem to notice his hospital gown yawned a little in the back, and he probably wouldn't have cared. We spent the next hour going from item to item, page to page, in the Five Wishes.

The trepidation I had felt on the long drive to the hospital floated away as if it was never there in the first place. The Five Wishes document helped make us both feel comfortable and

relaxed. I read a question, and Dad read descriptions of what needed to be considered. He was at times thoughtful and at other times his responses were quick and sure.

"Nope, I don't want that."

"Yep, that's important to me."

"If you see that I won't have any quality of life, then I want to go. I don't want to be a vegetable. I don't want to be in pain, and whatever they have to do, do it. I've heard that pain killers could bring the end on more quickly, but at that point who the hell cares."

I asked what he wanted for his funeral.

"I want a Mass at St. Agatha's, and you kids can choose the readings. I don't want the priest to ask the congregation to share memories about me. If they haven't said it to my face while I was alive, then I don't want it said at my funeral. You and your husband will sing, and I want the 'Lord's Prayer', 'Amazing Grace', and the 'Ave Maria.'"

Okay then. That was settled. I smiled inwardly. To Dad, I nodded gravely, taking notes.

"I want to be remembered for my work with the Red Cross."

I was surprised at that. "What about your service in the war?"

"Well, that too. I want to be remembered as a father of wonderful children, a husband, and oh, how I loved a good story and a good joke."

Once every question was asked and every blank filled in, I gathered two hospital staff who were willing to witness Dad's signature. He was still seated on the side of the bed, and I sat down beside him again. He put the Five Wishes on the bedside table and signed it, his thick fingers firmly holding the pen. The signature was bold and every letter legible. He handed the papers to the two witnesses, one after the other, for their signatures.

When it was just the two of us in his room again, he held the document in his left hand, and I held it in my right. We looked at it as we leaned into each other. With our free hands clasped, we prayed the prayer that glued us together as a family. "Our Father, who art in heaven, hallowed be thy name; thy kingdom come; thy will be done ..."

I made copies of the Five Wishes for myself, my brother and sister, and each of his physicians. I found a manila envelope and taped the

original to the side of the refrigerator in his kitchen. I wanted the Five Wishes to be close by if he was seriously in distress and had to call an ambulance.

Looking back, the Five Wishes opened another door. Because I was willing to wade into the murky waters of death and dying with him, he began to confide in me.

It was my experience as a psychotherapist that helped me understand how to be with him and hear what he was saying. I didn't have to counter what he said or shut him down. I just had to listen and validate where he was and what he was feeling. It was difficult for me to hear some of these things, but I think it helped Dad voice what was swirling around in his head and heart.

"I wasn't always nice to your mother in the end. I sometimes feel so guilty about it."

Dad said he regretted yelling when her dementia prompted her to ask the same questions over and over again. He wished he could have been different or that he'd found a different way.

He told me that he wanted to have been different with her when she passed away. He wanted her back. He said he'd started having

dreams about her and he relished her presence in them.

"Have you ever talked to a friend, or the priest at church, about it?"

"Do you think that would help?"

"It might," I said.

Sometimes it was the missing of her that would have Dad talking about his own desire to go. Sometimes it was his lack of energy after a dialysis treatment that prompted the conversation. Sometimes it was out of the blue.

"You know, Yvonne, I'm ready to go. It's time. My only wish is that I would be carried out of the house feet first on a stretcher. That's the way I'd like to go."

My answer was the same as I'd given my mother. "It's okay. Let God know that you are ready, and the two of you decide when. I get that you don't want to be around anymore, but I will miss you like crazy."

*M*y parents had always made the holiday season magical for us kids. By comparison, I realized how stark and lonely it was now for Dad. I was not at all surprised that this Christmas he landed back in the hospital. When the rest of us were fully occupied creating magical experiences for our own children and grandchildren, it was where he could be surrounded by people who treated him like the special person he was.

He went to the hospital because he was nauseous and couldn't keep anything down. After his stomach was empty, his body would wrack with the dry heaves, causing intense pain in his

upper back. Doctors helped Dad's symptoms subside, but they kept him in hospital well after he was eating again without vomiting. They were controlling his pain with medication and wanted to help him rebuild his strength through physical therapy while making sure the nausea didn't return.

My sister, brother, and I kept in daily contact with the hospital by phone, monitoring his care. As I had done many times before, as soon as I knew he was hospitalized, I called his unit to make sure that the Do Not Resuscitate (DNR) order was included in his chart.

I asked the nursing station to transfer me to the phone in Dad's room.

"Dad, we need to talk about your DNR. Remember when we worked on the Five Wishes?"

"Of course, I remember. Isn't it still on my hospital record?" Dad's voice was weak but steady. I could picture him in his blue cotton gown, the distinct "hospital" smell emanating from the bed linens, the creak and crinkle of the vinyl-wrapped mattress betraying his attempts to get comfortable.

"No, apparently a new one is needed each time you come in. It's the kind of thing people

can change their minds about," I told him. "If you still feel the same way, I'll ask the nurses to bring in the paperwork for you to sign."

"Yep, have them bring it in."

I hadn't yet gotten Dad a Christmas present. Each year it became more and more difficult to think of a gift he might need or want. I called the local florist in Meadville and asked if they had a small artificial Christmas tree suitable for a hospital room.

They described one eighteen inches tall, its branches covered in sparkling ice. They said they'd add some colorful glass balls, a bright red bow at the top, and a ribbon cascading down the tree. It would be delivered the same day.

By the time I called Dad again, it was after supper and I'd forgotten about the little tree. Before I could even say hello, he was off.

"Hon, the Christmas tree arrived. It's just beautiful." He sounded much better. "It really feels like Christmas now."

My heart was in my throat, my cheeks wet and salty. He'd seen so many Christmases, he was ill and in hospital, yet he made me feel like my little gift of a silly decorated tree had made all the difference to him and his day. I won-

dered if he knew how much his thanks meant to me.

"Hey Dad, Kirk and I've decided to come to Meadville," I said once I'd recovered my composure. "Your nurse says you'll be there for a while yet. We'll drive in one day, spend two, and drive home on the fourth day. Is there anything you need?"

"Nope, a visit from you would be just great."

Once the car was packed, I made one last tour through the house to check that all things were in order. The small appliances were unplugged. The thermostat in the house was set just high enough to help prevent the pipes from freezing, and each faucet was opened to keep water moving at a slow drip. My last task was to water the plants. I noted that none of my three Christmas cactuses on the dining room windowsill were in bloom. Not even the white one.

The drive was uneventful. From the passenger seat, I drank in the gray skies and lapped up the stillness and peace that only the snow can bring. Despite the bitter air, I felt light-hearted and easy when we parked the car and walked into the hospital.

Dad's face brightened as we entered the

room. His hospital gown, not so different from the one I imagined on the phone, had seen better days. Frayed, thinning, and limp. His bed was raised so that he was in a semi-sitting position, and his color seemed good. He winced as he tried to rearrange himself on the bed, but once settled his smile returned.

"So, how are you? And what's the latest from the doctors?" I asked, perching on the chair nearest the bed.

"I'm much better. The stomach thing seems to have resolved itself, but my back still hurts. I can't get comfortable, and I can't sleep. The meds take the edge off, so that helps."

"Do they know what caused the nausea and vomiting?"

"They aren't totally sure. Maybe an interaction between some of the drugs I've been taking. They've switched them up,"

"How about physical therapy? How's that going?"

"They're helping me gain back some strength in my legs and arms," Dad explained. "If I'm going to be able to manage my own bathroom visits, I need all the help I can get." He started to laugh at that, which brought on a coughing

spell, which triggered his back pain. He tried to hide the grimace, but I could see the pain etched on his face.

We chatted for a little longer, about not much in particular. My mind wandered. I remembered the look of my dad's clean strong hands on the steering wheel from my little-girl vantage point in the back seat, his thumbs toward the center. I heard his booming Saturday morning voice, *"Let's get crackin', times a wastin', the day's half over!"* And I could still feel the strength of his arms as he reached around me to show me how to cast, and how to hold my thumb just so to hold the line against the fishing pole. I came back to the portly, wizened, bald old man in front of me, so different than he was and yet so much the same, and realized the room had gone quiet.

We visited for the next two days in the early afternoon and then again after supper. When Kirk and I weren't at the hospital, we ran errands for Dad. We bought new cleaning supplies and made sure the house was spotless for his return. I spoke to Terry and Charlene, who lived across the road from Dad and who had been taking care of driving him to and from dial-

ysis, doctor's appointments, and grocery shopping, as well as keeping his driveway clear of snow.

"How has Dad been lately, before this last hospitalization?" I asked Terry, standing on his front step, bundled up against the crisp air.

"He's as cantankerous and ornery as a bull sometimes," Terry admitted. "But he makes up for it by being kind and thoughtful. Just when I think I've had enough he'll pull out some sweetness and I'm putty in his hands."

I smiled and told him I knew exactly what he was talking about. "I know the hospital is going to want to release him soon, and we have to be heading home. Can they call you when it's time to pick him up from the hospital?"

Terry agreed. Back at the hospital, I informed the social worker that we had everything in place for when Dad was ready to be released. Kirk and I were planning to leave Meadville and head for home the next morning, which was New Year's Eve.

While Kirk checked the oil, topped up the windshield washer reservoir, and filled up the gas tank, I spent a little alone time with Dad. It was time for me to give Dad his second

Christmas present. I motioned for him to move over, and I sat beside him on his bed. I propped the first draft of my book on his copious belly, the burgundy of the three-ring binder perfectly matching the tiny print of his hospital gown. I leaned back against the bed, and we began to flip through the pages.

I knew he was tired, but I read just a little bit to him. When I finished, I put the book on the bedside table and turned around to face him. "Dad, I want you to know how very proud I am of you. I am so proud of your service."

Dad's eyes misted up as he ran a papery hand over the closed binder cover. He told me he was the one to be proud, because his little girl had written a book.

Back home in Pennsburg, the phone rang on the evening of New Year's Day. We'd been home just over twenty-four hours. When I picked up the phone, Dad started yelling.

"Why the hell did you tell them I could go home?" I pulled the receiver a few inches from my ear to protect my eardrums. "I'm in agony! The damned hospital sent me home with no pain pills!"

It was his back. He couldn't sit, stand, or lie

down, and all he wanted was to sleep. Which he couldn't do.

"I'm scared, Yvonne," Dad had lowered his voice. "I don't want to be alone. Can you take a leave of absence from work?" That's when I knew how serious this was.

"Of course, Dad. I'll leave tomorrow morning as early as I can. When we get off of the phone, I'll find someone to come and stay with you until I get there. I'll also call the hospital to see about getting you some medication."

I took a deep breath to steady myself and said as clearly and firmly as I could muster, "This is it Dad. You can't live at home alone any longer. When I get there, we will have to go to plan B."

He agreed, and then ended the conversation with, "Honey, I'm so sorry I yelled at you. I didn't mean it."

I was used to his gruff ways, and sadly I was used to him yelling. I was not used to receiving an apology from him for his yelling.

For the next several hours, I made phone calls, my left ear burning from the constant pressure. I called the hospital and learned it was against the law to send Dad home with pain

medication. I called Dad's pharmacy, which was closed. I called Charlene, who would run right over, but couldn't stay the night. Terry, however, was going to clear more snow from Dad's driveway. A stalled lake-effect snow storm meant the white stuff was accumulating at an inch an hour. I called my friend Barb, who said her granddaughter was a certified nursing assistant and might be able to help. Fifteen minutes later, it was all arranged. I called my brother and sister to update them, and then called Dad.

"Char just got here," he said, his voice dripping with relief. "That makes things better. I'll see you when you get here."

The immediate tasks out of the way, a wave of emotion crashed over me and pushed me into a chair. Buffeted first with worry, then relief, then fear, it was as though heavy winds swirled around me, changing temperature, direction, intensity. I felt the crushing weight of all the changes and decisions that filled the days ahead.

The snow had stopped by the time I arrived at Dad's mid-afternoon. Barb greeted me at the door. She'd come over earlier to stay with Dad while her granddaughter picked up Dad's new medicine from the pharmacy. Now that Dad

had the drug in his system, he seemed much better. I hadn't realized how tightly the muscles between my shoulder blades were clenched until they released when I saw that Dad was better.

Dad was sitting in his favorite spot in the kitchen, in the cracked brown vinyl chair with wheels, the doughnut cushion firmly under his butt. For a flash I was catapulted back to all those nights we talked on the phone, him sitting in the same chair in the same spot, telling me about his life before I was born. Today, though, no phone. Today, I was standing in the same room. He looked up at me, the hint of a soft smile playing at the corners of his mouth, his eyes telegraphing he was happy I was here.

I asked how he was feeling. "The pain is better now, tolerable. But I haven't been able to sleep. I'm so, so tired."

He pointed to the nursing aide. "She's good. Candy's her name. Just what the doctor ordered."

Despite her youth, Candy had taken charge. She made sure Dad took his meds and his insulin and she checked his blood sugar. When Dad got pushy, she pushed back. She was calm,

confident, and Dad said he'd relaxed around her immediately.

Barb pulled me aside as she and Candy were leaving. She told me that when she was alone with Dad and Candy had gone to the pharmacy, a strange thing happened.

"Your Dad was sitting at the end of the couch, and I was in that chair by the window," Barb said. "He looked at me, then pointed to the other end of the couch." Barb raised her arm and pointed, the silvery winter light from outside waning. "He said, 'Can you see Teddy, sitting there?' I told him I couldn't."

I looked at the couch, both ends now empty. As I pondered Dad's vision and what it meant, Barb said, "Your dad then said that perhaps he was just tired. But he seemed changed, somehow. More peaceful."

We said our goodbyes, and once I'd closed the door, I called Terry and Charlene. Char answered.

"Dad's having trouble sleeping. It's hard to lie down. If we move his recliner up to the living room that might help. Would you and Terry be able to come help me move it?" The chair was too big and heavy for me to move myself. I hated

to ask for yet another favor, but it was for Dad, and Char said they'd be over shortly.

When I hung up, Dad said his stomach was upset, and he asked for a blueberry yogurt. When he'd finished that, he stood up somewhat shakily and announced he needed the bathroom. After several minutes, when he didn't return to the kitchen, I found him trying to lie down on his bed.

He winced in pain as he carefully lowered himself on his side. I lifted his feet from the floor and swung them onto the bed. Then I covered all of him, except his feet, with a blanket. That's the way he slept, all his life, with his feet outside the covers. He asked for another pillow, which I gave him. I tucked the blanket around him, turned off the light, and quietly left the room.

There was a knock on the door announcing that Terry and Char had arrived. As we discussed how we would move the recliner to the living room, we heard a thud.

"Sounds like he's fallen," said Char into the silence that followed. We tore up the stairs and down the hall. In the bedroom, Dad was on his face in the narrow space between the bed and the dresser.

"Dad! Dad!" I'm not sure what I hoped he would say, but he didn't answer me. I froze, terrified. What was I supposed to do now?

I heard Char's voice, but it seemed disconnected from her face, like it came from the other side of the room. "Call 9-1-1!"

Grateful for a task, I picked up the phone beside Dad's bed and dialed. The emergency medical technician, the EMT, lived just a few doors down and was there in minutes.

"You'll have to help me move him," he said. Again, I was grateful for instruction. "I'll lift under his shoulders, and you lift his feet and pull back."

It took several maneuvers, but we finally had Dad lying face up at the foot of the bed, no longer in the tight squeeze alongside the bed. The EMT started doing CPR. Presence of mind returned to me and I yelled, "Stop! He's DNR!"

The EMT kept up the rhythm on Dad's chest and said, "We have to work on him."

Then I remembered the Five Wishes hanging on the refrigerator door. I grabbed the papers and thrust them into the hands of the second EMT who had just arrived.

"These aren't any good," he told me.

"They're six years old. You need to update these things every year."

Frustrated and worried we were not doing as Dad wished, I called the hospital.

"I'm Mike Caputo's daughter. He is on his way by ambulance to the emergency room. Can you please get the DNR there?"

I wanted to do the right thing, to do as Dad wanted, to respect his Five Wishes, including his request that we "do not resuscitate."

By the time I called my sister, there were two more EMT's on the scene. One of them came to me just as I hung up the phone to say they'd received authorization from the ER physician to stop working on Dad. "You have only a few minutes...."

I walked back into the bedroom, and the EMTs quietly left, gathering just outside the door. Dad lay face up on the floor, his bare feet protruding from his old pair of jeans. His T-shirt had seen better days, his beard in need of a trim. He was absolutely still.

I felt an eerie calm. I lay down on my right side, the length of my body right next to Dad's warmth. I put my left arm over his chest and murmured into his ear. "It's all right. I love you

and I will miss you, but you will be with Mom." And then I recited the Lord's Prayer. "Our Father, who art in heaven, hallowed be thy name; thy kingdom come; thy will be done on Earth as it is in heaven…" When the prayer ended, I said, "It's okay Dad, you can go."

The phone rang, and I got up from the floor. I returned to the kitchen to take the call from my brother Michael. As I was filling him in, one of the EMTs came in. When I saw his face, I knew.

The EMTs put Dad on a gurney and carried him out to the ambulance that would take Dad to the ER to be pronounced. It had begun to snow heavily again, big fat white flakes light against my skin.

For a moment my personal grief gave way and I threw my arms in the air with fists clenched in the sign of victory. To the EMTs who were now staring at me quizzically, I said, "Yes, guys. You have given my dad his wish. He did not want to die in hospital. He wanted to be carried out of his home feet first, and that's just what you've done."

I stood at the end of the gurney, pulled back the cover, and stroked my dad's smooth, bald

head. It had begun to grow cold. The journey had been awful. The journey had been beautiful. Dad's face bore a peaceful expression that said, *I'm home. I'm no longer in pain, and I'm with your mother.*

As the ambulance doors closed, I lifted my face to the inky sky, the snowflakes falling from heaven melting and wet on my cheeks.

ANGELS ON MY SHOULDERS

During one of our regular phone calls, I had told Dad that I was taking voice lessons.

"Your mother would be so proud," he said. "This is great. You'll sing at my funeral."

It wasn't what I wanted. I wasn't taking lessons to be a soloist. I had no desire to stand alone in front of an audience and sing. There were things I was frightened of that I was willing to learn how to face. This wasn't one of them. I knew I had a good ear, and that I could hit and hold the right notes. But I loved the comfort of being surrounded by the other altos in my section of the choir. My lessons were

about learning how to more comfortably contribute to the choir and the wonderful music we produced.

As we prepared for the funeral, I struggled with how I was going to honor my father's request. It came to me in a flash. I'd been focusing on my own performance anxiety. But I didn't have to do this alone because, thankfully, Dad had also asked Kirk to sing at his funeral. Kirk, with his glorious tenor voice, was proud to have been asked. Dad asked me to sing, he didn't ask me to sing solo. Since one of the songs Dad requested was "Amazing Grace," Kirk and I could do it together. I had sung it so frequently I knew I could handle it as long as Kirk was by my side. It would also be lovely to have the congregation accompany us on some of the verses. The solo work could be Kirk's. I would be honoring Dad's request without crashing through my comfort zone.

I must have had angels sitting on my shoulders. Perhaps one of them was Mom. When it came time, Kirk and I walked up to the podium. We stood and announced we would sing the first verse together, and we requested the congregation sing along to the remaining verses.

We sang the first verse, and my voice, though soft, was clear and deliberate.

Amazing Grace, how sweet the sound...

Kirk struggled a little through the second and third verses, the tears gathering in the corner of his eyes. Mine were dry throughout. I was calm and assured. As I looked at the casket in front of me, draped with the ivory pall with the gold cross in its center, it seemed to lift and undulate and shimmer.

*T'was grace that brought me safe thus far
And grace will lead me home...*

The voices of the congregation rose, filling the church with the harmony of love, of farewell. I raised my eyes heavenward, singing clear, crisp notes, Kirk's hand warm and soft in mine behind the podium. I felt my father all around me, within me, watching me from above. In a sense we were flying together.

*I once was lost but now am found
T'was blind but now I see...*

PILOT'S LICENSE

e needed to get Dad's house ready to sell. We all participated. The nieces and nephews selected model planes that would soon hang in their children's rooms. My step-daughter and son selected bedspreads and afghans my Mom had made. My brother, sister, and I chose mementos that would remind us of childhood.

Room by room we cleared away clutter. We ordered a dumpster for things in bad shape or of no value to anyone. My sister took great delight in heaving the cracked Naugahyde-and-chrome wheeled chairs, including the stained doughnut

cushion, up and over the side of the dumpster. She had offered several times to get Dad something new and more comfortable, but he would have none of it. "That damned chair is just what I need," he'd say.

I placed empty boxes in each room for personal documents and paperwork. I was the family historian, so all of that was going with me. They found their place on an old table in the basement of my home. I was still working full time, and I knew I needed more hours than I had available to sort through the contents. I promised myself that my first task in retirement would be to take care of them.

I kept my promise. Four years later, I carried all the boxes up three flights of stairs to my office. I had no idea what was in each box. Like my mom, I hated disorganization. As I sorted through each box, I heard Mom's voice in my ear. *"Yvonne, a place for everything and everything in its place."*

I emptied the contents of each box into piles. One pile for photo albums, another for deeds, powers of attorney, and wills. A third pile was for the cards and letters we children and grand-

children had written to Mom over the years. The fourth was for scrapbooks and cassette tapes from Mom's days in Sweet Adelines. And the fifth pile was for Dad's service records, books, old photos and mementos. Each pile then went back into a box of its own.

I started with the largest box and the thirteen photo albums inside. Dad loved taking pictures, and Mom loved having the recorded history. I opened each one and carefully peeled pictures from the sticky pages. I sat in the middle of my couch. In an arc around my feet I made separate stacks of photos, each meant for my brother or sister, a niece, nephew, or a cousin. To each pile I added cards and letters they'd written to Mom. Each stack of history went into a large manila envelope and mailed.

The deeds and copies of my parents' last will and testament found space in my file cabinet. I sent all of the memorabilia from the Sweet Adelines to a chapter member.

Finally, I had a chance to look at the expandable binder full of Dad's service records. Hours flew by as I leafed through books and papers he had saved from his time in the service. The text-

book he used to learn navigation. The carbon copies of his pre-deployment flight record. The card from Rackheath detailing every one of his bombing missions. Documentation on everything he'd told me during our weekly phone calls. Glorious.

I reached into the bottom of the last box and pulled out a four-by-seven-inch, black, hardcover *Pilot Logbook* with Dad's name inscribed on it. I ran my finger down each of the yellowed pages, which held a record of every training flight he had taken beginning on April 13, 1947 and ending on September 2, 1947. A flimsy, torn, and delicate piece of paper fell out of the back of the book.

Dad never told me he had earned his private pilot's license, but here was the proof. I sat there with faded license on top of the open logbook, my eyes looking at but not seeing the trees outside my office window. Had he flown solo? How many times? When? How could I not have known?

One summer in my early twenties I worked the breakfast shift as a waitress at a local restaurant. Mom would drop me off on her way to work, and Dad would

pick me up at the end of the shift. Waitresses on that shift would rotate responsibility for serving new customers that came in during the last hour of the shift, between two and three in the afternoon.

One beautiful day, nearing the end of my shift, I was anxious to go home. The late rotation was mine. My feet hurt, and I was sitting on the floor in the kitchen with my back against the wall. I was ready to sit in the lounge chair in the back yard with my book until it was time to prepare supper. Another waitress came into the kitchen and announced that I had a new customer. I was annoyed. My plans for the chaise lounge went up in smoke.

Seated by the front window of the restaurant was a man in his mid-thirties. He was rather plain, but he had a pleasant face. He asked to see the dinner menu, flashing a genuine smile as he said that he knew it was early, but he wanted a full meal. I put on my best customer-service

face, tucking my disappointment away in the pocket of my server apron. After I had placed his order with the kitchen, I called Dad.

"Don't come to pick me up for another forty-five minutes," I told him. The last thing I wanted was to have Dad waiting and fuming when I finally got in the car to go home.

When I went back to check on the young man, he said, "I've asked about you and I know you're single. Would you like to go out to dinner?" But he's just had dinner, I thought, flattered and confused at the same time.

The white lie came out of my mouth unbidden. "I'm sorry, but I have other plans." Yeah, like an appointment on a lounge chair in the backyard.

"Okay," he said. "How about I take you for a ride instead?" The prospect of this was even less pleasing than a meal. "My airplane is out at the Meadville Airport," he continued. "I also know your Dad is coming to pick you up. When he gets here, I'll ask his permission." He held out his hand and told me his name was John. How did he know my Dad was coming? How could he know my father was cautious about where I went and who I dated? I was pretty

sure Dad would say no, so I figured it was safe to agree.

When John had finished his meal, he paid his bill and he left me a nice tip. And he came out with me to talk to Dad. My father didn't look at me. He didn't ask me if I wanted to go. He just started smiling and said, "Sure."

I could have kicked him. This was not something I was comfortable doing. Why in the world had he responded so quickly? What was he thinking? How did he know this guy was legit? But I didn't speak up. I was too stunned. Was I going to be safe with John? I realized that as the pilot, John would be busy. His hands would be safely where they were supposed to be.

On the way to the airport, John explained that he owned the plane. He piloted businessmen to and from meetings, and often that would take him to small regional airports like the one in Meadville. On the tarmac was his single-engine Cessna. John opened the passenger door and gave me a hand as I climbed up and in. He radioed the control tower, started the engine, and we taxied down the runway. Take off was smooth, and we flew low enough for me to see

places that were a familiar part of my life. I loved the view of the trees and rolling farmland stretched beneath us.

John asked if I wanted to take the controls. He showed me how to pull back on the yoke, and up we went. Push the yoke forward, and the plane descended. Turn the yoke right or left, and the plane banked in those directions. It was liberating to be in control of a flying aircraft. But I was content to make this a one-time experience.

With John safely in control again, I started pointing out landmarks. "Can you find your way to your house?" John asked. It only took me a couple of minutes to locate the aqua water tower off in the distance, next to a road far above the tree line. Our house was on that road. Follow it, and we would get there.

My dad must have heard the plane. When we approached the house, Dad and Mark were standing in the front yard. Dad was waving his red and white baseball cap to beat the band. We were flying so low I could see the ear-to-ear smile on his face.

Closing the *Pilot Logbook*, I understood what was behind that smile. He was sharing his joy of

flying with someone he loved deeply. And I was flying with Dad.

MY LAST VISIT to Rackheath a few years after Dad died, Kirk and I were standing at the doors to the old air control tower. It was now occupied by an information technology business. The doors were locked, but there was a bell. Once again, I heard Dad saying, "*If you want to do something, go ahead and do it. Ask permission later.*" I pressed the buzzer and a young man came to the door. I asked if it would be possible to go up on the roof.

The reception area was a little museum with photos taken during the renovation of the building. There was one of the original crews of the Witchcraft, a DVD of the 467th bomb group, and a plaque dedicating the building to Colonel Shower. Tears welled in my eyes as I signed the guest book. Above my signature was Gina's, my niece. She'd been here four months prior. I knew she had visited the Second Air Division Memorial Library, but I didn't know she had

come to Rackheath. She too wanted to touch the soul of the man she called her grandfather.

We walked through narrow halls, glancing into the rooms on the first floor. The manager giving us a tour said, "We haven't changed the layout at all. We took one wall down on the second floor, but that's it."

We climbed a narrow metal staircase on the outside of the building and stepped onto the flat gray roof, still wet from last night's rain. The skies were overcast, and a strong breeze prompted me to pull my sweater tighter. Near the edge of the roof was a small shed with windows on all four sides. This was where the Rackheath air crews would huddle as they scanned the horizon for incoming and outgoing planes.

As I stood there, a shiver ran through me and the hair on the back of my neck stood on end. Dad was whispering in my ear, *"This is where we stood when we knew a mission was returning. We counted the planes. It let us know how many of the group were returning and how many had been lost."* The stark, bleak reality of the war.

. . .

I PUT the pilot logbook back in the box and reached into the box containing letters. I picked one out at random, unfurled the fading paper, and saw it was a letter Dad had written to Mom while she was pregnant with my older brother.

Do you think I shall be a good father, honey? Golly, I hope so.

You were, Dad. You were.

VENOSA AND POTENZA

Kirk and I joined our choir on a trip to Italy and France. We sang at Notre Dame in Paris and the Normandy American Cemetery. We also sang at St. Peter's Basilica in Rome and St. Mark's in Venice. This trip was the perfect chance for me to visit Venosa and Potenza, the towns where my grandparents grew up.

Being in a car and on the roads in Italy is one of the most nerve-wracking things I have ever done. Kirk agreed to do the driving. There didn't seem to be any rules, lanes weren't important, and there were no speed limits. A two-lane road could easily have three lanes of cars with

motor scooters coming up between the cars. A scooter whizzing past my window made me jump.

We took the four-lane autostrada as far as we could, then exited to smaller roads. Our route took us through the Apennine Mountains, dotted with honey-colored brush and deep-green scrub bushes and short pines. Venosa and Potenza are both perched on hilltop plateaus. The homes and buildings, in all shades of sand and topped by orange ceramic tile roofs, are nestled closely together and attached. The cobblestone streets are so narrow it felt like I could spread my arms and touch both sides.

It was hot, most days 100 degrees. We had air conditioning in the car, but to truly experience these villages we had to walk. The inescapable heat bounced off the cobblestones and buildings and hit us like a wall. We found very few trees to provide shade.

Seeing both Venosa and Potenza has helped me imagine the journeys my grandfather and grandmother embarked on when they left. I can picture the stage coach Grandpa took from Potenza, alone, or the one Grandma took when she left Venosa with the children, and how few

belongings they would have had with them. It must have taken days to come down off the mountainside and into Naples.

Dominick Caputo was born in Potenza, Italy in 1871. Grandma Angelina was born in 1882 in Venosa, thirty-six miles northeast of Potenza. A spunky young woman, she and my grandfather Dominick were engaged when she was fifteen years old and he was twenty-six. At seventeen, Angelina gave birth to her first child, Josephine. Dominick left for the United States in 1905, alone, when Angelina was pregnant with Constance. Angelina refused to leave Italy until they could afford to bring the children.

Dominick made his way to Scranton, Pennsylvania, and found work as a stonemason. Every time Dominick returned to Italy, which he did three times before the whole family emigrated, Angelina would become pregnant again. So, the cost of bringing the family to the US kept escalating. Angelina was literate and educated, and she managed to earn a living by turning her home into a school for the children of the village. This, in turn, allowed the other village mothers to go to work in the fields.

So, there was Josephine, born in 1905, Con-

stance, born in 1906, Rose, born in 1910, and Joe, born in 1912. It wasn't until 1921 that the Caputos could afford the five extra tickets for the emigration journey to the United States.

The stagecoach trip from Venosa took several days, creaking and bouncing and winding down mountain trails and through valleys to reach the port of Naples. There, they boarded the grand ship, the Fernando Palaciano, that would take them to their new home in the USA. Their tickets were in steerage, below deck and crowded in foul and unsanitary conditions. The voyage lasted ten days, an experience vastly different from their lives in the village in Italy. They suffered nausea, claustrophobia, and the constant fear of the unknown waiting for them.

Ellis Island was closed for quarantine when they arrived, and the ship was ordered instead to dock in Philadelphia. Grandpa had been waiting in New York to welcome his wife and children, but they were processed and cleared at the immigration inspection station in Philly, where there was no one to greet them. A kind stranger read the identification tags pinned to their clothing and helped them buy tickets and board

a train to Scranton, where the joy and relief of a reunited family awaited.

At the age of forty, Grandma Angelina gave birth to her fifth child, my father, on February 10, 1922, who automatically became a US citizen.

On one of our summer trips to Scranton as children, Dad took us to see St. Lucy's Church. "My dad helped to build this church," he explained, running his hands over the pulpit and communion rail as he spoke. He told us about Grandpa Dominick's work as a stonemason using marble brought from Italy. That white marble, streaked with gray, kept the inside of the church cool even on the hottest summer day.

Fifty years later, I revisited St. Lucy's Church. The parish priest was giving us a tour and I told him about my grandfather and his role in the construction. The priest explained that much of the original marble had to be removed. When they built the church, between

1924 and 1928, nobody knew that underneath were the remnants of coal mines. The timbers supporting the tunnels had begun to deteriorate. The weight of the church was causing it to slide down the hill. To save the church, the marble in the pulpit, some of the altar, and the belfry were removed in 1956.

In Potenza, I stood at an iron railing looking out over those mountains and I knew my grandfather had probably been at that very same spot, looking out with his intense pale blue eyes at the view he would never see again. What was he thinking and feeling the last time he stood there? Excitement? Fear? Regret? Was he relieved that in America he might be better able to feed his family?

Venosa is an hour north of Potenza. I clearly remembered my Uncle Joe saying they lived right off the square. "I can close my eyes and know my way to my house."

I thought I'd be able to go straight to the street where my grandmother and her children lived. But the square was more of a rectangle. I stood in the middle of it, amazed to see a dozen narrow lanes leading off of it, each no more than the width of a car. Which one was theirs? What

was the street name? What was the house number? When I was sitting with Uncle Joe, I never thought to ask for a specific address.

I wish Dad and I had made that journey together. I wanted to stand at that railing in Potenza and in that square in Venosa with him. I wanted to reach for his hand and hold it while together we experienced the places and people who made us who we are.

I had never given the fact that I'm Italian much thought. Our meals weren't Italian. We didn't attend the Italian Catholic church in town. And I rarely heard my father speak the language. Growing up I felt more of a connection to the Scotch-Irish, Welsh, and English side of me. My phone calls with Dad caused a shift in my self-perception.

WHEN WE RETURNED to England in 2015, our granddaughter was with us. Emerson, Em for short, stood on what remained of a runway, much of it covered in overgrown grass or weeds.

"What do you think, Em?" I asked.

"It's hard to believe what happened here,"

Em said. "It's not a museum, and there's not really anything here. But I can feel the impression of it."

We, our children, and our granddaughter have all stood on that runway. Two more generations standing where Mike Caputo helped win the war, thinking about him, who he was, and what he did for us all those long years ago.

EPILOGUE

Mickey snapped me with a wet dishtowel. So, I pushed him out the window. We were in the midst of one of our normal spats over who was going to wash the dishes and who was going to dry.

I was certain I was in line for the washing detail; he was adamant that I was the dryer. We both felt the dryer had the harder job because that person had to clear the table, dry the dishes, wipe the table down, and sweep the floor. The washer only had to wash.

Mickey was standing right beside the kitchen window when he snapped the towel. It stung when it hit, and I reacted. I pushed him

with all my might, and he went sailing, tucked up into the fetal position, rear first out the window.

When Dad heard the crash of glass, he came flying up the cellar stairs roaring about our allowances being cancelled until the window was installed and paid for.

"Mickey started it!" I barked as I backed into the counter, trying to avoid the broken glass all over the floor.

"I don't give a damn who started it," Dad hollered. "There's a broken window that has to be replaced and you're both paying for it."

Mom was none too pleased either, her face set with displeasure.

"I hope he cleared my iris bed." She peered into the backyard, seeing that Mickey had, indeed, landed on the grass just beyond the flower bed. Mom loved her irises, weeding and tending and separating the rhizomes to start a new bed elsewhere in the yard. And sighing happily when they were in full bloom.

Thirty years later, I drove across the state to visit my parents. Mom took me into the garage and handed me about a dozen iris rhizomes to put in my own garden. I was thrilled. I did my

research and planted them with care. I was disappointed the first year when green leaves appeared but no blossoms. Year two, nothing. The years passed, and I forgot all about them.

When the water problems started in our basement, we had to tear up the concrete patios at the front and back of the house. We dug trenches all around the foundation and installed French drains, adding new gutters along the roofline that tied into the new drains. We graded the land and built a new patio onto the back of the house. Red and grey pavers created an outdoor room under the huge red oak tree.

We finished the work in March, about a month before Mom passed away. In May, standing proud at the edge of the patio, was a lone lavender iris in bloom.

That one iris divided, and I kept planting the new rhizomes. I'd send extra rhizomes to family members. Every May I look out over a sea of gentle lavender.

The May after Dad's passing, the lavender sea was punctuated with crests of large, deep purple irises. I pointed them out to my daughter-in-law, incredulous as to how they got there.

"They're from your Dad!"

ACKNOWLEDGMENTS

My relationship with my father continues to deepen even after his death. I believe this book is responsible.

After he was gone and I couldn't call him up to ask for more details about a specific story, I personally visited many of the places he spoke about, from the bases here in the US to Rackheath in the UK. I felt him there with me.

When writing section two, I had to dig deeper and think more about who Dad was, so that I could portray his point of view with as much accuracy and integrity as I could. All of this helped me understand Dad on a deeper level.

Whenever I struggled with a particular passage, or wondered how to treat a particular subject, I'd receive little signs from him. A blue jay would perch on the windowsill of my study, looking in at me and staring. An airplane would fly overhead. Or I would hear his voice, clear as a bell, telling me to trust my instincts and it would be fine.

On the morning I delivered the final two chapters to my editor, signifying the end of an eleven-year journey with this manuscript, my dad's story, and this book, I hit send and then walked down to the kitchen to refresh my coffee.

On the windowsill in the dining room sat my Christmas Cactus, one white flower in bloom.

As messy as Dad's work bench was, the bookcase behind it wasn't much better. While I might have uttered a cuss or two clearing it all out after his death, I'm grateful because it led to the discovery of two large, worn, and expandable manila folders. Inside were all of his USAAF

personnel files. Dad had also saved two volumes of *Navigation Manuals,* by the Department of the Air Force, *The 467th* by Allan Heally, and *The Flight Manual for the B-24 Liberator.* These documents were immensely helpful in my research.

Mom always vowed she'd never throw anything out. She had to clean up after us all of those years, so when she was gone, we could clean up after her. The letters between her and Dad during the war were tied in blue satin ribbons in the back of the ugly, bright-red speckled filing cabinet. Writing from Dad's point of view only became possible by reading and re-reading what he'd written. Mom had also saved photos of her and Dad's time together during the war. When I'd left home, from time to time an envelope would arrive with a newspaper article of Dad's volunteer work, sent to me by my mother. Like my mother, I saved it all, and I could not have written *Flying With Dad* without it.

I have come to appreciate the struggles of Grandma Kate and Aunt Josephine. They reacted to a world that had been created for them in the only way they knew how. Thank goodness for Aunt Ada, the role model Mom so dearly

needed. Each of them cared for my parents the best way they knew how, and in understanding them I have a clearer picture of my parents and of myself.

I have to thank my husband, Kirk. Seeing his face in the door watching as I typed or re-searched, I sensed his enduring support for the work I was trying to do. From day one he has listened to my stories, and he has been coura-geous in saying things to me that I needed to hear. Thanks for providing us an opportunity to co-parent our wonderful children, Deborah, Pe-ter, and Kate. We now have grandchildren to add richness and exhaustion to our lives. Most of all, thank you for being my best friend.

Together with my siblings, Michael and Connie, often my rivals, we can now laugh at some of our antics. I don't think Mom and Dad were laughing at the time. I could not have written this book without you. You were always on the other end of the phone filling in the gaps of my memory, adding your different perspec-tives to help make the story come alive for me. I am most impressed by, and grateful for, our ability to take care of Mom and Dad in the end, because we are a team.

Mary Catherine Desmone, we joke that we have been the best of friends longer than we have been in our marriages. You were Mark's dearest friend for a while and your memories of he and Dad made their stories richer.

If someone would have told me that I would write a book and that it would take me eleven years to complete, I would have laughed until my sides hurt. But once I heard the first story from Dad, I was driven. The story just had to be written. I've had conversations and help from Mark Malatesta, Girl Friday Books and their associates, and Jane Friedman. They helped me build the confidence that I could do this. *Self-Publishing's Legal Handbook* by Helen Sedwick, and *Choosing the Best Self-Publishing Companies and Services 2018* by Jim Gimmatteo and John Doppler from the Alliance of Independent Authors helped me get to know what I don't know.

My deepest gratitude goes to Ingenium Books and John and Boni Wagner-Stafford. John has helped me with so many technical issues involving this machine in front of me called a computer. Just finding a way to get emails back and forth was an adventure I'd rather not repeat.

Boni has been the angel sitting on my shoulder. She won me on our first phone call. She listened—really listened—to what I wanted this book to be. She took the draft and worked magic on it. She helped me to find my own voice and the voice of my father. What could be better than that? She has been one of the best teachers I could have asked for and a therapist that I am not sure she knows she is. We now share a deep and abiding respect for each other.

A very special thanks to Dr. Richard Gromen, sadly deceased. When I was a sophomore in college, I was told by friends to get out of his World History Class because he was just too demanding. I stuck it out, which turned out to be a blessing. He made history come alive because he always wanted to know what things meant and why they mattered. I can trace my love of history back to his class.

I wanted the background of this story to be as accurate as possible. Andy Wilkinson and Brian Mahoney of the 467th Bomb Group have been invaluable in giving me the facts. I met Perry Watts in England when I handed the first draft of the book to the Second Air Division Memorial Library in 2009. His book, *The 467th*

Bombardment Group (H) in World War II has been a treasured resource.

Great Britain has become a second home because of the friends Kirk and I have made. There is a lovely dinner waiting for us with David Hastings and his wife Jean every time we visit England. David was the Vice Chairman of the Memorial Trust of the Second Air Division USAAF when Dad proposed sending the model of the Witchcraft to the library. We met David in 2009 and he took us to every conceivable place Dad would have known when he was at Rackheath. Ian and Sue Denny have also made sure I have seen all there is to see around what is left of the air base.

Every request I have made to the Second Air Division Memorial Library has been met with thoughtfulness and time. A special thanks to Libby Morgan, Jenny Christian, and Orla Kennelly. Allen and Heather Morton require special mention. Not only have they housed and fed us on our many trips to England, but they have stood side-by-side with Mom and Dad on what was left of the runway at Rackheath.

When I felt stuck on a chapter or an event, I got in a car or on a plane to get to what I consid-

ered to be the best source possible. Being provided with brochures and photos, and seeing the countryside itself, made Dad's journey real in unexpected ways. I visited the Allegheny Region Red Cross Office in Reno, Pennsylvania; a special thanks to Ashley Keener. She dug through file cabinet after file cabinet looking for something with Dad's name on it—and found it.

Jim Cihon and Arden Hughes, both of Meadville, took my phone calls. They filled me in on Dad's work with the Red Cross, the Repeater Council, and the Emergency Services Council.

The National Personnel Records Center in the National Archives sent me records that contained reports about Dad during his reserve time. One particularly glowing report was signed by Major Dave A Wettstein. I loved reading someone else's assessment of Dad's integrity, loyalty, and meticulous appearance. Those documents also supported Dad's promotion to captain.

Ruth Andel, archivist at Allegheny College in Meadville, Pennsylvania found things I'd given up hope had existed. I must also thank

Pennsylvania State Archives in Harrisburg, Pennsylvania; the Middletown Pennsylvania Library; Stefani Miller at the Harlingen Arts & Historical Society; Rosalie Pecina at Kelly Field at Port, San Antonio; John Tosh at the Texas Air Museum, San Antonio; Sacred Heart Cathedral in Austin Texas; Hunter Chaney at the Collings Foundation; and Clint Epley at the Commemorative Air Force Museum in San Marcos, Texas.

A very special thanks to Wilson Noden, navigator for the 467[th] Bomb Group. He arrived in England in February of 1945 and was there at the same time as my father. He didn't know Dad, but he gave me details that helped me picture things that Dad had done. Sitting across from him and listening to his tales was a pleasure.

Life is richer when surrounded by supportive friends, and you know who you are. If I heard it once I have heard it a thousand times: "When is your book coming out?" Sometimes when I was at a real low point, daunted at my own undertaking, that question was all I needed to re-energize and continue to plow ahead.

Lastly, I thank the God that I have come to know through my own personal journey. I am grateful for the pain of life and the richness of its lessons, and I am soothed by how deeply anchored I feel to whatever is next.

*If you enjoyed **Flying With Dad**, please consider leaving a brief review on the website or with the retailer where you bought the book.*

Reviews are very important to every author. Your feedback doesn't have to be long or detailed, just a sentence saying what you enjoyed.

Please accept my thanks if this is something you'd like to do.

ABOUT THE AUTHOR

Yvonne Caputo has been a teacher, the head of human resources in a retirement community, a corporate trainer and consultant, and a psychotherapist. She has a master's degree in education and in clinical psychology. Her book, *Flying with Dad,* is a story about her relationship

with her father through his telling of World War II stories.

She has always been a storyteller. She has used stories to widen the eyes of students, and to soften the pain of clients. It's her stories that result in rave reviews as a presenter and a speaker.

Yvonne lives in Pennsylvania with her best friend (who is also her husband). Together they have three children, three grandchildren, and a labradoodle.

BIBLIOGRAPHY

"Second Air Division in East Anglia, The," *Second Division Memorial.* Rackheath, Norfolk, England, Alpha Press. 2003, 5-16.

"A Narrative History of Lackland Air Force Base," accessed Fall 2018, 1 – 3, https://www.37trw.af.mil/Portals/57/Documents/History/AFD-061212-028.pdf

Air Navigation, Volumes 1 and 2, Department of the Airforce, Washington, DC, 1954. Volume 1, 1-47, 139-163,185-237, Volume 2, 1-29.

Air Navigation for Pilots, Department of the Air

Force, St. Louis Missouri. Universal Printing Company, 1952: 2-44, 5-1, 5-9, 5-48.

"Airplane Dead Reckoning Navigation Procedure," WWII Training Film 33974, 1942, accessed Winter 2019, https://www.youtube.com/watch?v=tEjJIhDanEY

Aircrewman's Gunnery Manual, Aviation Training Division, Office of the Chief of Naval Operations, US Navy in Collaboration with U. S. Army Air Forces, 1944.

"American Memorial Chapel – 1958," St. Paul's Cathedral, accessed Summer 2019, https://www.stpauls.co.uk/history-collections/history/history-highlights/american-memorial-chapel-1958

Allen, Don. "The Library Fire of 1994," Second Air Division Memorial Library, accessed Summer 2019, https://2ndair.wordpress.com/2018/08/01/the-library-fire-of-1994/

"A-Ration" *Wikipedia,* accessed Summer 2019, https://en.wikipedia.org/wiki/A-ration

Arbuckle, Alex Q.C. 1942-1945: "Reach Your Boys Overseas," unknown, accessed Summer 2019, https://mashable.com/2017/03/19/v-mail/

"B-24 and Its Crew: Navigator, Principle Duty," accessed Winter 2019, http://freepages.rootsweb.com/~webermd1/family/Liberator-Info.html

"B-24 Liberator & Its Crews, The," accessed Spring 2019, http://www.heritageleague.org/b24.htm.

"B-24 Liberator Willow Run Assembly Plant," Airplanes of the Past.com, accessed Summer 2017, https://www.airplanesofthepast.com/b24-liberator-willow-run-assembly-plant.htm

"Basic Training and Classification of Personnel," The Army Air Forces in World War II, accessed Fall 2018, https://www.ibiblio.org/hyperwar/AAF/VI/AAF-VI-16.html.

Barbash, Fred. "Britain's Blitz of Memories," The Washington Post, accessed Summer 2019,

https://www.washingtonpost.com/archive/
politics/1995/05/08/britains-blitz-of-memories/
97344c89-6d71-420c-a5d6-28bdef22752d/?
utm_term=.c2ea4beb0b44

Bombardiers Information File, Army Air Force,
March 1945.

"BonAir Hotel, 2101 Walton Way," Historic Au-
gusta Incorporated, accessed Fall 2018, http://
www.historicaugusta.org/properties/bonair-
hotel-2101-walton-way/

"Building the B-24 Bomber During World War
II, Story of Willow Run", accessed Summer
2017, https://archive.org/
details/74182StoryOfWillowRun

"Cadet Classification, U.S. Army Air Force
Training Film, 1942-43," Ronald Reagan Presi-
dential Library, accessed Fall 2018, https://www.
youtube.com/watch?v=X415Ofsqxjk

Callanan, Luke and Jenny Higgens. "Goose
Bay," Newfoundland and Labrador Heritage
Site, accessed April 2016, https://www.

heritage.nf.ca/articles/politics/goose-bay-base.php

"Camp Miami Beach WW2," WWII Miami Beach Veterans, accessed Fall 2018, http://www.miamibeachvets.com/

"CAPT Robert M. Knox," 100[th] Bomb Group Foundation, accessed Summer 2019, https://100thbg.com/index.php?option%3Dcom_bombgrp%26view%3Dpersonnel%26Iemid%3D334%26id%3D2861

Christopher, Dewey. "Bloody Hundredth, The Most Famous Heavy Bomb Group in World War II, accessed Winter 2019, https://100thbg.com/index.php?option=com_content&view=article&id=255:bloody-hundredth&catid=25:group-history&Itemid=581

"Cirrhosis," Mayo Clinic,, accessed Fall 2018, https://www.mayoclinic.org/diseases-conditions/cirrhosis/symptoms-causes/syc-20351487

Coles, Dr. David J. "Keep the Homes Fires Burning: Florida's World War II Experience,"

Museum of Florida History, accessed Fall 2018, http://www.museumoffloridahistory.com/exhibits/permanent/wwii/history.cfm

"Combat America with Clark Gable," Zenos Warbirds, accessed Spring 2019, https://www.youtube.com/watch?v=7SJQYG_GskY

"Comparison Prices over 70 Years," The People History, accessed Fall 2018, http://www.thepeoplehistory.com/70yearsofpricechange.html

Conn, Stetson, Rose C. Engelman, and Byron Fairchild. "The Western Hemisphere – Guarding the United States and Its Outpost, United States Army in World War II," Center of Military History, United States Army, Washington DC, 1964. 451 – 452, https://en.wikipedia.org/wiki/Narsarsuaq_Air_Base

"Consolidated B-24 Liberator Heavy Bomber," Airplanes of the Past, accessed Winter 2008, https://www.airplanesofthepast.com/b24-liberator.htm

Craven, W. F., and J.L. Cate, eds. *The Army Air Forces in World War II, VI, Men and Planes*, 527-556, (Fall 2018), https://www.ibiblio.org/hyperwar/AAF/VI/AAF-VI-16.html

Crosby, Harry, Michael Faley, and Jan Riddling. "History Summary," accessed Summer 2019, http://www.8thairforce.com/legacy_100thbomb.htm

Dechow, Douglas. "The Bloody 100[th]," Aviation History Magazine, accessed Summer 2019, https://www.historynet.com/the-bloody-100th.htm

"Detailed History Second Air Division Memorial Library," accessed Summer 2019, http://www.americanairmuseum.com/place/136527

Dresser, Laura J., and Sherrie A. Kossoudji. "Working Class Rosies: Women Industrial Workers during World War II," *The Journal of Economic History*, Vol.52, 431-446, accessed Summer 2019, https://www.jstor.org/stable/2123119?read-now=1&refreqid=excelsior%

3Ac6fa893ce93c8c0ad2fa29197a125357&seq=
14#page_sca n_tab_contents

"Duties and Responsibilities of the Navigator,"
Stalag Luft I Online, accessed Winter 2019,
http://www.merkki.com/navigators%20of%
20usaaf%20in%20world%20war%20II.htm

Dwyer, Larry. "Consolidated B-24," Aviation
History Online, accessed Winter 2008, http://
www.aviation-
history.com/consolidated/b24.html

"Flexible Aerial Gunnery: Making a Gunner,"
US Army Air Forces Training Film, WWII,
1943, accessed Fall 2018, https://www.youtube.
com/watch?v=Ts5gsZy8JH0

Flight Manual B-24, Aviation Publications, Ap-
pleton Wisconsin, 1942, V-XXII

Forsyth, Robert. *Jagdgeschwader 7 'Nowotny,'* ac-
cessed Summer 2019, https://www.google.com/
search?q=Robert+Forsyth%2C+

Jagdgeschwader+7+%27Nowotny%27+
(Osprey+Publishing)

"General Henry H. Arnold," U.S. Air Force, accessed Winter 2009, https://www.af.mil/About-Us/Biographies/Display/Article/107811/general-henry-h-arnold/

"General Henry 'Hap' Arnold," National Museum of the US Air Force, accessed Winter 2008, https://www.nationalmuseum.af.mil/Visit/Museum-Exhibits/Fact-Sheets/Display/Article/196848/gen-henry-h-hap-arnold/

"German Prisoners of War in South Carolina," Old Ones Dream, accessed Summer 2019 https://www.oldonesdream.com/my-blog/2013/05/german-prisoners-of-war-in-south-carolina.html

Giddens, Paul. "History of the 31st College Training Detachment (Aircrew) Meadville," Pennsylvania, 1944.

Gohl, Stanley. "The Founding of Charleston Air Force Base," Joint Base Charleston, (Winter

2019), https://www.jbcharleston.jb.mil/News/ Commentaries/Display/Article/1156851/the- founding-of-charleston-air-force-base/

Harlingen Army Air Field; Brochure, Army Air Forces Training Command, 1943, 30.

"Harlingen–Decade 1940 to 1949, accessed Summer 2019, http://www.myharlingen.us/ upload/page/0338/docs/07%20Decade% 201940%20to%201949.pdf

Hatfield, Edward A., "WWII in Georgia," *New Georgia Encyclopedia, accessed* Winter 2006, https:// www.georgiaencyclopedia.org/articles/history- archaeology/world-war-ii-georgia

"Heat and Cold," WWII U.S. Army Air Forces Pilot's Information File, accessed Summer 2019, https://books.google.com/books?id= XTyBFuWtesUC&q=Heat+and+Cold#v= snippet&q=Heat%20and%20Cold&f=false

Helmrich, Jonathan E. *Through All the Years: A History of Allegheny College,* (New Castel, Penn- sylvania, Commercial Printing Company, 2005.)

"History of Charleston AAF (113th AAF Base Unit)" *Historical Research Division*, Maxwell Air Force Base. 7, 13, 16-17

History of Crawford County Pennsylvania, (Chicago, Warner, Beers, and Co., 1885), 660.

"History of Male Circumcision, The" (Fall 2018) http://www.cirp.org/library/legal/QLRC/02.html

"History of Meadville, Pennsylvania, The" Official Website of the City of Meadville, accessed Fall 2018 https://www.cityofmeadville.org/? SEC=5F136313-AF30-4906-B3FE-6F88E1CE2114

"History of the Norfolk Broads," Accessed Summer 2010, https://www.broads-authority. gov.uk/learning/for-students/history

"History of Wesleyan College, The" First for Wesleyan, accessed Winter 2008, https://www. wesleyancollege.edu/about/wesleyan-college-history.cfm

Kibble-White, David H. *Airfield Focus 55:Rack-heath*, (Peterborough, England, GMS Enter-prises, 2002) 3 – 7.

"Lockheed C-130 Hercules: Fact Sheet," *The Aviation Zone*, accessed Summer 2018, http://www.theaviationzone.com/factsheets/c130_specs.asp

Lorenzi, Rossella. "Flying Coffin Wreck Found," *Seeker.com*, 2014. Accessed Spring 2019, https://www.seeker.com/flying-coffin-wwii-wreck-found-1769179012.html

Middletown Air Service Command, Its History and Contribution to Victory, Middletown Air Service Command Publication, Middletown Air Mate-rial Area Records; William K. Sowers Collec-tion, Manuscript Group 363, Pennsylvania State Archives, Harrisburg, PA., 2009.

Miller, Donald L. *Eighth Air Force, The American Bomber Crews in Britian*, (London, England: Aurum Press Ltd., 2006) 65-96, 111-151, 274-275.

"Napalm," Encyclopedia Britannica, accessed Winter 2009, http://www.britannica.com/EBchecked/topic/402801/napalm.

National Youth Administration and Aviation Film, National Archives, circa 1937. WPAToday, 2014. https://www.youtube.com/watch?v=8R6u-jvrnVs

Nored, Ed. "WWII Uniforms and Flight Gear," Hell's Angels, 303rd Bomb Group (H), accessed Spring 2019, http://www.303rdbg.com/uniforms-gear3.html

"North American AT-6, Texan, The Skytamer Archive,
accessed Fall 2018, http://www.skytamer.com/North_American_AT-6.html

Papp, Jozesf, "Azaleas Should Be in Full Bloom for the Master's Tournament," *Augusta Chronicle*, April 1, 2019, accessed Spring 2019, https://www.augusta.com/masters/story/news/2019-04-01/azaleas-should-be-full-bloom-masters-tournament- 01/azaleas-should-be-full-bloom-masters-tournament

"Park Spotlight: Pymatuning State Park,"Pennsylvania Department of Natural Resources, accessed Summer 2018, http://www.dcnr.state.pa.us/news/resource/res2005/05-0830-pymatuningsp.aspx

"Physiology of High Altitude Flight, B-17, B-24," Archives, San Diego Air and Space Museum, accessed Winter 2019, https://www.youtube.com/watch?v=3_2_CiCN21o

"Rheinmetall MK 108 3 mm Cannon," *National Museum of the Air Force*, April 23, 2015, accessed Summer 2019, https://www.nationalmuseum.af.mil/Visit/Museum-Exhibits/Fact-Sheets/Display/Article/196224/rheinmetall-mk-108-30mm-cannon/

Ross, David, ed. "Norwich Cathedral," *Britain Express*, accessed Summer 2019, https://www.britainexpress.com/attractions.htm?attraction=124

"San Antonio: Geography and Climate," City-Data.cpm, unknown, accessed Fall 2018, http://

www.city-data.com/us-cities/The-South/San-Antonio-Geography-and-Climate.html

Shettle, M. L. Jr., *Army Air Fields of World War II*, (Roswell, Georgia: Schaertel Publishing Co., 2005) 48 – 55, 56 – 63.

Brannon, Barbara A. "China's Soong Sisters at Wesleyan," Wesleyan College, 1997, accessed Fall 2018, https://www.wesleyancollege.edu/about/soongsisters-home.cfm.

Spicer, Mary. "Meadville No Stranger to Flooding in Its Storied History," *Meadville Tribune*, June 3, 2012, accessed Spring 2018, https://www.meadvilletribune.com/archives/meadville-no-stranger-to-flooding-in-its- storied-history/article_20e53b1c-dfac-5a4d-ae0b-d5fd-c79ccbaf.html

"Straddle Trench Latrines," *Integrated Publishing*, Medical Reference and Training Manuals, accessed Fall 2018, http://armymedical.tpub.com/MD0008/Straddle-Trench-Latrines-Introduction-to-Military-Preventive-Medicine-114.htm

Stibbe, Matthew. "Flying Legends, Pilot Safety and A Live in Aviation." Forbes.com, published Oct 5, 2012, accessed Winter 2019, https://www.forbes.com/sites/matthewstibbe/2012/10/05/janeen-kochan/#156e84a4500c

Swinhart, Earl. "North American AT-6," *The Aviation History Online Museum*, updated November 9, 2013, accessed Fall 2018, http://www.aviation-history.com/north-american/at6.html

"Teaching Eleanor Roosevelt Glossary, National Youth Adminstration," *Eleanor Roosevelt Papers Project*, George Washington University, unknown, accessed Winter 2008, https://www2.gwu.edu/~erpapers/teachinger/glossary/nya.cfm

"Training the American GI," *National World War II Museum New Orleans*, unknown, accessed Fall 2018, https://www.nationalww2museum.org/war/articles/training-american-gi.

Watts, Perry. *The 467th Bombardment Group (H) in World War II*. Atglen, Pennsylvania: Schiffer

Publishing Limited, 2005. 43, 199-202, 215-223, 284-294.

Wu, Brian. Reviewed by Weatherspoon, Deborah, PhD, RN, CRNA. "Diabetes: Past Treatments, New Discoveries." Updated April 26, 2019, accessed Winter 2009, https://www.medicalnewstoday.com/articles/317484.php

Williams, Aubrey W. "National Youth Administration: The College and High School Aid Program," Speech, September 23, 1937. Accessed Fall 2018, https://socialwelfare.library.vcu.edu/eras/great-depression/national-youth-administration-college-high-school-aid-program/

Yoder, Anne, archivist. *Military Classifications for Draftees*," Swarthmore College Peace Collection, accessed Fall 2018, https://www.swarthmore.edu/library/peace/conscientiousobjection/MilitaryClassifications.htm

CPSIA information can be obtained
at www.ICGtesting.com
Printed in the USA
LVHW091703280320
651507LV00004B/1038

9 781989 059326